W9-BAN-923

REVISED EDITION

New Jersey
Gardener's Guide

Copyright © 2003 Pegi Ballister-Howells

All Rights Reserved. No part of this book may be reproduced or transmitted in any form, or by any means, electronic or mechanical, including photocopying, recording, or by any information storage and retrieval system, without permission in writing from the publisher.

Published by Cool Springs Press, a Division of Thomas Nelson, Inc., P. O. Box 141000, Nashville, Tennessee, 37214.

Ballister-Howells, Pegi.
    New Jersey gardener's guide / Pegi Ballister-Howells.--Rev. ed.
        p. cm.
    Includes bibliographical references (p.   ).
    ISBN 1-59186-067-9 (pbk.)
    1. Landscape plants--New Jersey. 2. Landscape gardening--New Jersey.
        3. Gardening--New Jersey. I. Title.
    SB407.B355 2004
    635.9'0949--dc22
                                                    2003021253

First Printing 2004
Printed in the United States of America
10 9 8 7 6 5 4 3 2 1

Managing Editor: Ramona D. Wilkes
Horticulture Editor: Ruth Rogers Clausen
Copyeditor: Sally Graham
Production Artist: S.E. Anderson
Cover Designer: Sheri Ferguson Kimbrough

On the cover: Peony, photographed by Pegi Ballister-Howells

Visit the Thomas Nelson website at www.ThomasNelson.com

REVISED EDITION

New Jersey
Gardener's Guide

Pegi Ballister-Howells

COOL
SPRINGS
PRESS

Nashville, Tennessee
A Division of Thomas Nelson, Inc.
www.ThomasNelson.com

Dedication

To my husband Tom Costantino, our children, Teejay and Kira, and our dogs, Holly Hock, Sweet William, Jacob's Ladder and Magic Lily. Family and gardening; Perfect Together!

Acknowledgments

I would like to thank Hank McBride from Cool Springs Press for the opportunity to update this book and Ramona Wilkes for her steady hand throughout the editing process. Holly Hock, my mostly border collie provided the constant support that only a dog can give. She stays by my side when I work which helps enormously through the rough spots. Without Laurie and our coffee breaks, the level of intensity would have often been unbearable.

From a gardening perspective there are three nurserymen that deserve my thanks. Mel Moss of Livingston Park Nursery, Mike Mendenko from The Village Nurseries, and Bill Griffin of Griffin Nurseries have all been invaluable in helping my collection of plants at Blooming Acres to expand and grow. These great plant professionals have worked continually to find me interesting and unusual plant specimens. This, in turn, has allowed me to accumulate much of the experience I share with my readers in this book. I would also like to thank my extended family of listeners on WCTC 1450 AM. Their constant encouragement and interest in what I have to say makes putting down words on paper feel more like writing a letter to a friend than a project. Finally, to all the people, friends and strangers, who told me they liked the first edition, my deep thanks. Without their words, I could not have done it again.

Table of Contents

Featured Plants *for New Jersey*

Welcome to Gardening
in New Jersey

If your home is your castle, then think of your yard as your kingdom. Your landscape is an extension of your personality and must fit your own concept of beauty and function. It must also fit with your lifestyle. As ruler of your kingdom, you decide if you want formal gardens or meadows of wildflowers or if you prefer low-maintenance evergreens or blasts of color. Plant the flowers that bring you joy and the shrubs that make you smile. Lots of shade trees do not make an area good for touch football games, but large areas of open ground require mowing. Delicate flowers in the back yard where toddlers play is asking for disaster, but to share a love of growing things with children is a gift for both teacher and pupil. You need to decide what you want and need from your yard. You should have a plan. It doesn't have to be a plan that has every tree and blade of grass outlined on a diagram but a general plan of open areas and private nooks. A major part of the plan should be a consideration of how much effort you intend to put into maintenance.

Consider planting shade trees on the south side for summer shade and winter sun. Plant hardy evergreens on the north side to give protection from winter wind. Border plantings and flowering hedges can create privacy. You will need a focal point or two, and be sure to consider plantings that unfold their own brand of majesty in the dead of winter. A snow-covered scene will make even a compost pile gorgeous, but a well-planned winter landscape will have a stark and regal beauty in the absence of snow.

If you are starting from scratch, you might consider planting groups of plants in a particular order—the order that they are presented in this introduction.

Shade Trees and Large Evergreens

Start by planting shade trees and large evergreens. These create the basic structure on which you will build your empire. Choose both plants and planting locations carefully. It is not easy to change your mind once these cornerstones become established. To reduce the risk of insects and/or disease wiping out an entire planting, avoid planting monocultures. Mixed evergreens add subtle variations to the landscape. It is like combining velvet with velveteen and suede; the textures are rich and cry out to be touched.

Think about what you are planting. A blue spruce outside the front door is a big mistake. It can reach 100 feet! Maple trees have tenacious roots that will wreak havoc on your septic system if planted

Tranquil Landscape Cloaked in White

too close. The beautiful native dogwood needs shade. Holly trees are lovely year-round, but if they are planted by the pool, bare feet will suffer from the fallen, prickly leaves. These are all fine trees, but in the wrong spot they can make you miserable.

Small Flowering Trees

Next it will be time to select small flowering trees, which is a little like choosing chairs for your living room. They can be similar in style to what is already there, or completely different. Maybe just one will make a perfect focal point in a small space, or scatter several about the yard to fill a larger area. Use all the same plants for impact or add diversity with plants that have different key features.

The joy of small flowering trees is their return engagement every year: same time, same place. It often takes a while before small trees bloom to their full potential, so plan carefully to have trees that behave according to the blooming needs of your landscape. But even if they do not thrive, or if they have pest problems or encounter some other disaster, it is not an overwhelming task to remove them and start over.

Mixing small flowering trees with evergreens can create a wonderful effect. Crapemyrtles are only borderline-hardy in New Jersey, but when protected by a clump of evergreens, they may endure and present their midsummer frills with enthusiasm. Dogwoods will be happier nestled into the shady boughs of evergreens and will brighten the evergreens' shadowy skirts with spring color. Plant one or two little beauties and see how they do. One or two may be just enough, or you may decide you need another one over here and another over there. You do not just plant a garden and walk away. You mold it, watch it grow, shape it, sculpt it, and grow with it. The planting of small flowering trees is one of the most satisfying of planting projects. These plants offer years of quiet joy.

Shrubs

Shrubs can be small or almost treelike. They may hold their leaves or shed their summer raiment. In a small yard, a single shrub may take center stage. On sprawling grounds, plant them in clusters or rows for impact. You need to know a lot about the particular plant you are considering; be sure to ask the right questions. Some yews grow straight up. Some spread out low and wide like a hovering pterodactyl. (A pterodactyl in a three-foot space is destined for extinction!) Euonymus get scale like an ice cream cone dipped in chocolate jimmies. Wisteria growing on a wooden porch will eventually crush the porch wood. Asking questions about size, habit, rate of growth, and pests *before* they are problems will help you have a peaceful co-existence with your landscape plants.

Most shrubs can be moved or pruned or replaced without destroying a long-term investment. It is not a good idea to move shrubs around like checkers on a checkerboard, but if you have a change of heart or find that a plant is not doing what you had hoped in a particular spot, get out your shovel and move it. If you follow reasonable planting procedures at an acceptable time of year, transplanting can be accomplished without too much trauma to yourself or the plant.

Stone Boarder with Hostas

Weeping Norway Spruce Decorating a Stairway

Vines and Ground Covers

After planting shrubs, you can fine-tune your grounds with vines and groundcovers. Vines can create vertical interest and sometimes a truly dramatic focus. They can be solutions to hide ugly fences, ramshackle sheds, or a concrete wall. Vines used to advantage in tight quarters can define spaces and even create the feeling of privacy in an urban setting. When planted in the wrong spot, some vines can get other plants all tangled up as if they were caught in a spider web. Ask, read, investigate, and observe before you plant anything creeping, climbing, twining, or spreading.

Ground covers are great work-savers that offer their own brand of beauty. The "Big Three" are English ivy, pachysandra, and periwinkle. These will all get the job done, but a little creativity in this arena will be most rewarding. If you don't cover the ground, Mother Nature will do it for you, so you might as well choose something that tickles your fancy.

Roses, Perennials, Bulbs, and Annuals

The leap to planting roses, perennials, bulbs, and annuals is like moving from building to decorating. The first major steps of landscaping (or creating a home) should create harmony, personal satisfaction, and a genuine level of comfort that makes you "fit" in the surroundings you have created. With that done, adding the trimmings can be rollicking good fun. Go for bold impact or delicate pastels. Be daring and experimental or elegant and refined. Plant, move, divide, change. Plan a color scheme or a riot of uncontrolled brilliance. Express yourself and have as much fun as possible doing it. Nothing is permanent, and everything generates new ideas for next year.

Know Your Garden

In this kingdom of yours, you need to spend time with your subjects. Your yard is full of wondrous delights, but you have to take the time to see them. If you wander about your kingdom only when trudging behind a lawn mower, you will not notice the new shoots on the weeping Norway spruce which are so bright they look like they have tiny lights inside, nor will you see the red anthers on the black pussy willows as the fuzzy buds begin to mature.

Although there is much satisfaction and true pleasure in taking time to appreciate what you have, there is more to be gained from spending time in the yard than simply enjoying its charms. If you do not know what your plant kingdom looks like when it is healthy, you will not recognize the subtle signs when all is not well. At some point, the leaves will yellow or the limbs become bare. You may notice something is wrong as you dash from the car to the kitchen door, but if you spot a problem only at a run, it is often too late to solve it. Time spent in quiet observation is time well spent. By being prepared to "nip it in the bud," you can keep a problem from becoming overwhelming. The occasional few minutes spent mingling with foliage and flowers can save you hours of pruning, battling bugs, and even replacing damaged plants.

When spending time in your garden, take a look at the leaves of your plants. Turn a leaf over and look at its underside. Sometimes it is the same color as the top of the leaf, but on some leaves the two surfaces are different. Look for bumps and ridges on the stems, look at the shape of buds, notice whether the flowers grow at the tips of the branches or farther back. The new growth often emerges one color and then matures to another shade. Flowers, fruits, and seeds come in an almost infinite variety of sizes and shapes.

Interesting Garden of Shapes and Colors

A novice Christmas tree grower once called me in a panic. There were horrible growths all over his trees. He was sure the growths were certain death for the trees and no one knew what they were. It was a new disease, he could lose everything, and "no one cared!" The poor man was borderline hysterical. Instead of heading to the beach for the weekend, I rushed out to his farm armed with reference books, a magnifying glass, sampling bags, and spray recommendations to stop the onslaught of the unknown enemy. His tree-destroying growths turned out to be the male cones. If he had taken the time to know his plants, there would have been no panic.

Walkway with Pachysandra

Choosing the Plant and the Right Spot

The plant and its spot have to be considered at the same time. Whether you want to plant a tree, a shrub, or even an herbaceous plant, first take a good look at the planting spot. Is there standing water? Sandy soil? Clay? Sun? Shade? Root competition? Air pollution? A septic system? If the spot receives blazing sun, a flowering dogwood will fry. You may have to tuck the dogwood into a shady nook and plant a sun-loving flowering cherry in the sunny front yard.

If the magnetism of a particular plant makes it irresistible, take the opposite approach. You might be able to find a spot in your landscape that has conditions suited for the plant. Find out if the plant needs sun or shade, learn its ultimate size and rate of growth, and learn

Row of Sugar Maples

about potential pest problems and soil and water requirements. There may also be a few unique characteristics such as fall color or your own preference for male or female plants that could affect your planting
decision. A female holly has berries and might be a perfect choice for center stage, but without a male
somewhere close by to provide pollen, you will be berryless, and then, what is the point?

Understanding Zones

The right plant in the right location will have the best chance for an uneventful, successful life. Anything
less than a good match could become a maintenance nightmare. The United States Department of
Agriculture (USDA) Cold Hardiness Zone map divides our country into minimum-temperature zones.
New Jersey zones are 5, 6, and 7, but only the northwest corner, up in the mountain, is Zone 5. The
hardy plants selected for presentation in this book are hardy in all three zones with the exception of a few
selected specifically for the warmer coast climate. Seaside conditions offer their own challenges and
require plants that are up to the task. Zone hardiness is only one factor that determines whether a plant
will survive the winter in your area. Other factors include wind, sunlight, rain, humidity, soil, drainage,
and exposure.

Digging In

When it's time to plant, dig a big hole. Make it much bigger than you need. Then make it a little bigger
than that. Look into the hole. Is it wet? Try filling it with water to see if it drains. If the water just sits,
you may have a drainage problem.

You can compensate for this by digging up a large area several feet down and incorporating organic
matter and sand throughout the area. If drainage is a serious problem, you can install a drainage pipe.
If it is minor, large rocks well beneath the rootball will provide a well for the water to collect away from
the roots. You can also plant with the rootball slightly above ground level to keep the roots out of the
soggy soil.

Winter Jasmine

Just about all New Jersey soils will benefit from the addition of organic matter: peat moss, well-rotted manures, or compost. Leaf compost is commonly available in large quantities from local composting facilities. Some towns make it available to residents for free; check with your department of public works or parks. You can always make compost yourself. It is neither difficult nor time consuming. If you mix your leaves and grass clippings, you can produce a fine quality compost that will improve your soils and reduce the waste management burden on your community. Compost is not a substitute for fertilizer, but because nutrients cling to the organic matter particles, the plants have more opportunity to make use of existing nutrients. Check with your County Extension Office for details on backyard composting. They can also provide information on testing your soil's nutrient levels, a good practice prior to planting as well as for maintaining your landscape.

Organic matter improves both sand and clay soils. In sand, organic matter helps hold soil moisture and nutrients. In clay, it opens air spaces and allows water to drain more effectively. The organic matter will hold on to residual moisture longer and so delay or prevent that rock-hard, water-repelling condition that occurs when clay soils get overly dry. It is possible to add both organic matter and sand to heavy clay soils to open up the soil even more. Never add sand to clay without also adding organic matter. Clay and sand makes something very similar to concrete, which is not something you want to encourage in your yard. If you add a 2:1 mixture of organic matter and sand, you will enjoy significant improvement in tilled soil, moisture content, and nutrient levels.

There is no exact rule for the amount of organic matter you should add. If you add one shovelful of organic matter for every one to two shovelsful of soil, you will be doing well. Mix the soil amendments with the soil you plan to put back into the hole and with the soil you will use to fill in around the plant. Then you are ready to plant.

How to Plant

Unless you are attempting to compensate for a drainage problem, place the plant at the same height it was previously in the ground or container. You may want to slightly mound up very loose soil since the soil will tend to settle, but experience with your own soils will give you the best guidance.

Do not throw fertilizer into the hole; this will burn the roots. For trees and shrubs you shouldn't even mix fertilizer into the soil you use to fill the hole. Wait until the plant has been established for at least one year before fertilizing with anything.

Garden Draped with Wisteria

Be very careful not to damage any roots in the planting process. When clumps of dirt fall away from the ball, tiny hair roots go with them. It is these tiny roots that are responsible for most of the plant's water uptake. Handle the rootball gently and shift it as little as possible once the plant is out of its pot. It is not necessary to remove burlap from around the roots of a balled tree or shrub if it is natural burlap. The roots grow right through the weave. By the time the roots get large enough to feel any restrictions from the fabric, it will have rotted away. Newer, plastic burlaps must be removed.

Always remove any wires, cords, or strings that encircle the trunk or branches. Even those made of natural materials may not deteriorate quickly enough to avoid damaging the trunk. If the trunk should become girdled, the tree is as good as dead. There is no doubt about that—it happens with a surprising suddenness. It is often a very clean, uniform death without spots or gaping wounds. The trunk continually expands, but at some point the restriction goes from letting small amounts of moisture through to completely cutting off moisture, killing the tree.

After removing the tags and strings and placing the plant, fill the hole with the amended soil. Tamp it down firmly, but do not hard-pack. You may want to stake trees or large shrubs, especially if you are planting in the fall. Winter winds can wreak havoc on newly planted material. Evergreens are even more likely to catch the wind or hold excessive amounts of snow—all the more reason to provide stakes for additional support. Water thoroughly.

Care and Maintenance

Some plants require division to stay healthy and productive. Perennial plants can be split into smaller segments to control their size or to increase the number of plants. There is a general rule that spring-blooming species are divided in the fall and fall bloomers can be moved or propagated in the spring. Transplanting woody ornamentals is best done in the early spring, but many are easily moved in the early fall as well.

Each of the plant entries in this book has a section on care, but there are a few general rules that are worth noting right away. To begin with, throw away your electric hedge shears. They are the most destructive piece of noise-making, plant-ruining equipment ever made. You think they save you time, but what they really do is make such a mess of a plant that you get trapped into using them over and over. Eventually the plant is worthless and you have to start all over again, or you must perform several years of meticulous hand pruning to allow the plant to recover.

A pair of long-handled loppers (with a ratchet mechanism for extra power if you need it) and good hand pruners are the best tools. Selective pruning, where you remove the offending branches at a joint or major "V," maintains the natural shape and beauty of a plant. If your plant requires removing half the branches once or twice a year so that it will fit in its space, you have the wrong plant for that location. Move it, or get rid of it, and plant something more appropriate.

The time to prune depends on the species. Never prune spring-blooming plants in early spring or you will remove all the flowers. Shade trees can have major limbs removed any time, but such removal is best performed during winter dormancy or in the middle of summer. If you cannot remove a branch while standing on the ground with a pole pruner, hire a professional. Climbing large trees and swinging from ropes is not for the inexperienced.

The need to control insects and diseases can be kept to a minimum with careful plant selection. If and when you have a problem, the window for effective control is often very limited. Early spring, when buds are just starting to open, is a critical time for the prevention of many diseases. Controlling insects while the pests are in juvenile stages or in smaller numbers is much more satisfactory than at any other time. Knowing your plants and being able to spot a problem early can make a big difference in successful prevention.

Watering is critical, especially for newly planted material or when drought makes growing in the garden difficult. To reduce the risk of disease, it is always better to water in the early morning than at night, and point the water to the ground rather than toward the leaves. Water deeply and thoroughly. Make sure the entire root system has a good drink. Shallow watering encourages shallow roots, which will dry out more quickly in the long run. One inch of water per week, put down all at once, is good for most plants. You can measure by using several tuna fish cans under the sprinklers. Shade trees may need more water, but less frequently. Newly planted trees and shrubs should be watered more frequently in really hot weather, especially the first year or two.

How much maintenance your yard requires is largely a result of the plants you have chosen and where they are growing. It is also a matter of your personal style. A soft, natural look is a lot easier than carefully groomed shrubs forced into the shape of meatballs and hockey pucks. It is your home, your yard, and your kingdom. Rule it wisely.

Mixed Planting with Fountain Grass

How to Use the New Jersey Gardener's Guide

Each entry in this guide provides you with information about a plant's particular characteristics, its habits, and its basic requirements for vigorous growth, as well as my personal experience and knowledge of it. I have tried to include the information you need to help you realize each plant's potential. Only when a plant performs at its best can one appreciate it fully. You will find such pertinent information as mature height and spread, bloom period and seasonal colors (if any), sun and soil preferences, planting tips, water requirements, fertilizing needs, pruning and care, and pest information. Each section is clearly marked for easy reference.

Sun Preferences

For quick reference, I have included symbols representing the range of sunlight suitable for each plant. "Full Sun" means a site receiving at least 6 to 8 hours of direct sun daily. "Part Sun" means a site that receives at least 6 hours of direct sun daily. "Part Shade" means a site that receives about 4 or less hours of direct sun daily. "Shade" means a site that is protected from direct sun. Some plants grow successfully in more than one range of sun, which will be indicated by more than one sun symbol.

Full Sun   **Part Sun**   **Part Shade**   **Shade**

Additional Benefits

Many plants offer benefits that further enhance their appeal. The following symbols indicate some of the more notable additional benefits:

 Attracts Butterflies

 Attracts Hummingbirds

 Produces Edible Fruit

 Has Fragrance

 Produces Food for Birds and Wildlife

 Drought Resistant

 Suitable for Cut Flowers or Arrangements

 Long Bloom Period

 Native to New Jersey

 Supports Bees

 Provides Shelter for Birds

 Colorful Fall Foliage

Companion Planting and Design

In this section, I provide suggestions for companion plantings and different ways to showcase your plants. This is where many people find the most enjoyment from gardening.

Did You Know?

The Did You Know? portions of the text provide interesting information about nomenclature and history, as well as little known facts about the featured plants. Share these facts with your neighbors and friends who stop by to admire your landscape!

USDA Cold Hardiness Zones

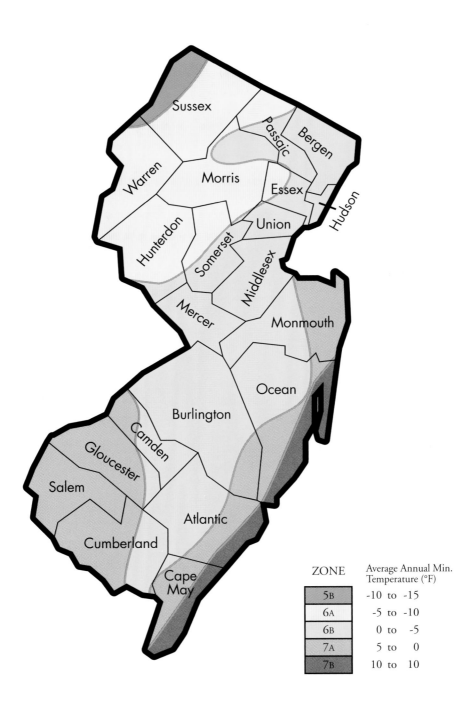

ZONE	Average Annual Min. Temperature (°F)
5B	-10 to -15
6A	-5 to -10
6B	0 to -5
7A	5 to 0
7B	10 to 10

Hardiness Zones

Cold-hardiness zone designations were developed by the United States Department of Agriculture (USDA) to indicate the minimum average temperature for an area. A zone assigned to an individual plant indicates the lowest temperature at which the plant can be expected to survive over the winter.

Annuals
for New Jersey

Annual flowers in the landscape are like accessories to a perfect outfit. You can try a single strand of short pearls or a floor-length feather boa with sparkles everywhere. You can do monochromatic elegance this year and all-colors-go-together-in-the-garden next year.

Cosmos

In all likelihood, however, you will find that you are a fairly consistent creature. If you wear bright colors and decorate your home in bright colors, you will probably do something similar in the yard. Your garden is an extension of your personality, and you can express that in a windowbox or on ten acres.

I once heard a distinguished landscape architect from Rutgers University give a seminar on landscaping principles. He stressed the importance of making the front yard, or "public space," very conservative and subdued. He said to save the big flower gardens and colorful displays for the more private backyard. I guess I was a bit of a gardening radical, because my very first thought was, "Why do all that work for only my family to see?" Years later, I would add to that, "Why do all that work for the kids to trample?"

Your own version of annual flower planting principles must be to plant what you want, where it makes you happy. Your garden is for your personal pleasure. That includes both the act of gardening itself and the results of your efforts. Make your garden work for your lifestyle.

A Good Start

First decide what you want your annual flowers to accomplish. If you are primarily concerned with cut flowers, you may want a separate bed allotted to the task. If your concern is summer color with as little work as possible, you need to choose plants that will shed their dead flowers and pack in close enough to keep weeds under control. There are a few species that come back from seed each year. These can be gorgeous and easy, but they come up where the mood suits them and usually have a free-spirited air about them. If you want something dignified, try something else.

Color is a tricky thing. Up close, most colors do go together in a garden, especially for a cutflower bouquet. From a distance, however, all colors together look like those bottles with layers of colored sand that someone shook too hard. If you plant colors in repeated stretches or use one as the foundation color with complementing splashes, it may be more effective. Even consider using all one color for each species, and soften it with another flower altogether. Dark-purple petunias and red salvia make an intense color combination with interesting variations in height and texture. Try white sweet alyssum and pink periwinkle for something more delicate.

Always keep in mind that gardening is an art form with four dimensions. It will change continually over time. Annual flowers will be the most consistent part of your summer garden in any one season, but the rest of the garden will be changing around them. Use your annuals to fill in gaps as spring bulbs fade, but remember that a misplaced giant marigold will conceal your spectacular Oriental lilies in August. Your perennial chrysanthemum plants can get bush-sized before they bloom. Annuals packed in too close will just get in the way.

As with all plants, be sure to match the growing requirements of the plants with the conditions in your garden. Prepare an entire bed if possible; it is better than just digging individual holes. Planting around spring bulbs or perennials makes that impossible, but you still want to improve the soil as best you can, even in tight spaces. All New Jersey soils will benefit from the addition of organic matter, such as compost. In heavy clay soils, the addition of compost and sand in a 2:1 ratio will help improve drainage. Never add just sand to clay soil as it makes something like concrete. The incorporation of 5-10-5 fertilizer during soil preparation is generally recommended, but do not put fertilizer directly into the planting holes as it will burn the roots. Side-dress, or sprinkle a small handful of 5-10-5 around the plants

Colorful Phlox

in midseason taking care not to get too close to the stem or it may burn. The use of water-soluble fertilize is another option. Follow the directions on the fertilizer you choose.

Succeeding with Seed

Growing your annuals from seed offers the advantage of an enormous selection of different flowers. Some will need to be started indoors during the winter in order to be large enough to plant out at the right time. Others can be direct seeded in the garden but will probably require thinning, or pulling, of some seedlings to create the desirable spacing for larger plants. This information is often contained on the seed packets. Transplanting is a bit of a shock, and transplanting immature seedlings into the garden is

difficult. Purchase transplants of the right maturity or grow them yourself to about the same size as you would find growing at the nursery in a pot or in six-pack cells. Just before or just after planting, you must remove all the flower buds. This may seem painful, but the plants will do much better during the long hot season if you allow the young plants to spend some time making a strong root system. Most plants cannot make both flowers and roots at the same time, at least not very effectively. Bud and flower removal frees the plant energy to make a more substantial root system, which will better support the plant in the long run. At the same time, pinching off the buds and the tiny new leaves will encourage bushier plants. Shorter, more compact plants require less staking and will provide more flowers.

Watching Them Grow

Once the plants are in the ground, you will need to water them thoroughly. An organic mulch will be helpful to keep down weeds as well as retain soil moisture. The amount of water needed after that depends on the annuals you have chosen, the exposure, the soil conditions, and of course, the weather. When you do water, it is best done in the early morning. It is always better to avoid getting water on the leaves as this encourages diseases, but if overhead watering is your only option, water applied in the morning will dry as soon as the sun comes out. Be sure to water deeply but not frequently. You want to encourage deep rooting of the plants to better endure summer extremes.

Deadhead, or remove dead flowers, as often as possible. This will keep the plants attractive as well as encouraging the plant to produce more flowers. The only exceptions to this are if you want to the plants to self-sow, in which case you should allow the seeds to mature in large numbers, or if you want to gather a few seeds to save for the following year.

Cut flowers for indoor enjoyment in the cool morning. Prune back leggy shoots at that time as well. Occasional pruning on a regular basis will help keep the plants productive. If they get messy, after you come back from vacation for example, prune back hard, leaving a few leaf nodes on each shoot to re-grow. Fertilize, and you should get a second burst of flowers before the end of the season.

The very best part of annuals is their transient nature. You can try anything. If there is a secret part of you that would love to go with the feather boa but you always wear pearls, the garden is a safe place to go a little wild. Circle the house with giant sunflowers! Mix purple and red and hot pink together! Grow morning glories up the porch rail! Plant enormous trumpet-shaped white moonflowers! Substitute ornamental peppers for petunias! Throw cosmos seed all along the edge of the property and let them go crazy!

You can have perfectly trimmed hedges, the obligatory dogwood, and a manicured lawn, but somewhere, somehow, sometime, let your annual flowers be at least a little outrageous.

Creeping Zinnia

Alyssum
Lobularia maritima

Soft, sweet alyssum is an excellent choice for edging beds. It can be grown from seed, but transplants are faster and easier. Sweet alyssum spreads in your garden like it's a sky of white clouds. The small round seed pods each hold a single seed. Long slender leaves are dark green. Sweet alyssum tolerates a light frost and generally blooms into late fall but will not survive a New Jersey winter. It self sows, so it may surprise you the following spring. Most varieties stay small, but others are tall enough to be cut flowers. In a sunny window it will make an agreeable houseplant. In containers, alyssum spills gracefully over the edge like a lace shawl. If winter growing conditions have weakened the plant, then toss it and look forward to spring.

Other Common Names
Sweet Alyssum, Snowdrift

Bloom Period and Seasonal Color
White or pink flowers bloom throughout the summer into fall.

Mature Height × Spread
12 in. × 18 in.

When, Where, and How to Plant
Start seeds for transplants indoors in early April. Direct seed in early May. Plant out in late May. You can also direct seed alyssum in the fall. A June seeding will ensure a late season display. Alyssum prefers a moist, loamy soil but is not fussy. Alyssum tolerates full sun, though shade in the hottest part of the day is ideal. Alyssum is perfect for edging, as filler, in front of shrubs, and in containers. The addition of organic matter is beneficial. When sowing seed, place it on the soil surface and do not cover. Space small varieties 6 to 8 inches apart; larger ones 8 to 12 inches apart. Germination takes five to fourteen days; it flowers in six weeks.

Growing Tips
Since alyssum seeds are laid on the soil surface, take care not to let them dry out. Keep alyssum watered during hot weather, watering transplants thoroughly and being extra generous with water in hot weather. If a midsummer shearing becomes necessary, apply fertilizer to help the plants bounce back.

Care
When needed, a midsummer shearing will rejuvenate the plant and encourage a burst of fall flowers. Just before frost, shear your potted alyssum and bring it indoors. Alyssum is an easy-care plant and is generally pest free.

Companion Planting and Design
Alyssum complements rather than taking center stage. In containers, mix alyssum with upright, larger blooms such as geraniums or petunias. In a garden, alyssum can edge any bed, but avoid straight lines. A staggered row creates a softer look. The contrast of soft fluff and hard rock is very satisfying. Taller varieties make great cut flowers with a honey-like scent.

Did You Know?
Alyssum is native to Mediterranean Europe. American gardeners became acquainted with it in the late 1700s. By the Victorian era, the use of flowers to communicate feelings and messages was refined to perfection. As a garden favorite, the popular sweet alyssum conveyed "worth beyond beauty." Today it is considered a true "heirloom" garden flower.

Annual Vinca
Catharanthus roseus

When, Where, and How to Plant

Sow seed indoors in early March. Cover the tiny seed lightly as seeds require darkness for germination, which takes fifteen to twenty days at 70 to 80 degrees Fahrenheit. Pinch at 3 to 4 inches. Transplant potted plants into the garden after frost, usually in late May. Direct seeding of annual vinca is not recommended in New Jersey. Full sun is best, but light shade is acceptable, unlike the popular vinca used as a ground cover, which requires shade. Prepare the soil to ensure good drainage (see chapter introduction). Add organic matter in heavy soils. Space plants 1 foot apart in a staggered row or in groups.

Growing Tips

Fertilize and water thoroughly at planting. While somewhat tolerant of dry conditions, vinca needs to be watered thoroughly when necessary. Applications of liquid fertilizer midseason will keep plants at their best. If used often for cut flowers, fertilize more often.

Care

Annual vinca is dependable and low maintenance. It thrives in heat and humidity, tolerates dry soils, is pest free, and generally low maintenance. Repeated early pinching will keep the plants compact. Cuttings taken in early fall can be rooted and wintered indoors.

Companion Planting and Design

Vinca is an excellent choice for mass planting. Use it in a mixed border, around shrubbery, or in containers. Pinks have very strong color and may not look best with oranges or corals but will look spectacular with whites, purples, and true pinks. It is excellent for cutting and effective in hanging baskets surrounded by sweet alyssum and a few dangling branches of *Vinca major*.

Did You Know?

For centuries, annual vinca has been used as an herbal medication in tropical countries. In the 1950s, it was learned that diabetes was being treated in Jamaica with a tea made from annual vinca. Research of vinca since that time has discovered anticancer alkaloids, one of which is useful in the treatment of childhood leukemia and alkaloids that reduce blood sugar.

Annual vinca is an underappreciated garden flower. It has a bushy habit and shiny dark green leaves one to three inches long. The pinwheel flowers and rich foliage have an elegant appearance as well as a long season. They sometimes last to Thanksgiving. The buds are unusual, about one inch long and lance shaped. Each unfurls into a flat bloom, often with a contrasting eye. Left in the garden, the dead blooms drop away so the onerous task of deadheading is eliminated. If pinched when young, the plants become compact and branch extensively. Annual vinca is native to Madagascar but has naturalized in most tropical parts of the world. It can even be found growing wild in southern parts of the United States.

Other Common Name
Madagascar Periwinkle

Bloom Period and Seasonal Color
Shades of pink and white, often bicolored, all summer.

Mature Height × Spread
2 ft. × 1 ft.

Bachelor's Button
Centaurea cyanus

This hardy, cheerful plant goes about its business without a care in the world. It self-seeds and can pop up anywhere. The pretty blue flowers arrive early and are useful and long lasting when cut. It looks fabulous mixed with Shasta daisies. During the Victorian era, this flower was popular as a boutonniere because of its lasting fresh look. This tradition gave rise to its common name. The plant is native to the Mediterranean, has been cultivated for centuries, and naturalized long ago in fields all over England. Bachelor's button has also naturalized in many places in North America. It was called "cornflower" because it grew wild in cornfields and "hurtsickle" because its strong stem damaged sickles during harvest. The flowers have straight, downy stems and silvery blue foliage.

Other Common Names
Cornflower, Hurtsickle, Bluebottle, Ragged Sailor, Blue Bonnet, French Pink

Bloom Period and Seasonal Color
Late spring through summer in blue, purple, pink, or white.

Mature Height × Spread
1 to 3 ft. × 6 to 12 in.

When, Where, and How to Plant
Start seeds indoors in early April. Direct seed in early May. Plant potted plants out in late May, after all danger of frost. Place in a sunny location where you don't need tidy straight rows. Bachelor's buttons planted around your tulips will bloom in time to hide the fading tulip leaves. It is happiest in cooler weather. Pick a spot with good air movement away from afternoon heat buildup. It is ideal for a wildflower meadow and is often included in wildflower seed mixes. In a more formal setting, space plants 6 to 12 inches apart in well-drained acidic soil.

Growing Tips
Water regularly and thoroughly. Bachelor's button will not thrive if allowed to dry out. Fertilize at time of planting and again in late spring.

Care
Cut fresh flowers regularly and/or remove dead flowers continually if you want blooms all summer. You can do successive seeding to keep the flowers coming. They bloom in eight weeks from seed. Store cut flowers upside down in a dry, dark place. They will retain the blue and make excellent dried flowers. Toss or transplant unwanted volunteers in early spring. Bachelor's button has minimal pest problems if any.

Companion Planting and Design
Try planting it in an open field and take advantage of its ability to reseed. Annual poppies, cosmos, and spider flower are good choices for mixing. In a more formal setting, they look great with Shasta daisies but mix well with other cutting flowers such as tall marigolds and zinnias. The blue color is treasured since it is limited in nature.

Did You Know?
There are several versions of how the genus was named, all relating to the centaurs of Greek mythology. In one tale, the name represents a centaur who was honored as the father of medicine. In another, the centaur Chiron used the flower 'centaury' to cure a wound on his foot. The last story is the best: The centaur Chiron was wounded by Hercules' poisoned arrows; he covered his wounds with cornflowers and was healed.

Begonia

Begonia Semperflorens-Cultorum

When, Where, and How to Plant

Growing begonias from seed is tricky. It may be more practical to purchase transplants. If using seed, start indoors in January or February. Mix the tiny seeds with sand to evenly disperse seeds on the soil surface. Keep at 70 degrees Fahrenheit and wait fifteen to sixty days for germination. Plant outside after the middle of May in well-drained soil with adequate organic matter, placing them 6 to 8 inches apart. Partial shade is ideal, providing the most attractive plant with the most flowers. In deep shade, the plants will stretch. If planting in full sun, choose darker-leaved cultivars and never let the soil get excessively dry. Provide shade from hot afternoon sun. In containers, begonias can be packed fairly tight. Provide adequate drainage.

Growing Tips

Water when dry, especially in containers. Fertilize regularly, according to directions on the container.

Care

More sun requires more water; however, even if they get overly dry, they have a great capacity to bounce back. If planted in deep shade, occasional pruning will keep the stretching plants neat. They self-shed dead flowers. In deep shade, good drainage is extra important to prevent leaf and/or root problems; avoid getting water on the leaves as this can make them more susceptible to mildew. For prevention, try a mildew fungicide and follow label directions.

Companion Planting and Design

Plant begonias along the edges of paths or tucked in around azaleas. They look wonderful mixed with ferns and can brighten up even the subdued hostas. Mass plant if it is not too sunny. Begonias can get a rigid "marching soldier" look, so avoid planting in very straight rows. Bring potted begonias indoors in the fall to enjoy the perky flowers well into winter while the rest of the garden sleeps.

Did You Know?

The original wax begonia, *B. semperflorens*, is native to Brazil. It has been crossed and re-crossed so often that the current botanical name has become a catch-all for the untraceable hybrids. They may not have an exact pedigree, but they are among the most popular garden flowers. In the Victorian language of flowers, they send an interesting message. A begonia means "dark thoughts."

Bright color in the shade garden is hard to find. If it were not for the dependable begonia, shade gardeners would despair. Plant begonias in late May, and they will bloom their little hearts out all summer. Wax begonia foliage does have a waxy quality. It helps retain moisture and makes this workhorse tolerate drier conditions than most. The almost round leaves are light to dark green or reddish to deep bronze. In partial shade the plants grow bushy and full. Foliage is packed tightly together on thriving plants, but the stems are quite brittle. Handle them gently. You will never have to worry about picking off dead flowers; they blow away in the wind. Planted in containers, they can be brought indoors to make satisfactory houseplants for the winter.

Other Common Names
Wax Begonia, Bedding Begonia

Bloom Period and Seasonal Color
White, pink, or red throughout summer.

Mature Height × Spread
8 to 12 in. × 6 to 12 in.

Black-Eyed Susan Vine
Thunbergia alata

At first glance, the flowers of the black-eyed Susan vine appear to have five petals and a dark central disc. Actually the center is a long, purple funnel. Black-eyed Susan vines are an excellent alternative to morning glories, which are lovely but self-sow to the point of invasiveness. There are new cultivars that lack the dark eyes, though these seem less distinctive. Black-eyed Susans are delightful plants that spread but are not aggressive. Even so, they like to twine around whatever happens to be handy and can smother smaller plants. They are sometimes suggested as a ground cover but will become vertical with the first shrub they encounter. Choose your location carefully so you can enjoy their charms.

Other Common Name
Clockvine

Bloom Period and Seasonal Color
Cream to deep orange with a deep purple throat in summer.

Mature Height × Spread
3 to 8 ft. × variable spread

When, Where, and How to Plant
When starting seeds indoors, sow in early April. Use peat pots to make seeding easier, and barely cover seeds with soil. They should be kept at about 70 degrees Fahrenheit and will take ten to twenty-one days to germinate. Transplant outdoors in May, spacing the plants 12 to 18 inches apart. Black-eyed Susans thrive in full sun or partial shade. In the garden, add plenty of organic matter to hold soil moisture.

Growing Tips
Black-eyed Susan vines need a lot of moisture, but they don't do well with wet feet, so avoid soggy soil and don't overwater. Mix a little fertilizer into the soil at planting time and side-dress at least once during the season.

Care
Monitor the vines to prevent them from overwhelming neighboring plants. If you can get the plants to overwinter in a sunny location indoors, you will have an even grander display the following year. Flowers self-shed so there's no need to deadhead them. Once established, they have few problems with pests or diseases.

Companion Planting and Design
Since this vine will climb over everything, it is best planted alone. Make use of its great rate of growth to cover a chain-link fence, or to soften a trellised gate or bare wall. Choose a spot where you can enjoy the blooms up close. If you give sunflowers a head start, black-eyed Susans growing up their stalks are very pretty. They are charming flowing over a split-rail fence or up a trellis by the porch. Grow them over the dog kennel to create summer shade as well as beauty. Hanging baskets bring the hanging gardens of Babylon to your backyard while the vine climbs up and spills over the edges.

Did You Know?
Black-eyed Susan vine is native to tropical Africa. The common name is often confused with species of North American rudbeckia, which are large and daisy-like with orange-gold flowers and a dark eye. They are, however, completely different in habit and not interchangeable in the garden. The confusion of common names (and sometimes botanical names) is a continual problem.

Celosia
Celosia cristata

When, Where, and How to Plant
Start seed indoors in late March or early April, using peat pots to minimize later transplant shock. Barely cover the seed with soil and keep at 70 to 75 degrees Fahrenheit. Germination takes six to fourteen days. Plant out transplants in late May. You can direct seed after danger of frost, but bloom will be delayed until mid August. Celosia will do well in full sun or partial shade. Prepare the soil with organic matter and lime. Celosia prefers a neutral pH. Space 12 to 18 inches apart, depending on cultivar or strain.

Growing Tips
Once the plants are established, they are very low maintenance. Water during dry weather. Side-dress with fertilizer once during the growing season.

Care
Flowers are long-lived in the garden, but remove them as the colors fade. Celosia has no serious pest problems.

Companion Planting and Design
Celosia's brilliant colors can be appreciated at a distance (sometimes better appreciated). Do a mass planting using different flower types to create an explosion of color. Plant in beds among spring perennials such as iris or peonies. Celosia will supply a second season of color. Use dwarf types as edging. For cut flowers, plant tall varieties in rows for easy access. For dried flowers, cut in full bloom and remove all unnecessary foliage. Hang singly upside down in a dry, warm, dark room. To shape the drying flowers, wire and bend while still fresh and pliable.

Did You Know?
Every year in North Brunswick, there is a gardener living on a main road who has a definite theme for the small yard. It always has outstanding drive-by impact. One year the entire yard was shades of purple. Included was a circular bed of enormous, deep-purple, crested celosia. The monochromatic use of color brought the height, habit, and texture of the different flowers into center stage. Though usually difficult to blend with more traditional flowers, the addition of celosia to this garden took it from interesting to outstanding.

People find celosia either fascinating or ridiculous. It has been described as an "acquired taste" or "an alien brain from outer space." Some find it "particularly brilliant." There is no doubt the colors are bright, even in the dark. If you seek elegance or subtlety, look elsewhere. For just a bit of fun, give celosia a try. There are two flower types. The first grows as a soft feathery plume, like a brilliantly colored flower spike on ornamental grasses. The second is a crested form that comes in the same striking colors but more resembles a "brain." Both are available in dwarf and tall varieties, and all are long-lived in the garden. Celosia resents transplanting. Direct seed, or handle plants with great care. If the plants go into shock, they wither away.

Other Common Names
Cockscomb, Woolflower

Bloom Period and Seasonal color
Various colors throughout summer.

Mature Height × Spread
1 to 4 ft. × 1 to 2 ft.

Cosmos
Cosmos bipinnatus

Cosmos is one of the most rewarding flowers for the not-overly-fastidious gardener. Cosmos drops seeds, so you can plant transplants or sow seed once and enjoy their exuberant return year after year. The free-spirited attitude of Cosmos may not fit with tidy rows of ageratum and geranium, but the airy lightheartedness brings joy wherever it sprouts up. The foliage is fern-like and open. The plants can get quite tall, and many sources recommend staking (although I think this is too much work). Cut big bouquets for indoor use when the plants start to get too tall. The flowers work well in an arrangement with almost anything, but a favorite is a large bunch of cosmos with a few pink roses. Cosmos is wonderfully low maintenance.

Other Common Name
Mexican Aster

Bloom Period and Seasonal Color
Summer to fall in white, and many shades of pink, and red.

Mature Height × Spread
3 to 10 ft. × 2 to 3 ft.

When, Where, and How to Plant
Sow seed indoors in late April $1/8$ inches deep and keep at 70 to 75 degrees Fahrenheit. You will see seedlings pop up in three to ten days. Plant out transplants in late May, 18 inches apart. Direct seeding can be done in mid- to late May. Cosmos requires full sun to do its best and will stretch in lower light, but this particular plant doesn't need to get any leggier. Don't fuss with the soil too much, as cosmos will flower more abundantly in poorer soils. Cosmos prefers an acidic pH, so there's no need to lime.

Growing Tips
Water at time of direct seeding and during dry spells. Fertilize during soil preparation, but fertilizing during the season may make plants taller and floppier.

Care
Thin seedlings if they are too thick. Pinching young plants will make them more compact and less likely to blow over. Continual removal of dead flowers will extend the bloom. Cut the plants back after frost or leave the seedheads for the birds to enjoy.

Companion Planting and Design
Plant cosmos where untamed plants will not seem unsightly. Big patches at the back of the property allow you to enjoy them from a distance. Plant in the back of borders, a meadow, or even scattered in foundation plantings. Don't try to force them into nice straight rows. They are excellent to seed or self-sow around spring bulbs for summer color. They don't injure the bulbs but help hide their dying foliage. Plants appearing in undesirable spots can be yanked out or transplanted. For arrangements, cut flowers in the early morning and place immediately in a bucket of water. Leave the larger buds intact and let them open indoors.

Did You Know?
Cosmos is Greek for "beauty," but the untamed species was first found flitting around the Mexican countryside in 1799. The wild type was available in the mid-1800s as 'Late Cosmos.' At 10 feet tall, it will blow over in a puff of wind. In 1930, 'Sensation' became available. It is shorter, sturdier, blooms earlier, and was the breakthrough needed to transform cosmos from a stubborn wild creature to a sweet thing with a mind of its own (rather like Shakespeare's *Taming of the Shrew*).

Garden Geranium

Pelargonium hortorum

When, Where, and How to Plant

Start seed indoors in late March or root cuttings in March or April. Dip the cuttings in a rooting hormone and insert them in a sterile medium. Plant out in late May in a sunny, well-drained location. They do well in containers, as edging plants, mixed among foundation plantings, or grouped outside the front door. Prepare the soil to ensure good drainage, adding organic matter and lime if necessary; geraniums prefer a neutral pH.

Growing Tips

Water regularly but avoid waterlogged soil. Fertilize monthly to encourage continual bloom.

Care

Remove the flower umbels as the blooms age. Geraniums can tolerate a very light frost, but bring them indoors at the first sign of frost damage on other plants. Provide as much sunlight as possible. By spring, geraniums will need hard pruning. Geraniums are subject to stem rot, so do not reuse soil from containers, and in the garden, skip at least one year in a diseased bed. Plant something else while the disease dissipates.

Companion Planting and Design

Geraniums are dependable bloomers in the garden or in containers. A group will cheer up a spot, but a single plant can easily get lost. A mass planting is very colorful. Geraniums are commonly planted with low growing annuals such as sweet alyssum or petunia. Try mixing them with hare's tail grass, asparagus fern, or gazania for a less traditional look. For edging, plant them in a staggered row. Geraniums are formal in appearance and therefore need to be presented in a way that avoids a "stiff" look.

Did You Know?

Garden geraniums are not true geraniums. The genus *Geranium* is known as "cranesbill," a lovely garden perennial but not as showy as *Pelargonium*. Scented geraniums are also *Pelargonium*, and they can smell uncannily like rose, peppermint, nutmeg, and even coconut. During the scented geranium boom in the 1800s, there were hundreds of varieties, but many were lost when they went out of fashion. Today, they are again gaining in popularity. There is even a "citronella" geranium used to keep away mosquitoes. A citronella fragrance is released when the leaves are rubbed or crushed.

Garden geraniums are extremely popular. One reason may be the very long season of bloom. Red is classic, but the intense pinks and salmon are spectacular. Geraniums are usually available in bloom, but if you remove existing buds at planting, they will produce more flowers throughout the summer. Each individual flower is about one inch across. It has five petals and is similar in appearance to an annual vinca flower or an impatiens. Unlike either of these two, however, geranium flowers develop in "umbels," or flat-topped clusters. The stems are stiff and hold the umbels erect, usually above the foliage. The leaves are rounded with a slight ripple. The entire plant is covered in a soft, fine fuzz.

Other Common Names

Fish Geranium, House Geranium, Bedding Geranium, Horseshoe Geranium

Bloom Period and Seasonal Color

Flowers in many colors from late spring to fall.

Mature Height × Spread

1 to 2 ft. × 1 to 2 ft.

Globe Amaranth
Gomphrena globosa

Globe amaranths are wonderful flowers in a range of colors from sweet pastels to bright, intense shades. In the garden the flowers stay lovely right up until frost. The round flower heads look more like a clover flower than true petals. Some varieties are quite round while others are oblong. Flowers appear at the tips of the branches as well as in the leaf axils. The heads are held very erect and look proud even on such a petite plant. Leaves are about four inches long. Gomphrena should be a welcome addition to any garden, large or small. It has much to offer, including plenty of dried flowers for winter bouquets. When cut and dried, they hold their color for years.

Other Common Name
Bachelor's Button

Bloom Period and Seasonal Color
Flowers appear all summer in many colors.

Mature Height × Spread
8 to 16 in. × 6 to 12 in.

When, Where, and How to Plant
Globe amaranth can be started from seed indoors or out. The plants transplant easily and do well in containers. Sow seeds indoors in late March or early April. For best results soak seed for twenty-four hours and then just barely cover with soil. Keep at 60 to 70 degrees Fahrenheit. Germination takes six to fifteen days. Plant out potted plants or direct seed in late May. Space 8 to 12 inches apart. Full sun is preferred, but they will tolerate light shade. Globe amaranth is not fussy about soil types but does not do well in soil that is overly rich. You will probably need to add lime to garden soil, since globe amaranth requires a pH of 6 to 7. Additional amendments are not required in average soils.

Growing Tips
Water when dry for the best results, but globe amaranth tolerates dry soils. Fertilize when it first starts to bloom (see chapter introduction).

Care
Pinch young plants to make them branch and stay compact. Deadheading is not usually necessary since the flowers last so long. The plants tolerate heat, humidity and dry soil. Globe amaranth forms a dense mass that minimizes the need for weeding. Use an appropriate fungicide at the first sign of mildew.

Companion Planting and Design
Gomphrena flowers are very small and are best seen up close, or you can plant them en masse to enjoy from a distance. Shorter varieties are engaging as edging plants or in front of foundation plantings. They work well in containers and can be brought indoors at season's end. Taller varieties make better cut flowers. Cut flowers for drying just before they reach their peak. Hang up to ten stems together, upside down in a dry, dark place to dry.

Did You Know?
Globe amaranth doesn't really take off until the weather warms up. In mid-May, shopping home-owners walk past the sluggish plants to the showy petunias and others that bloom their hearts out in a store cell pack. Once planted in warm summer soil, globe amaranth will provide care-free flowers until frost.

Impatiens
Impatiens walleriana

When, Where, and How to Plant

Start seed indoors in March. Plant out transplants in late May. Late May direct seedings will not bloom until midsummer. Impatiens need some shade to thrive. If impatiens dry out in full sun, they rapidly become toast. Better to plant in woods, under trees, along shadowy paths, as edging, and en masse in the shade. They do well in containers. Impatiens prefer woodsy soil that is high in humus with excellent drainage. Add organic matter and lime to achieve a pH of 6 to 7.

Growing Tips

Keep impatiens well watered during hot weather but avoid waterlogged soil. Fertilize once or twice.

Care

Pinch young plants to encourage bushiness. In deep shade, pinch during the summer to reduce legginess. Before frost, take cuttings or bring in potted plants and place in the sunniest spot in the house. Toss them if they stretch, or take cuttings and start over. Avoid rootrot—don't overwater.

Companion Planting and Design

Impatiens form an effective ground cover. In a woodland setting, where impatiens wind their way through ferns and around hostas, under a spreading dogwood and up to the azaleas, a single color of impatiens looks like a meandering stream. Because of the small flowers, mixed plantings lose color impact. Multiple colors can be effective only if each color is grouped and concentrated enough to stand on its own. When planted in a circle, the center plants stretch, creating an attractive mounded effect.

Did You Know?

In a narrow alleyway in New Brunswick, hidden between the houses, the sun shone overhead for only twenty minutes. Not even weeds grew. It took a pickax to break up the red shale. We added compost, and several years passed before carefully chosen plants took hold. There were ferns, azaleas, a witchhazel, and even an evergreen skimmia. Among these, we planted impatiens in a different color every year. The bright flowers lit the alleyway like neon lights. Visitors were shocked to come upon this out-of-the-way garden. The alley went from barren to bountiful, and it was the impatiens who infused it with energy. It was Mary Lennox's Secret Garden in the city and a very special place.

Impatiens and begonias play tag in the shade garden. Between them they are responsible for most of the summer color in a garden's shadowy nooks. Impatiens have a broader color range but are slightly more fragile than begonias. The flowers are abundant and self-cleaning. Blooms resemble those of the annual vinca. The five petals open flat in front of a single "spur," or wispy, petal-like sepal. This wisp is unique to impatiens. It is easier to see when the plant is in bud. Once the flower has unfolded, its stretching petals hide the dainty thread. Impatiens brings light and joy wherever it goes, even into the darkest corners of your garden.

Other Common Names

Busy Lizzie, Patient Lucy, Zanzibar Balsam, Patience Plant, Sultana

Bloom Period and Seasonal Color

Summer blooms in many colors.

Mature Height × Spread

2 ft. × 2 ft.

Lobelia

Lobelia erinus

Lobelia is delicate, airy and billows gracefully. There are upright and trailing varieties, both of which are suitable for containers. The trailers are particularly lovely in a hanging basket or tumbling over a wall. Both forms do well meandering through a rock garden. Although a pleasant alternative, lobelia's small flowers and limited range of colors cannot replace the look of impatiens or begonia. Still, it blooms on slender stalks with enthusiasm, has a very long season, and requires little or no attention. The blue color can be intense. I once photographed a lobelia blossom up close using slide film. When I saw the image projected onto the screen, I could not identify the gorgeous flower. The intricate detail is incredibly lovely but impossible to fully appreciate on the Lilliputian scale Nature has given us.

Other Common Name
Edging Lobelia

Bloom Period and Seasonal Color
Small tubular flowers in blue and purple all summer.

Mature Height × Spread
4 to 8 in. × up to 12 in.

When, Where, and How to Plant
Start seeds indoors in early March. Place seed on the soil surface since lobelia requires light to germinate. Use a sterile soil-less mix and water from the bottom. Maintain temperatures at 65 to 75 degrees Fahrenheit. Seedlings should appear in fifteen to twenty-one days. Expect flowers about one hundred days after sowing. Plant out transplants in late May in very light to moderate shade. Lobelia does best with shade during the hottest part of the day. Space 6 inches apart. Apply an organic mulch to retain soil moisture. Lobelia prefers a rich moist soil with a pH of 6 to 7.5. This means you should add both lime and organic matter at the time of planting. Pinch transplants to encourage bushiness.

Growing Tips
Keep lobelia well watered in hot weather. The plants will shrivel up if the soil becomes excessively dry and will rot quickly in soggy soil. An occasional application of a diluted water-soluble fertilizer will help them stay lush.

Care
A light pruning in midsummer will encourage a strong re-bloom come fall. Lobelia has no insect pests. Be sure to provide drainage if in containers, as root rot sets in quickly under soggy soil conditions. The many flowers disappear on their own when spent. A light shearing in midsummer is about the only attention these plants may require.

Companion Planting and Design
Lobelia is common for edging beds or paths since it softens the straight lines of walkways. It can be grown in containers or the crevices of a rock garden. Trailing varieties draped over walls and spilling out of containers are very effective. The tiny flowers need mass planting in a bed for color impact, but they are perfect for edging walkways where passers-by will see them up close.

Did You Know?
The genus is named after Matthias L'Obel, a Flemish botanist who served King James I of England around 1600. In the Victorian language of flowers, lobelia means "malevolence." This seems inappropriate for such a sweet flower.

Marigold

Tagetes spp.

When, Where, and How to Plant

Start seeds indoors in early April, using a sterile potting medium. Barely cover the seeds with soil and maintain 70 to 75 degrees Fahrenheit. Seeds germinate in four to fourteen days. Plant outdoors in late May. Direct seed in early May. Add lime to get soil pH up to 6 or 7. Adding organic matter at planting produces more flowers. Space small cultivars 6 inches apart, medium 12 to 15 inches apart, and giant ones up to 24 inches apart. Marigolds prefer full sun. Small varieties tolerate some shade but will not produce as many flowers.

Growing Tips

Marigolds endure dry soil but are less forgiving of soggy ground. Provide good drainage, especially in containers. Water when dry, preferably in the early morning. Fertilize at planting and in midsummer.

Care

Remove dead flowers routinely. Pinch young plants to encourage bushiness. Slugs may munch on seedlings but don't usually bother larger plants. If you have a serious slug problem, do not direct seed. Avoid overhead sprinklers to keep buds dry. Gray mold is not a serious problem but is more likely to appear in soggy flower buds. For cut flowers, collect them in early morning after a soaking rain or a deep watering. Strip all the foliage; it rots quickly and fouls up the water.

Companion Planting and Design

Small marigolds do well in containers, edging areas, rock gardens, or in front of foundation plantings. The contrast of blue ageratum or red salvia with yellow marigolds is striking. Plant taller cultivars in rows for cutting, in informal gardens, in the back of borders, or en masse for impact. They look great with large-flowered, tall zinnias. Even most of the smaller ones can be cut for indoor use. All marigolds bloom profusely once they get started, continuing until frost.

Did You Know?

The marigold's popularity must be credited to the W. Atlee Burpee Company. David Burpee took over the company in 1915 and began developing marigolds to compensate for waning interest in sweet peas. The company introduced many strains and cultivars, including the first hybrid in 1939, and later, a white marigold.

Marigolds are garden favorites with an interesting history. All are native to Mexico and have been cultivated for over four hundred years. They were introduced to Europe by Spanish explorers in the 1500s and cultivated in monasteries. They then went to Africa and France, then to India, and from India were introduced to England by Huguenot refugees. By the time marigolds made it back to America, they had become African and French marigolds. Exactly when they returned is questionable, though we know Thomas Jefferson grew them. How you use marigolds depends on the types you choose. Tall African types do best in the back of a bed, making outstanding long-lasting cut flowers. French marigolds and many modern hybrids are used as edging plants.

Bloom Period and Seasonal Color

Shades of yellow and gold, sometimes with splashes of burgundy, all summer until frost; cream color has been recently introduced.

Mature Height × Spread

6 to 36 in. × variable spread

Ornamental Cabbage
Brassica oleracea

Ornamental cabbages look like giant flowers. That makes these upscale cabbages a gift in cooler climates as they tolerate even heavy frost and remain colorful through most of the winter. Cabbages are a confusing group: broccoli, cauliflower, cabbage, kale, Brussels sprouts, and kohlrabi all belong to the same genus and species. The edibles are raised for flowers, stem, leaves, or buds; ornamentals are grown strictly for beauty. Leaves form low growing rosettes, with an open habit and contrasting pink, white, or purple centers. Flowering kale has frilly leaves in tighter heads; its center is also pink, white, or purple. Because these plants are the same species, the differences are sometimes minute. They bring joyful color while the rest of the garden fades into gray. They often stay perky till Christmas and may resprout after a mild winter.

Other Common Names
Flowering Cabbage, Flowering Kale

Bloom Period and Seasonal Color
Colorful foliage from early fall to winter.

Mature Height × Spread
12 in. × 18 in.

When, Where, and How to Plant
Start seed outdoors in late June or early July in a seedbed or flats. Seeds germinate readily; thin plants to 2 inches apart. Transplants are commonly available at nurseries when ready for fall planting. Plant as early as September. Color does not develop until after frost. Choose a sunny spot where you will be able to feast your eyes on the cheery plants when there isn't much else to see. They are not fussy about soils, though fertile, deep, well-drained soils are preferred. The pH is best at 6.5, which means most New Jersey soils need supplemental lime to provide optimum growing conditions.

Growing Tips
Water at planting. Cooler fall weather often means there's no need to water, but do so if the ground becomes dry. A light application of fertilizer at planting should be all that is necessary.

Care
You must thin seedlings, or they stretch out and are worthless. Use a "collar" (try a cat food can with both ends removed) around the stems or wrap the stems in a strip of newspaper to protect the young plants against cutworms. Keep an eye out for cabbage moth caterpillars; *Bacillus thuringiensis* (Bt) provides adequate control. These pests usually slow down when the weather gets cold.

Companion Planting and Design
Plant ornamental cabbage around the mailbox, outside the front door, or in a patch in clear view of the kitchen window. Mix cabbages with pansies for color and durability. Both make excellent container plants but may not fight off the cold as well above ground. The timing for planting cabbages works well with fall mums.

Did You Know?
Cabbages can surprise you. One fall we planted cabbages along the steps up to the front door. It was a mild winter, and the plants grew into January before they gave up. In early spring, the long stems lay along the soil surface and appeared dead. With the first spring air, the ugly stems sprouted all along their length, thick and colorful like a mat of pink and white roses. Their return was very welcome. They lasted through spring and until early summer.

When, Where, and How to Plant

Pansies are not easily grown from seed. Most gardeners are happier purchasing transplants. To start seed, sow ¹/₄ in. deep and keep seeds in the dark at 65 to 70 degrees Fahrenheit. For fall planting, sow in early July and plant out transplants in late September through October. For spring planting, sow in January and plant out well-hardened transplants in mid-April. Prepare the soil deeply, adding plenty of organic matter. Lime is probably not necessary since pansies prefer a pH of 5.5 to 6.5. Space plants 6 inches apart. An organic mulch will help plants survive both winter's worst cold and summer's heat.

Growing Tips

Water at planting. Fall, winter, and early spring watering is usually not necessary unless the ground is unusually dry. Water deeply during hot weather. Fertilize at planting, after pruning, and in early spring for those plants that overwintered.

Care

Continual removal of dead flowers will extend the bloom season significantly. Prune leggy plants and give a light sidedressing of fertilizer. If they get ugly, just pull them and start over the following fall. Pansies are incredibly durable and generally pest free.

Companion Planting and Design

You can plant pansies in every nook and cranny in your garden, including in rock gardens, around roses, and between daffodils. Plant in patches or staggered rows to show them off at their best. Grow under shade trees where they will bloom in early spring sunlight but benefit from the summer shade. Use containers for the balcony and deck. Pansies bloom with the earliest spring bulbs. The solid color flowers have more impact. Try pink or white or even black.

Did You Know?

Pansies are an excellent flower for pressing. Simple, inexpensive plant presses are available in many garden centers. You can also make a simple press with newspapers and a few heavy books. Pick the flowers at their prime. Make sure they are completely dry on the surface before pressing. Keep pressed for a few weeks until dry.

Pansies are extremely underappreciated. Few gardeners recognize them as one of the most cold hardy flowers available. Plant in October and enjoy flowers until Christmas or longer. They often bloom right through snow. Then they erupt into color early in the spring. Pansies planted in the fall are more heat tolerant because they have deeper roots and are well established. The patches get thick with foliage and are covered in flowers all spring. The blooms last well into summer. Pansies keep company with such stalwart fellows as crocus, dwarf iris, and snowdrop. Those with variegated petals resemble faces. The seemingly delicate flowers look up at you with smiling faces of innocent cheer. Their slender stems bely the threads of steel that run through their veins.

Other Common Names

Ladies Delight, Heartsease, Stepmother's Flower

Bloom Period and Seasonal Color

Flowers from autumn into winter and spring into summer; many colors, including almost-black; some are multi-colored.

Mature Height × Spread

6 to 12 in. × 12 in.

Petunia

Petunia × hybrida

Petunias are versatile, non-stop blooming machines. They are relatively new to cultivation. Most modern petunias are a crisscross of varieties, but the two species of primary importance are of South American origin. In 1830, P. violacea was found in Argentina, and P. axillaris was discovered in Brazil in 1923. The flowers are large and richly hued. They can be edged in white or have bars of contrasting colors. Eyes can be dark or light. Flowers are single or double, ruffled, fringed, or plain. Some of the old-fashioned "balcony" petunias are supposed to cascade nicely but are not easy to find. The leaves are narrow and small, covered in a fine fuzz, and slightly sticky. The plants get leggy, so a midsummer pruning keeps them blooming until fall.

Other Common Name
Common Garden Petunia

Bloom Period and Seasonal Color
Blooms all summer in many colors.

Mature Height × Spread
6 to 36 in. × 1 to 4 ft.

When, Where, and How to Plant

Start seed indoors in March. Saved seed can be started outdoors in late May, but start expensive hybrid seed indoors to avoid loss. Plant on the soil surface as petunias need light to germinate and temperatures of 70 to 80 degrees Fahrenheit. Seeds pop up in seven to twenty-one days. Plant potted plants out in late May. Petunias will give you the best results if you let them bask in sunshine. Plant outside in moist, well-drained soil, amended with plenty of organic matter. Petunias prefer a pH of 6.0 to 7.5, so you probably need to add lime. Space most varieties 7 to 10 inches apart.

Growing Tips

Keep well watered to maintain flower production, particularly in containers which dry out quickly. Fertilize at planting and once or twice during the season.

Care

Pinch young plants to keep them bushy. Remove dead flowers regularly. Prune in midsummer to revitalize the planting or trim long branches regularly to avoid a scalped look. Watch out for tobacco budworm, which feeds on the flower petals. *Bacillus thuringiensis* (Bt) may give some control, but if it doesn't help, contact your Cooperative Extension Office for options.

Companion Planting and Design

Taller petunias can go in a mixed border. Plant lower growing plants in a staggered row for edging, or group several together to get color impact. Don't mix too many varieties or the colors will run together like a madras shirt. Most petunias spread to varying degrees. This makes them pretty in a rock garden or scrambling over railroad ties. The cascading types, such as the new 'Wave' varieties, are perfect for windowboxes and hanging baskets.

Did You Know?

If you save seeds from hybrid petunias, they will not produce plants close to the production or size of the parents. On the other hand, some of the early varieties had the interesting ability to produce different shades of patterned flowers on the same plant. In *The Heirloom Garden*, JoAnn Gardner suggests trying to recreate the charm of the easy care, small flowered species of yesteryear. They may show up in the offspring of a modern hybrid.

Poppy
Papaver rhoeas

When, Where, and How to Plant
Direct seed poppies in the early spring in an open, sunny area. They do not transplant happily. Seeding again in late spring and early summer will keep poppy flowers blooming until the season's end. You can also seed in the fall. Since poppies prefer a pH of 6 to 7, add lime to soil. In prepared soil, spread the seed fairly randomly and then rake lightly for a natural look. Barely cover the seeds with soil. Poppies bloom from seed in sixty days. Thin the seedlings to about 12 inches apart. Provide well-drained but moist soil.

Growing Tips
Water seeds to ensure germination. Fertilize at the time of soil preparation, but otherwise poppies are not heavy feeders. Water thoroughly during hot weather to prolong bloom.

Care
Deadhead frequently, especially to avoid self-sowing. Save seed to replant elsewhere. Pull plants as they fade in hot weather or let the seedpods remain and use in dried arrangements. Avoid pre-emergence weed control if you want the poppies to return. Poppies are generally pest free.

Companion Planting and Design
Poppies are wonderful around spring flowering bulbs. Mixed with cosmos, poppies hide the bulbs' fading foliage then the cosmos take over as the poppies finish. Poppies are not suitable for formal gardens. Plant where self-sowing will be an advantage, not a nuisance. Try open meadows, wildflower gardens, or along fences—any place they can be free spirited. Poppies make beautiful, if not long-lived, cut flowers. To prolong the life of the cut poppy, sear the cut end immediately. You can also cut them in early morning just as the buds are about to open.

Did You Know?
The Shirley poppy is a selection of corn poppy. It was developed in the late 1800s by Reverend Wilkes, who found a single flower with a white edge. He replanted year after year, gathering seed only from those flowers that exhibited the variegation. The lovely Shirley poppy is named after the town where Wilkes lived and worked: Shirley, England.

Poppies will forever be associated with Dorothy and Toto from The Wizard of Oz. *That far-reaching field of red was a beautiful sight, even if it was the work of the wicked witch. This particular poppy is a self-seeding annual that is often included in wildflower mixes. One of its common names originated from growing wild in the cornfields of Europe. It is, in fact, the poppy of Flanders Field. Poppy flowers appear on tall, straight, leafless but hairy stems. The buds nod shyly and tilt upward just as they are about to open. Some flowers open with dramatic dark blotches at their centers. Foliage is hairy and finely divided. Double corn poppies are gorgeous and last longer, but they don't have the simple magic of the old-fashioned poppies of the field.*

Other Common Names
Shirley Poppy, Corn Poppy, Flanders Poppy

Bloom Period and Seasonal Color
Blooms late spring into summer, commonly in red but also in white, pink, salmon, and purple.

Mature Height × Spread
3 ft. × 12 to 18 in.

Portulaca
Portulaca grandiflora

Portulaca blooms profusely under brutal conditions. It spreads out cheerfully in hot, dry locations where few others survive. Portulaca is an outstanding container plant that holds up on those inevitable occasions when everyone thought someone else did the watering. The small flowers are stunning. The doubles look like miniature roses. Portulaca is a succulent, holding a reserve supply of moisture in its stems and needle-like leaves. The foliage is light green, and the stems sometimes have a red blush. They form a thick mat that is covered with flowers while the sun is out. The blooms close at the end of the day, and on cloudy days you may not see a single flower. Plant them indoors from seed for earlier flowers. Let them self-sow from the previous season or direct seed for later blooms.

Other Common Names
Rose Moss, Moss Rose, Sun Moss, Wax Pink

Bloom Period and Seasonal Color
Summer single or double flowers in many bright colors.

Mature Height × Spread
1 ft. × 1 ft.

When, Where, and How to Plant
There are differing opinions on seeding portulaca. One is to direct seed in late May, but direct-seeded flowers will bloom later and the tiny seed may wash away. Starting seed indoors in March gives you a head start on summer flowers, but the brittle plants resent handling. Transplants can be purchased. If starting with seed, sow them on the soil surface. Portulaca germinates in seven to twenty-one days. Plant out in hot, dry places with unimproved sandy soil and lots of sunshine. Avoid soggy soil. Do not fertilize or lime. Portulaca tolerates a pH of 5.5 to 7.5. Space plants 12 to 15 inches apart.

Growing Tips
Portaluca thrives without fertilizer. Only water in extremely dry conditions, over-watering will likely kill it. Container plantings require excellent drainage and may need water on occasion.

Care and Maintenance
Spent portulaca flowers drop on their own. Portulaca self-sows, but volunteers bloom later than transplants. Pinch young plants to make them bushier. If the plants get leggy in late summer, yank them. They will not recover once the weather cools. Other than that, it is problem free.

Companion Planting and Design
Portulaca does well as edging along hot driveways and concrete sidewalks and is ideal for rock gardens. A dense planting will do double duty as a ground cover. Weaving between boulders or spilling over a rock wall shows the brilliant flowers to perfection. Plant in any container that has drainage. Try a strawberry pot (a vase-like planter with holes on the sides); plants tucked into the small side pouches won't mind its inherent tendency to dry out.

Did You Know?
Portulaca oleracea is the common weed, purslane. It has stems and habit similar to *P. grandiflora*, but its leaves are flat and spatulate. Purslane can be troublesome, although there are several ornamental varieties. This native of India is quite edible and has an interesting flavor. It is used fresh in salads or cooked. Some think it tastes like mushrooms when stir-fried (though I disagree). If you can't beat it, eat it!

Snapdragon
Antirrhinum majus

When, Where, and How to Plant

Purchase rust-resistant varieties of snapdragon seed. If using seed, sow indoors in March in a sterile medium, such as vermiculite, to avoid damping off (a fungal disease that causes seedlings to flop over). Sow on the surface and water from the bottom. Provide light and keep at 55 degrees Fahrenheit. You will see signs of life in ten to twenty-one days. Pinch seedlings when they have four or five leaves. Plant mature transplants in late May to ensure early summer blooms. Snaps do best in full sun but will endure a bit of shade. In heavy clay soils add a 2:1 mixture of organic matter and sand. Snaps prefer a pH of about 7, so you probably need to add lime. Spacing is 6 inches for the smallest varieties and up to 12 inches for the intermediate and larger ones.

Growing Tips

Water at planting and when soil gets dry. Fertilize at planting and after a midsummer pruning.

Care

When night temperatures get above 50 degrees Fahrenheit, buds may not set. Prune dead stems. If plants stop blooming, prune hard (somewhere between cutting to the ground and removing the spent flowers), fertilize, and water deeply. They will bloom again at a later date, when the weather cools. Watch for brown spots on the leaves; this is a symptom of rust. To prevent the disease, plant your snaps in different locations each year or plant every other year. Although treated as annuals, snapdragons can overwinter with protection.

Companion Planting and Design

Taller snapdragons go in the back of a border or in clusters. Intermediate varieties do well in mixed borders, especially with tall zinnias and marigolds, in larger containers, along a fence, or in a cutflower garden. The shortest snaps are used in edgings, containers, and rock gardens.

Did You Know?

The flower shape is part of the whimsical fun of growing snapdragons. The upper and lower petals form the "jaws" of the mythical dragon. If you pinch the sides of the flowers, the dragon's mouth will open and close. Snaps are a delight to children (and to the child within).

Snapdragons are a welcome addition to any part of the garden and come in a variety of sizes. They provide a big blast of flowers in late spring or early summer. With a little extra attention in summer, the plants will give another show as the weather cools. The tallest ones need staking, at least until they bush out. The tiniest varieties may also be a little floppy. Snapdragons add character to a bouquet of cut flowers. Those in the intermediate two-foot range usually stay upright on their own and provide stems long enough for an impressive arrangement. All snapdragon flowers open from the bottom of the spike and work their way up. This results in an extended bloom in the garden or vase.

Other Common Names
Common Snapdragon, Toad's Mouth

Bloom Period & Seasonal Color
Spring through fall in a range of colors.

Mature Height × Spread
6 to 36 in. × 8 to 18 in.

Spider Flower
Cleome hassleriana

Spider flowers are absolutely charming. The wispy stamen and especially the stretched-out seedpods are the foundation of its common name: spider flower. They bloom from early summer until frost without any fuss. Flowers develop into slender seedpods that grow perpendicular to the main stem. New flowers continue to appear at the top, making the plant taller, more bizarre, and more wonderful with each passing day. There are many blooms at any one time, forming a large sphere. The bright medium-green leaves are palmately lobed, which means they resemble rounded fingers. Spider flower does well planted in an iris bed. By the time the irises have taken their last bow, the foliage of the spider flowers will be lush, with flowers not far behind.

Other Common Name
Spider Plant

Bloom Period and Seasonal Color
Pink, white, or lavender blooms appear all summer.

Mature Height × Spread
6 ft. × 4 to 5 ft.

When, Where, and How to Plant
Sow seed indoors in late March or early April. Direct seed in late May. For best results, refrigerate seeds in a plastic bag with slightly damp peat moss for two weeks before sowing. Sow on the soil surface and keep at 70 to 75 degrees Fahrenheit. Germination takes ten to fourteen days. Plant out in early June, in a sunny location, but give plants plenty of room. Spider flowers do fine in average soils and tolerate dry soils. They prefer a pH of 6 to 7, so you probably have to add lime. Space 1 to 2 feet apart. Spider flower often reseeds.

Growing Tips
Spider flowers rarely require watering. Fertilize lightly at planting and perhaps once mid season to encourage flower production. Heavy feeding may result in excessive leaf growth. If you want the plants to self-sow, remember to let the seedlings come up. Be aware that a pre-emergent weed killer used in the spring to prevent weeds will effectively prevent spider flowers from germinating as well. Thin seedlings to 1 foot apart.

Care
If you do not want the plants to self-sow, remove the wispy seedpods before they open. If you have selected a location for self-sowing, don't do anything. Spider flowers have few if any problems.

Companion Planting and Design
Try spider flowers as the back of a border. If you scatter these plants throughout the peony or iris beds, they will take over when the perennials finish. They have tremendous drive-by impact and are excellent for planting along the road. You can also plant a large bed at the back of the property and let them go crazy. Spider flowers make impressive cut flowers. As side shoots develop, you will have more, but smaller, blooms. Sometimes secondary flowers blossom while the primary cluster is intact.

Did You Know?
Spider flower seedlings can come up with such enthusiasm that you may think they are weeds. Look for the unusual palmate leaves to sort the wheat from the chaff.

Strawflower
Helichrysum bracteatum

When, Where, and How to Plant
Start seed indoors in early April or direct seed in late May. Sow seed on the soil surface. Provide light and maintain at 65 to 75 degrees Fahrenheit. Germination will take place in five to twenty days. Plant potted plants in late May to early June. Strawflowers will tolerate poor soils and are great for planting at the shore. They are not fussy and do fine in average sandy soil with a pH of 6 to 7. Plant short varieties 8 to 10 inches apart and tall ones up to 18 inches apart.

Growing Tips
Water transplants and fertilize at planting. After that, strawflowers rarely need water or fertilizer. They are very drought tolerant.

Care
If you like larger blooms, remove all but one developing flower bud per plant. If you leave the plants in the garden, they may reseed the following year. Self-sowing is more likely in sandy soil. Strawflowers are pest free.

Companion Planting and Design
Plant tall types of strawflowers at the back of the border. Use smaller types in mixed borders, rock gardens, and containers. They are excellent cut fresh, and so, they can join marigolds, zinnias, gladiolus, and snapdragons in the cutting bed. A mixed planting of strawflowers, celosia, and globe amaranth provides an abundance of material for drying. To do this, cut the flowers just before they open fully. Remove the leaves, bundle five or six together with a rubber band, and hang upside down in a warm, dry, dark place.

Did You Know?
Strawflower's rich shades of yellow, orange, gold, and red can be stunning. I once visited a farm in Bergen County that had a field of flowers to cut for the farm stand. There was an enormous bed of strawflowers in the field, and the sun streamed through the beautiful patch. As I looked through the flowers, I could clearly see the New York skyline. It was breathtaking.

Strawflower is an old-fashioned flower that fits perfectly in today's world. It is pretty in the garden and is one of the best flowers for drying. Even when fresh, the flowers have a dry, papery quality. Strawflowers bloom in many colors, though all of them hint at the colors of fall. There are many shades of yellow, gold, orange, bronze, and red, as well as a few shades of white and pink. Each flower has a central disc that is sometimes hidden by the petals. The medium-green leaves are two to five inches long and strap-like. The plants branch but maintain a very stiff upright habit.

Other Common Names
Everlasting, Immortelle

Bloom Period and Seasonal Color
Flowers all summer in a variety of colors.

Mature Height × Spread
2 to 3 ft. × 12 to 18 in.

Sunflower

Helianthus annuus

Everyone loves sunflowers. There is tremendous satisfaction in producing such spectacular results in a single gardening season. It touches that "Jack-and-the-Beanstalk" magical place in the hearts of all gardeners, but especially children. While classic yellow reigns supreme, varieties are available in dark red, orange, cream, and bicolor. Semi-double flower types are fun; full doubles look like giant pompons. Branching varieties make sensational cut flowers. In addition to being spectacular garden flowers, every part of these North American natives has value. The seeds, oils, flower buds, leaves, and even the inner stalk material has been harvested for specific uses. American Indians used sunflowers for everything from dye to medicine to soup. Sunflowers have all these qualities and are incredibly easy to grow, too.

Bloom Period and Seasonal Color
Late summer flowers in shades of yellow and gold with occasional dark red or cream.

Mature Height × Spread
12 ft. × 3 to 4 ft.

When, Where, and How to Plant
Direct seed in late May. Plant in a sunny location and cover seeds with $1/4$ inch of soil. Starting seed indoors doesn't offer much advantage as the seeds sprout and grow but plants will be set back after transplanting. Move volunteers while the plants are about 8 inches tall, taking a ball of soil with them. They grow almost anywhere, but a deep, rich, well-drained soil gives the best results. Sunflowers tolerate a pH of 5 to 7, so lime is seldom necessary. Seedlings pop up in ten to fourteen days. Thin to 12 inches for shorter types and 24 to 36 inches for tall ones.

Growing Tips
Water transplants thoroughly to help get them established. Water deeply whenever the soil gets dry. Fertilize at planting and side-dress with fertilizer midseason.

Care
Pinch branching varieties to encourage bushiness. To save seed, wait until all the disc flowers have been pollinated. Bees can be seen pollinating as they work from the center of the disc in a spiral. Cover the flower heads with a paper bag and tie around the stem. After the seeds develop, cut the head. Remove the seeds for storage or keep intact. Smear peanut butter on the surface of a dried flower head and hang it in a tree as a winter treat for birds. Sunflowers have few, if any, problems.

Companion Planting and Design
The shorter, branching types work in the back of a border or cutflower garden, but those that reach 8 or 12 feet may be difficult to mix with other flowers. A single plant becomes a focal point. Plant along the road for drive-by impact or to hide an ugly fence, or group sunflowers in a bed by themselves.

Did You Know?
Squirrels like sunflower seeds almost as much as birds do. I once saw a squirrel hanging by its toes from the edge of a large flower head weighted down by seeds. The squirrel did stomach curls to reach up and grab the seeds and ate them dangling upside down.

Verbena

Verbena × hybrida

When, Where, and How to Plant

Think carefully before growing verbena from seed. The germination rate is never great, sometimes very poor, and can take up to three months. If you are determined to try, sow seeds after two weeks of refrigeration in damp peat moss and cover lightly with soil. Keep them dark at 65 to 75 degrees Fahrenheit. Do not direct seed. Plant out potted plants in late May in any sunny spot. Take advantage of its heat tolerance by growing verbena in extra-hot areas, such as next to a driveway or in front of a south or west facing wall. Verbena will give its best performance in better soils. It requires a pH of 6 to 7, so applying lime to the soil is recommended. Spacing varies, but 12 inches apart is usually suitable.

Growing Tips

Water and fertilize at planting. Water deeply when the ground becomes dry. Fertilize midseason for a boost. Containers need water on a regular basis.

Care

Pinch young plants to make them branch and become bushy. Regular removal of dead flower clusters will keep flower production enthusiastic. Spider mites and leafminers can both be problems which get worse in hot weather. A strong spray of water, especially on the underside of the leaves, will reduce mite populations. Remove leaves infested with leafminers and dispose of with the trash. If problems persist, it may be necessary to resort to an insecticide. Be sure to use one that is labeled for both the pest and the plant. Follow label directions to the letter.

Companion Planting and Design

Use verbena as a summer ground cover. If you direct the branches to bare spots and pin them to the soil, they will root and fill in gaps. It's lovely flowing over a wall or wandering in a rock garden. Use as edging if you have room for it to spread; it can be lovely softening railroad ties, bricks, or even sidewalks. Verbena is an excellent container plant by itself, or mix with salvia, petunias, or dwarf marigolds.

Did You Know?

Verbena is an old-fashioned flower and was considered a favorite in Victorian gardens. In the Victorian language of flowers, a white verbena means "pure and guileless." A scarlet verbena means "sensibility."

Verbena is underappreciated. The flowers are vivid, and the plants bloom all summer with little complaint in the hottest, driest weather. The individual flowers are five petaled stars. Those with a contrasting white eye are very flashy; the solids create rich mats of color. Though the plants stay low to the ground, the stems get long as they spread out. Verbena makes a surprisingly effective cut flower. The grayish-green leaves are opposite, two to four inches long, narrow, and coarsely toothed. The leaves are hardly noticed, especially since verbena's brilliant flowers attract all the attention. Verbena is almost as tolerant of brutal growing conditions as portulaca. Try using these two plants in the same spot in alternate years for a little diversity.

Other Common Names

Vervain, Sweet Verbena, Rose Verbena

Bloom Period and Seasonal Color

Flowers all summer in bright colors, including white, red, yellow, and purple.

Mature Height × Spread

6 to 12 in. × 12 to 18 in.

Wishbone Flower
Torenia fournieri

This shade-loving plant provides an alternative to the workhorse shade plants, impatiens and begonias. The blooms are not as bright and showy, but they are lovely little flowers that are produced in large numbers all summer. In the fall, torenia can be brought indoors as a potted plant. Place it in a sunny window, and it will add color well into winter. Wishbone flower gets its name from the arrangement of the threadlike stamens and bulbous anthers (the male flower part). Together they form what looks like a tiny wishbone. The flower itself resembles a smaller version of the snapdragon flower. The petals are variegated; often the upper lip is one color and the lower lip a darker shade or a different color altogether, with a yellow throat. New varieties have larger, showier flowers.

Other Common Names
Blue Torenia, Blue Wings

Bloom Period and Seasonal Color
Usually violet, blue, white, or rose with a yellow throat, all summer.

Mature Height × Spread
12 in. × 6 in.

When, Where, and How to Plant
Sow seed indoors in early April or outdoors in late May. Seed requires light to germinate; sow on the soil surface at 70 to 75 degrees Fahrenheit. Germination time varies; you may see tiny leaves in anywhere from seven to thirty days. Plant transplants in late May in a cool, shady spot. In the garden, be sure to add plenty of organic matter when you prepare the bed for planting. Torenia needs moist, well-drained soil. Space plants 6 to 8 inches apart.

Growing Tips
Water at planting and regularly throughout the season, especially during hot weather. Fertilize at planting and in midsummer.

Care
Pinch young plants to encourage bushiness. Spent flowers drop on their own. A light pruning midsummer may revitalize the plants. Pot up a few plants from the garden in early September. This will give them a chance to get acclimated before you bring them indoors in early October. They will bloom for months before fading away. Torenia has no serious insect or disease problems.

Companion Planting and Design
Its compact size makes it a good choice for shaded rock gardens. In a woodland setting, it will mix well with ferns and hostas. Use it to edge a shady path or in the front of a mixed border, or tuck it under azaleas and rhododendrons. Plant under shade trees or in any shady nook that needs color. Wishbone flower makes a great container plant for a shady spot in the summer or a sunny window in wintertime.

Did You Know?
Torenia is native to Vietnam and not yet common in New Jersey gardens. I assumed its introduction to North American gardens could be traced to the time of the Vietnam War. However, I found torenia in a 1937 Inter-State Nursery catalog (for the bargain price of 10 cents a pack). It is more likely they are overlooked because they require warmer weather to bloom and don't look like much in cell packs at the nursery.

Zinnia

Zinnia elegans

When, Where, and How to Plant

Start seed indoors in early April. Barely cover seeds in the flats and keep at 70 to 80 degrees Fahrenheit. They should germinate in a week or less, though it may take up to twenty-four days. Plant out transplants or direct seed in late May. Direct seeding is usually just as effective. Plant zinnias in any sunny spot. In the garden, zinnias will appreciate extra organic matter, though they will grow in almost any soil. Adding lime is recommended since zinnias require a pH of 6 to 7. Spacing is variety dependent, but don't crowd them. Good air circulation is essential.

Growing Tips

Water regularly, but to prevent mildew problems, avoid getting water on the leaves. Fertilize when plants start to bloom.

Care

Regular deadheading will keep the flowers blooming and the plants attractive. Watch out for powdery mildew, zinnia's one real problem. Spray with an appropriate fungicide at the first sign of white blotches on the leaves.

Companion Planting and Design

Use tiny varieties as edging and in containers. Try intermediate zinnias in a mixed border, cutflower garden, larger containers, in front of larger foundation plantings, along fences and buildings, or at the base of the mailbox. The tallest plants should be in the back of a row or bed, with clear access to them for cutting bouquets. Zinnias are stiff, which detracts from aging, taller varieties. These show best if something smaller with a looser habit grows around them, such as petunias or dwarf snapdragons.

Did You Know?

This remarkable plant is a native American. It can be found from Colorado down to Mexico. More colorful versions come from South America. The Aztec Indians had long been cultivating the flowers by the time the Spanish came upon them. Zinnias traveled to Europe in the 1700s, where breeders began to develop the almost limitless number of strains and cultivars we have today. Crossing and backcrossing continues, and in recent years even green flowers have appeared in the cultivar 'Envy'.

If you had nothing but zinnias in your garden, you would still have a full plate. They are essential, dependable, and magnificent, like the air and the sun and the rain. The wonderful smile-generating flowers are what make them treasures. Zinnias are one of the easiest flowers to grow and are great for beginners, especially children. Even gardeners who have come to know Mother Nature on a first name basis plant zinnias for their pure joy. In even the worst of seasons, zinnias will happily provide generous armfuls of flowers. Flowers can be anywhere from 3 feet tall and 6 inches across to 6 inches tall and 1 inch across. There are small flowers on tall stems and large flowers on compact plants. Singles, doubles, wavy-petaled cactus types, and pompons add more fun.

Other Common Name

Youth-and-old-age

Bloom Period and Seasonal Color

Many colors all summer, including pastels, vibrant shades, or bicolored.

Mature Height × Spread

3 ft. × 1 to 2 ft.

Bulbs, Corms, Rhizomes and Tubers *for New Jersey*

Bulbs, corms, rhizomes and tubers are some of the more magical aspects of the plant world. You take a little brown lumpy thing, stick it in the ground, wave a magic wand, and, POOF, you have flowers. A true bulb is technically a modified stem and has layers, like an onion. A tuber is a fleshy root, like a potato. A corm is part of a stem, underground like a bulb but solid like a tuber.

Fall is the time to plant many bulbs for flowers in the spring. It doesn't matter how many you plant, come spring you will always wish you had planted more. The actual planting is almost an act of faith. You know that if you plant these structures, you truly believe in your heart that spring will come. It is a hex sign against Old Man Winter. No matter how hard winter may try to hang on, these bulbs are going to push out of the ground and burst forth in spring. The thrill of seeing the tiny green tips poking up in spring and the first hint of purple crocus, sometimes right through the snow, is an incredible lift to sagging spirits. Winter doldrums fly out the window. It *proves* that spring is coming: the rebirth of life, a fresh start.

So Many Choices

It is hard to pick a favorite spring bulb. Crocus bloom first and thus are very powerful little flowers in the battle against winter. Plant hundreds, even thousands in your lawn. They will bloom a sea of color

Ring of Crocus

while the rest of the world barely stirs. By the time you need to mow the grass, they will be long gone. Add snowdrops, winter aconite, and miniature iris as an army to fight back winter.

Daffodils offer the next big push. Daffodils can go under shade trees since they bloom before the leaves come out. They will naturalize and spread; each year you will have more than the year before. Try pink ones, and butterfly flowers, and tiny 'Rip Van Winkle' in the rock garden. Daffodils are easy and make the best cut flowers. Mix them all together or plant a patch of a single kind.

Stunning Color with Tulips

The daffodil season overlaps the tulip season. There is nothing like tulips for an explosion of color. You get your biggest impact if you plant a mass of one kind. You get your longest season of bloom if you plant in small patches with carefully selected varieties for early- through late-season bloom. A big bed of one kind with patches scattered about gives you the best of both worlds. Watch out for bunnies, deer, and squirrels. Rabbits and deer will eat the flower buds and maybe the leaves, too. Squirrels dig out the bulbs, but this can be avoided by laying a large gauge chicken wire over the bulbs. The flowers will come up between the wires without much difficulty. Deer and rabbits may limit your bulb options to daffodils, crown imperials, and many of the alliums, all of which must taste awful since they are generally left alone. When planning your tulip beds, be aware that tulips do not naturalize and need to be replaced at least every three to five years. If you plant by the hundreds, this is a lot of work.

Tulipmania!

The history of tulips is worth mentioning. They are of mysterious beginnings, have been the cause of wars, created major economic collapse, and prevented starvation for many during WWII.

Tulips appeared in Turkey in about 1554 where they were under cultivation in the Sultan's garden. Less than one hundred years later, one of the biggest economic collapses in the history of the modern world took place. Tulips had become such a craze that they were being sold on speculation. Bulbs were sold and resold, sometimes before they had ever bloomed. Prices for a single bulb were phenomenal. One bulb was traded for 12 acres of land. When this artificial economic structure collapsed in 1637, many people suffered tremendous financial loss. This catastrophe has been equated with the stock market crash of 1929. Although tulips lost favor as a result, breeding and selection continued, particularly in Holland but also in Europe and America. The tulip went through another crisis during the German occupation of Holland during World War II. Tulip bulbs were ground and mixed with flour for food. The Dutch were able to spare the best varieties so that after the war the tulip industry resumed its growth. All of that, and they are beautiful, too.

Seasons of Beauty

Follow your tulips with ornamental alliums. These are close cousins of the onions we eat but are grown for the fabulous flowers, not the bulbs. Yes, many do smell like onions, but this is a small price to pay for long lived, easy care flowers throughout the month of June. Mix up your spring display with crown imperials, foxtail lilies, hyacinth, grape hyacinth, scilla, and some other little secrets like glory-of-the-snow and dogtooth violets.

When spring warms to summer, you enter the domain of the lilies. True lilies have bulbs that look like artichokes and flowers that look like the brass instruments of Glenn Miller's band. Asiatic lilies open in June, Aurelian hybrids in July, and Oriental hybrids finish the season in August. Plant them once and watch them return year after year.

The season ends with fall blooming bulbs such as the true fall blooming crocus and the *Colchicum* species called autumn crocus. The pink flowers of the hardy cyclamen are treasures in the October garden and the yellow *Sternbergia* bloom in September and October.

All this, and then there is another universe of summer bulbs to plant in spring and store in winter. The gorgeous calla lily and the giant canna fall into this group. There are no better cut flowers to bring to a dinner party than an armful of gladiolus or a basket full of dinnerplate dahlias. The exotic Peruvian daffodils look like nothing else on this planet or any other, and the enormous leaves of the *Colocasia* or elephant ears allow you to take a bit of tropical rainforest and transplant it into your backyard.

The Importance of Healthy Soil

Bulbs are like nothing else in gardening. You can get spectacular results in a very short period of time. One of the most critical components of bulb gardening is good soil preparation. You want to be able to enjoy your bulbs for many years to come. One of the important ways to do that is to get them off to the very best possible start. Good drainage is critical, but they also require a significant amount of soil moisture. That means adding copious amounts of organic matter and often double digging the soil, especially in heavier ground. Preparing an entire bed is more effective than working each individual planting hole, but in beds with other established plants you have to do the best you can in small patches.

Bone meal is sometimes added during soil preparation as an enduring fertilizer that breaks down and releases its nutrients slowly over time. After planting, the use of 5-10-5 fertilizer in the spring or a bulb fertilizer in the fall will encourage the longest possible enjoyment of the bulbs you have in the ground. Always allow the foliage to ripen and yellow before removal to give plants the greatest chance to be revitalized for the following year. Planting depth and spacing varies from species to species as well as for different varieties of the same species. This information is generally contained in the package or shipped with the bulbs when you purchase them.

Mulch your bulbs for winter protection, summer weed control, and moisture retention. If green leaves pop up prematurely over the winter or early spring, this is rarely a problem, but a heavy mulch can prevent it from being an issue.

The non-hardy bulbs which must be dug in the fall will benefit from the same careful soil preparation, but rotating planting beds and fresh soil preparation each spring allows a bit of extra TLC that is not easily given to long term, hardy bulbs.

All combined, the mixture of hardy spring bulbs from tiny crocus to dramatic alliums, with summer bulbs (both hardy lilies and outrageous but tender bulbs such as *Hymenocallis*, Peruvian daffodils), followed by fall blooming crocus as well as other well kept secrets, can provide color from late winter to late fall. The diversity of size, color, flower type, and drama is vast. So consider moving beyond the lovely but safe haven of daffodils and tulips. There is a world of bulbs just waiting for your imagination to kick in.

Cactus-Flowered Dahlias

Autumn Crocus
Colchicum autumnale

Colchicum is a wonderful surprise for the autumn garden. It lasts for years and blooms bright pink when most of the garden is turning the earthy tones of fall. All the plant parts of an autumn crocus are poisonous, so you will need to wear gloves when handling them. Despite its common name, the flowers look a lot like oversized crocus flowers, but are not. The flowers and bulbs of crocus are much smaller than those of Colchicum. One really fun aspect of autumn crocus (true crocus, too!) is they are planted in summer, as late as early September, to have flowers that same autumn. The blooming becomes more prolific as the bulbs mature. In spring the leaves appear looking like a loose head of lettuce. Foliage dies in the summer, and bulbs lay dormant until flowers pop out in fall.

Other Common Name
Meadow Saffron

Bloom Period and Seasonal Color
White or pink flowers in September or October.

Mature Height × Spread
6 to 10 in. × up to 12 in.

When, Where, and How to Plant
Colchicum plants are poisonous; be sure to wear gloves. Plant Colchicum during summer dormancy. Plant any time from when the foliage dies back until early September, but be sure to do so before the plants start to bloom. Plant colchicum in ordinary, well-drained garden soil in a sunny to lightly shaded site; they do best when left in their original spot. Place the bottom of the bulb 3 to 4 inches deep in well-drained soil. Space bulbs 6 to 9 inches apart. Leave enough space around the bulbs for the substantial spring foliage. You can also start seed from the previous year's flowers. Seed-grown plants may sit dormant for one or two years, blooming after three or four.

Growing Tips
Water at planting. They are dormant during the heat of summer, so they rarely require additional water. These plants are hardy, but a layer of mulch is suggested. Fertilize the bulbs in early spring (see chapter introduction).

Care
The most challenging part of maintaining autumn crocus is tolerating the foliage when it starts to get ugly, which usually occurs in June. Plants can be divided during the summer dormant period and will take two years to bloom. Slugs can be a problem. Hand picking is one control option—ask your garden center for more.

Companion Planting and Design
Plant in rock gardens or where the plants can be appreciated up close. Remember spring foliage will take up more space than the flowers. Autumn crocus works nicely planted beneath a ground cover of periwinkle or with low ferns.

Did You Know?
All the plant parts of colchicum are poisonous, so always wear gloves when handling. The chemical "colchicine" is derived from the plant for medicinal purposes, but it is highly toxic even in small doses. It can be absorbed through the skin. As a novelty, you can place a dormant autumn crocus bulb on a plate or in a cup, where it will bloom without soil or water. Make sure it is out of reach of pets and children.

Calla Lily

Zantedeschia spp.

When, Where, and How to Plant

Plant out in spring after danger of frost has passed. Mid-May is generally safe in New Jersey. Choose a location where your callas will get partial shade. Plant where you will be able to appreciate the flowers up close. Callas require a soil with good drainage. One advantage to digging tender bulbs in the fall is that no location has to be permanent. If you try a spot that turns out to be less than ideal, choose somewhere else the following year. Dig deeply to ensure adequate drainage and add plenty of organic matter. Plant roots 3 inches deep and 6 to 12 inches apart. Apply a heavy layer of organic mulch over the top.

Growing Tips

Water at planting and regularly during the summer. Fertilize at planting with 5-10-5. Be sure to mix fertilizer in thoroughly with amendments during soil preparation.

Care

Dig plants after a light frost has damaged leaves (usually in mid-October). Gently remove much of the excess soil. Allow the plants to dry in a shady spot for two or three days. Make sure they are not exposed to frost but receive good air movement. Pack in slightly damp peat moss and store in a dry place at 40 to 50 degrees Fahrenheit until planting time. Rootrot is the only serious problem and is generally eliminated with good drainage.

Companion Planting and Design

Planting annual lobelia all around callas can make for an outstanding combination. Lobelia's delicate flowers and foliage complement calla's big leaves and flowers, and they will thrive in the partial shade callas prefer.

Did You Know?

My parents were married in 1934. Mother's wedding picture hangs in our hallway. In her arms is an absolutely enormous bunch of large white calla lilies. The flowers are said to represent "magnificent beauty." Every time I look at that picture, I understand why.

In New Jersey, calla lilies must be grown as tender bulbs. Plant in the spring and dig in the fall for winter storage. Tender bulbs are tedious to dig and store, but calla lilies are so spectacular they are worth the effort. The classic white calla is Z. aethiopica. Very few things in this world are close to perfection—this pure white calla is one of those things. The classic calla is unfortunately one of the more difficult to grow. Winter storage is tricky. Starting with fresh rhizomes each spring might be simpler. To have white callas from one year to the next, try Z. albomaculata. The foliage is spotted and the lovely white flowers are smaller versions of the classic. Because beauty is subjective, every gardener must decide which calla is the most exquisite.

Other Common Name
Lily of the Nile

Bloom Period and Seasonal Color
White, pink, or yellow blooms (or many new shades of unusual colors) in summer.

Mature Height × Spread
1 to 4 ft. × up to 3 ft.

Canna

Canna × generalis

New Jersey gardeners generally treat cannas as summer bulbs. New varieties are listed as hardy through Zone 7, but many references only credit them as far north as Zone 8. The fantastic growth cannas achieve in a single season, up to eight feet, is so extraordinary that the hassle of digging them up in the fall is bearable. Cannas look "tropical." They appear to best advantage when planted in big patches by themselves. New selections may have very large petals on compact plants, some reaching only two to three feet. The big banana leaves are usually green but can also be a dark bronze. New varieties include variegated foliage. Variegated flowers start one color then open to a completely different color. Cannas are giant workhorse plants that are quickly evolving into Shetland ponies.

Other Common Name
Indian Shot

Bloom Period and Seasonal Color
Showy spikes in yellow, pink, red, or orange all summer.

Mature height × Spread
8 ft. × variable spread

When, Where, and How to Plant
Plant cannas after danger of frost, usually in early to mid-May. Plant in full sun. Prepare the soil deeply, adding plenty of organic matter. Cannas require constant moisture but don't do well in soggy soil. Plant 4 inches deep and 18 inches apart. An organic mulch helps maintain soil moisture and keep weeds under control until plants are thick enough to squeeze out the weedlings themselves.

Growing Tips
Cannas benefit from a regular application of fertilizer (see chapter introduction), but in better soils they will do fine with just a spring boost. Water deeply and regularly in hot or dry weather.

Care
The nifty little spherical seedpods eventually become unattractive. Remove dead flower stalks as the flowers fade, but don't cut too far back. The next flowers emerge just below the one that is finishing up. Watch out for Japanese beetles, who love cannas. After frost, cut back the stalks and dig up the tubers. Allow to surface dry and store in slightly damp peat moss at 40 degrees Fahrenheit. Grow them in a container for a bit of the tropics "à la terra cotta" on your deck.

Companion Planting and Design
Mounded, circular plantings of cannas in the middle of the yard or driveway can be very effective. Plant around the compost pile. The tubers will thrive while hiding the pile. A border planting, in front of a wall, across the front of the property, or next to a building will be dramatic, elegant, and a little outrageous. Smaller cannas are a better choice with more traditional garden flowers out in the yard.

Did You Know?
If you want to experiment, dig out and store all the tubers you will need for next spring, throwing in a few extra to make up for winter loss. Cover the rest with 6 to 8 inches of wood chips. If tubers are close to the house on the sunny south side, they may overwinter just fine. If it works, you have eliminated a big job. If not, plant the ones you stored.

Crocus
Crocus spp.

When, Where, and How to Plant
Plant spring-blooming crocus in fall any time from mid-September until Thanksgiving. Plant in sun or partial shade. The earliest flowers appear in warm, sunny locations. Crocus is not fussy about planting conditions but requires good drainage. Plant in groups or drifts to get the best effect. Good soil preparation is beneficial, though that may be difficult if you are planting through sod. Make a deep hole and refill it with improved soil. Plant corms 3 to 4 inches deep and 3 to 4 inches apart.

Growing Tips
Water at planting and throughout the fall if dry. Fertilize with bonemeal or bulb fertilizer in the fall.

Care
You can leave crocus in the ground for years. Each plant will spread into a thick clump. Crocus will be happiest, however, if you divide the clumps every three or four years. Divide in late spring when leaves are fading but are still attached; replant immediately. You can also divide in early fall, though the bulbs may be difficult to locate. Crocus are virtually pest free.

Companion Planting and Design
Plant bulbs in the lawn right through the sod or plant groups of crocus under deciduous trees and shrubs; they will be gone before the trees leaf out. Crocus are ideal for rock gardens. You can plant them with peonies and irises, or in the rose garden. Crocuses fit in anywhere and everywhere. While mixed colors are very pretty up close, large patches of one color are far more dramatic from a distance.

Did You Know?
While crocus are by far the most popular of the early spring bulbs, there are other bulbs to add diversity. The miniature iris blooms very early in the season and has large flowers for such a little plant. It may even beat the crocus to bloom, though it does not spread and so never has quite the same impact. Winter aconite has cheerful yellow flowers that resemble a cross between a crocus and a buttercup. The foliage is very pretty. Snowdrops are white and look a little like dainty, drooping airplane propellers. Both naturalize readily.

Crocus are the first line of attack to free the world from winter's icy grip. Gardeners are building fires and looking for lost mittens while crocus prepare for the primeval battle. Onward, upward they fight. Strong. Steady. Brave. A few get trampled by the dog. Another succumbs to a pair of snow boots. It doesn't stop them. They keep coming. Then it happens. They burst forth like a cannon shot, and winter goes down with a crash. The little soliders wave their victory flags in a sea of color. For just a second our hearts stop. The crocus are blooming! The crocus are blooming! It doesn't matter what feeble attempts winter will make now. Crocus have taken the ground, and the battle is won. Spring is ours! After that, any flower announcing spring is yesterday's news.

Bloom Period and Seasonal Color
White, yellow, lilac, purple, or striped cup-shaped flowers appear at the first sign of spring.

Mature Height × Spread
4 to 12 in. × 12 in.

Crown Imperial
Fritillaria imperialis

The crown imperial looks like something Mother Nature would wear to Mayfest. The circle of blooms appears on top of three- to four-foot stems with a tuft of short pointy leaves poking out through the center of the ring. The flowers resemble upside-down tulips, and the foliage is often compared to lilies. The short, swordlike leaves emerge all around the stem like lily leaves, only wider. The leaves appear from ground level to about two feet up the stem, which is bare from that point up to the top, where the flowers form a "crown." Crown imperials are native to Persia (now Iran) and were introduced to Europe in the 1500s. They are old-fashioned garden favorites that are long lived once they become established. The flowers are tall and regal.

Other Common Name
Imperial Fritillary

Bloom Period and Seasonal Color
A ring of red, yellow, or orange blooms appearing in April.

Mature Height × Spread
3 to 4 ft. × 1 ft.

When, Where, and How to Plant
Plant bulbs in the fall as soon as possible after they arrive in the mail or the same day they are purchased locally. Crown imperials are hardy to Zone 5, but to ensure that you have flowers and not just leaves, plant in a spot out of intense wind and cold. A little protection from midday sun is preferred. Prepare the soil down at least 12 inches and backfill the hole with a bed of pebbles and loose soil. Good drainage is critical. Plant the bulb 6 inches deep. Be very careful not to injure any roots that may have begun to grow during shipping. The top of the bulb has a natural depression.

Growing Tips
Fertilize every fall (see chapter introduction for information on fertilizing). Water in spring if the ground is dry.

Care
Mulch heavily for winter protection. Remove the flower stalks as they yellow. Crown imperials are generally long lived but are subject to botrytis, which can cause the plants to shrivel up in spring. Just replace and plant elsewhere if it appears. It's not worth spraying for. Be careful to ensure good drainage at the time of planting to help avoid this problem.

Companion Planting and Design
These plants get tall, so plant the bulbs at the back of the spring garden. Remember: crown imperials do not do well if relocated, so pick a permanent spot. Plant a few together both for appearance and the well-being of the bulbs. They seem to do better in groups. To camouflage the fading leaves, plant Asiatic lilies. Their foliage is similar enough to blend with the crown imperial, and they bloom in June, just in time to draw attention away from the crown imperials as they decline. *Monardas* (bee-balm) will grow bushy enough to hide the foliage and does quite well with midday shade.

Did You Know?
Crown imperials are not as commonplace now as they were at one time. Perhaps they went out of favor because of the way they smell, which is something like skunk cabbage. The odor is supposed to be extremely effective in repelling rodents, moles in particular. Deer avoid them also.

Daffodil
Narcissus spp.

When, Where, and How to Plant
Plant from mid-September until Thanksgiving in well-drained soil. They do best in sun but can take some shade, especially light shade from trees whose leaves have not yet emerged. Daffodils do best when they are left in one place; provide extra soil preparation before planting to get them off to a good start. Add organic matter and bonemeal at the time of planting. Don't break up bulbs that have multiple stems—each "nose" will produce another flower. Daffodils look best planted in bunches. Plant 6 to 8 inches down from the base of the bulb and 6 to 8 inches apart.

Growing Tips
Fertilize with bonemeal at planting and with 5-10-5 in the early spring. Water if the spring weather turns unseasonably hot and summer-like.

Care
Remove dead flowers as soon as they get ugly. You don't want to waste plant energy on producing seed that will never be planted. Allow the foliage to mature before you cut it off. This year's leaves feed the bulb for next year's flowers. Divide bulbs when they become crowded and bloom less prolifically. Lift the bulbs as the last of the foliage fades, then divide and replant immediately. You can divide in the fall, but locating the bulbs when there are no leaves is tricky. Daffodils are marvelously free of pests.

Companion Planting and Design
Daffodils (the miniature varieties in particular) are terrific for rock gardens. They work well in borders, mixed with shrubs as part of a foundation planting, scattered in a meadow, at the edge of woods, or in any nook that needs a splash of spring color. Daffodils and daylilies make an excellent combination; daylilies will conceal the daffodils' aging leaves.

Did You Know?
Neither deer nor rabbits will eat these plants. This makes daffodils invaluable in those parts of the state where deer can be a major problem. They must taste really horrid, since deer will eat almost anything if they are hungry enough.

Daffodils are joyful flowers. They have a simple elegance that is irresistible. The flowers appear early, but not so early that you can't enjoy a walk in the garden to appreciate them. Daffodils are among the first spring blooming garden flowers that can be cut for an arrangement. A bunch in a vase, leaning this way and that, radiates cheerfulness all around. The flowers are long lived in a vase, even longer lived in the garden, and the plants seem to last forever. Daffodils naturalize, or spread, and eventually seem to have been planted by Mother Nature herself. Since the flowers bloom before foliage emerges on the trees, bulbs can even be planted under shade trees. They will bloom right through a groundcover of myrtle, creating a pretty display while the myrtle is in bloom. The selection of available daffodils is extraordinary.

Other Common Names
Jonquil, Narcissus

Bloom Period and Seasonal Color
Early to mid-spring blooms; usually yellow and white but can be cream, orange, pink, or even green.

Mature Height × Spread
4 to 20 in. × variable spread

Dahlia
Dahlia hybrids

Dahlias include many different flower types, from small single blossoms suitable for containers to enormous "dinner plate" flowers that reach eleven inches across. Some require staking to hold the weight of the fully double blooms. There are pompon types, formal and informal doubles, and spiderlike cactus-flowered dahlias. The simpler types include single, anemone, and "collarette." Smaller dahlias generally produce lots of blooms. The largest may produce only fifteen blooms per season. A single huge bloom is very dramatic. Dahlia tubers resemble bunches of skinny potatoes. They are not tolerant of cold weather and must be dug and stored after the first frost. The flowers are so intense that once you grow them, you will do whatever it takes to include these beauties in your garden.

Bloom Period and Seasonal Color
Blooms all summer in many colors, including pink, white, cream, yellow, and red.

Mature Height × Spread
15 in. to 6 ft. × variable spread

When, Where, and How to Plant
Plant dahlias in mid-spring after the soil has warmed. Planting by April 30 will give you early blooms without much risk of a setback from the cold. Don't plant later than mid-June or you will miss a large part of the blooming period. Plant in full sun with excellent drainage. Add a significant amount of organic matter. The depth and spacing of dahlias depends on the type and is usually given on the package. Larger varieties will require staking. Staking should be done at the time of planting to avoid damaging the growing roots later. Dahlias also benefit from a dose of fertilizer at planting time, such as 5-10-5 or a water-soluble fertilizer according to directions.

Growing Tips
Keep plants well watered during the season. Take care to not over feed. Excess nitrogen makes for lush foliage and fewer blooms.

Care
Mulch for weed control. Cultivation and even hand weeding can damage surface feeder roots. Remove faded blooms when they get ugly. Dig tubers after the tops become frosted. Remove excess soil and allow tubers to dry for several days where they are protected from frost. Store over the winter in a cool, dry location. Divide tubers in spring at the time of planting. Aphids may need control. Check with your Cooperative Extension Service for currently recommended insecticides.

Companion Planting and Design
The largest flower types are difficult to blend with other flowers but look truly sensational in a bed by themselves. They can be effective in the back of a border. The smaller varieties are much more flexible; use them in borders or in shrubbery beds, plant them in containers or mix them with annuals or perennials. Cut almost fully open blossoms in the early morning for indoor use, placing in warm to hot tap water and allowing the water to cool.

Did You Know?
While all dahlias are lovely, the dinner plate varieties are like nothing else. A single flower is spectacular, and a bouquet is unbelievable. Six plants in a bed take your breath away every time you walk by.

Dogtooth Violet
Erythronium americanum

When, Where, and How to Plant
Plant as soon as the corms are received in the fall—before they quickly dry out. Plant in part shade to deep shade in well-drained humusy soil that holds moisture but is never soggy. Soil preparation is very important. Dogtooth violets require excellent drainage with constant moisture. Add plenty of organic matter. Plant corms 3 inches deep and 4 to 5 inches apart. Take care not to let the corms dehydrate while handling them for planting. Use an organic mulch to keep the soil from drying out. Dogtooth violets can also be started from seed, but will take five years to bloom.

Growing Tips
Water at planting and whenever the soil gets dry. Fertilizer is seldom necessary, but an application of 5-10-5 or a water-soluble fertilizer in the early spring will be beneficial in poorer soils.

Care
Corms can be left in the ground for years. They prefer not to be divided and have no serious pest problems. Remove spent flowers to direct energy toward the plant rather than into the production of seed. Keep plants well watered during the summer, especially if it is hot and dry. If you must divide dogtooth violets, do it in late summer and replant immediately. Take care not to let the plants dry in the process.

Companion Planting and Design
Plant dogtooth violets at the edge of ponds or streams, along woodland paths, in shaded rock gardens, around azaleas and rhododendrons, or under needled evergreens. Tuck them into any shadowy nook that will benefit from a splash of color. They will blend beautifully with ferns, Jack-in-the-pulpits, trilliums, violets, and bloodroot.

Did You Know?
Years ago, someone brought me a sample of a pretty little woodland plant for identification. I was sure it was a dogtooth violet. My coworker was absolutely sure it was a trout lily. He had thirty years more experience than I, so I didn't want to argue. This was the first in a career-long state of confusion caused by the inconsistency of common names. It gets really complicated when botanical names are just as bad.

The dogtooth violet is a gentle woodland flower that thrives in moist, rich, humusy well-drained soil. When planted in the right spot, it will reward its keeper for years with dainty, care-free, long-lasting yellow flowers. This is not a plant for a big show. It is well suited to the shaded rock garden or to a naturalized woodland setting. It is delicate and small but quite noble, holding its shy, nodding flowers up on straight slender stems. It produces five to ten flowers per stem and is quite hardy. The flowers look more like tiny tiger lilies with oversized anthers than violets. The foliage is mottled or speckled in patterns that are supposed to resemble the scales of a trout. Perhaps trout lily is the best of the common names for this plant.

Other Common Names
Trout Lily, Fawn Lily, Yellow Adder's Tongue

Bloom Period and Seasonal Color
1 to 1 1/2 in. yellow flowers in April and May.

Mature Height × Spread
1 ft. × 6 to 12 in.

Fall Blooming Crocus
Crocus spp.

These happy little plants with cup-shaped flowers are particularly convenient to plant. They are available locally and in catalogs in late summer. Plant as late as the middle of September for flowers in a matter of weeks. Fall blooming crocus also naturalize, rewarding you for your efforts for many years to come. It is important that these fall crocus not be confused with autumn crocus, the common name for the Colchicum species. Flowers of Colchicum are similar in appearance but larger than true fall-blooming crocus. There are over twenty species of fall blooming crocus, but not all are hardy in New Jersey. In general, however, those commonly available will do just fine here in the Garden State. C. sativus, the saffron crocus, is one of the more popular species. It will do well in all but the cold northwest corner.

Bloom Period and Seasonal Color
Flowers with brightly colored stamens in white, pink, lilac, or blue appearing in September and October.

Mature Height × Spread
3 to 6 in. × 12 in.

When, Where, and How to Plant
Plant fall-blooming crocus in late summer or early fall, preferably by mid-September if you want to enjoy blooms the same season. Plant as soon as possible after receiving the corms. Choose a location where you can see the flowers up close, in full sun or light shade. Good drainage is critical. Add organic matter to loosen heavy soil. Clusters of the same variety will have more impact than a mixture of colors. Plant 3 inches deep and 4 inches apart.

Growing Tips
Water at planting and if the weather is unusually hot or dry in spring or fall. Fertilize with bone meal at planting and with 5-10-5 in the early spring.

Care
Crocuses should be divided every three or four years to keep them vigorous. They make new corms on top of the old ones and will eventually push their way up to the surface. It is very important that you allow the foliage to mature before cutting it back. Fall crocus are virtually pest free.

Companion Planting and Design
A swathe of fall blooming crocus will be visible from a distance, but if you are planting just a few, they need to be up close and personal. Rock gardens are an ideal location. Although fall blooming crocus naturalize and spread, they are not as suitable as their spring cousins are for lawn planting. They bloom while the lawn is actively growing, which can make mowing a problem.

Did You Know?
To harvest your own saffron, plant *C. sativus* corms (the saffron crocus) where they will be easily distinguished from other fall crocus. Check the patch daily while in bloom. The stigma is located in the center of the flower and is bulbous at the top. Pluck it out of the flowers while they are fresh. Allow the stigma to dry on a paper towel and then store it in a glass container in a cool, dry place. It takes thousands of flowers to make a pound of spice, but saffron is generally used in tiny amounts.

Flowering Onion

Allium spp.

When, Where, and How to Plant

Plant alliums in fall in full sun. Deep, sandy loam soil is best, but alliums are not particular; they tolerate dry soils better than many other bulbs. As a general rule, plant 2 to 3 times as deep as the height of the bulb itself. For specific instructions, check the packaging of the bulbs you have purchased. Loosen heavy soils by adding a 2:1 mixture of organic matter and sand. Avoid soggy soils.

Growing Tips

Fertilize in the spring (according to chapter introduction). Water only if the ground becomes excessively dry.

Care

Allium will die to the ground after blooming is over, but don't remove the foliage until it fades. The flowers can be cut for indoor use as fresh flowers, they can be cut fresh and then dried, or they can be dried on the plant and then cut. Alliums will naturalize or can be divided. Bulbs can stay in place for years, but divide them in the fall if they become overcrowded. Alliums are generally pest free.

Companion Planting and Design

The smaller species of allium snuggle well into rock gardens, but the colossal types need a spot all to themselves. They make excellent cut flowers, but many smell like onions. When cut fresh and dried upside down, they often retain their color.

Did You Know?

For years I had a patch of *A. giganteum* planted in front of my home. Every spring I waited impatiently to see the large magenta spheres appear, but every spring, just as the flowers were about to open they would disappear. I never saw those plants in full bloom. When I was moving, a police car stopped in front of the house. The officer informed me that it had been a little old lady who had been stealing my flowers, to take to church. He thought I would want to know. That's where my tulips had gone as well, but she always left some of those.

Flowering onions offer a little-known world of spring bulbs. They pick up right where tulips leave off and carry spring right into summer. Alliums include some of the best "Ooh" and "Aah" generators in the garden, with flowering clusters or spheres. The ten-inch spheres of 'Globemaster' are so flamboyant they could be from a Dr. Seuss book. A patch of A. giganteum will produce six-inch spheres on top of four-foot tall, very straight, very naked stems. Allium flowers last a long time. If left long enough, they will dry to a light brown and can be saved for dried arrangements. Not all alliums are large. The one inch A. caeruleum is a lovely shade of dusty blue that reaches eighteen inches. Smaller alliums produce flat clusters in white, pink, or yellow.

Bloom Period and Seasonal Color

White, pink, blue, magenta, or yellow flowers in May or June.

Mature Height × Spread

1 to 4 ft. × 12 in.

Gladiolus
Gladiolus × hortulanus

The common garden gladiolus is far from common in an aesthetic sense. Glads make outstanding cut flowers and are embarrassingly easy to grow. Their colors are any-where from subtle to vibrant. Three stems of its tall narrow spikes in a vase make a statement. A dozen is powerful. It is possible to have as many as fourteen flow-ers open on one stem at a time. Because of the successive bloom, each stem makes a very long-lasting cut flower. Today's glads have been crossed with so many species and cultivars for so many years that the origin is completely obscured. There are now hundreds of named varieties available. The newer tall ones do not require staking, even though they reach four feet. This is a big improve-ment. Smaller varieties reach only two to three feet.

Other Common Names
Garden Gladiolus, Corn Flag, Sword Lily

Bloom Period and Seasonal Color
Flowers in many colors appearing 65 to 100 days after planting.

Mature Height × Spread
2 to 5 ft. × 1 ft.

When, Where, and How to Plant
Start in late April to early May. Plant every two weeks until mid-July. Choose a sunny location with good drainage. Rotate your gladiolus beds each year to minimize disease. When taking corms out of storage, you may see the shriveled old corm at the base of a fresh, new corm. Twist off the old one and compost it. Small "cormlets" may be found around the corm. These will produce flowers in two to three years. Plant corms of taller varieties 4 to 5 inches down and 3 inches apart. Incorporate organic matter and fertilizer into the soil at planting.

Growing Tips
Do not toss fertilizer into the planting holes. It burns the corms. A sidedressing of fertilizer is recommended when the plants have five leaves (see chapter introduction for more on fertilizer). Water deeply once a week if the ground is dry.

Care
Keep weeds under control with organic mulch. Cut flowers when the first bud is fully open. Leave at least four leaves to nourish the corms. Remove blooms when they fade. The corms can be dug when the leaves have yellowed, usually about six weeks after flowering. It is not necessary to wait until frost. Cut the leaves back to 2 inches. Dig the corms, shake off the soil, and allow to dry for a few days, out of the sun where they will not freeze. Store at 40 degrees Fahrenheit in a dry location. If planted with good drainage, glads have few if any problems.

Companion Planting and Design
Glads, especially the tall ones, are difficult to blend with other garden flowers. Plant in rows for cut flowers or in groups of the same color in the back of a mixed flower garden. Five to ten of the same color make an attractive display.

Did You Know?
Gladiolus look spectacular all alone in a vase. Arranging is easy in a large vase with a narrow opening. This allows the stems to crisscross in the vase. The flowers will then fan out to show off the blooms. Try it—you will look like a pro.

When, Where, and How to Plant

Plant glory-of-the-snow in September or October, as soon as you have the bulbs in your possession. Plant in a location with sun or partial shade. Glory-of-the-snow needs moist soil with good drainage. The addition of copious organic matter will be beneficial, especially since the plants should not be disturbed for many years. Plant bulbs 3 inches deep and 2 to 3 inches apart. These small plants do best in clusters of at least twelve, preferably all of the same variety.

Growing Tips

Water at planting. A light application of 5-10-5 in early spring, but not while in bloom, may be beneficial.

Care

Glory-of-the-snow has few needs and prefers to be left undisturbed. Your biggest problem will be waiting for them to come into their own. It doesn't bloom well its first year, so be patient and be sure not to move it too soon. The results are worth the wait.

Companion Planting and Design

Rock gardens are ideal, but any place where the plants will not be disturbed is fine. They look particularly lovely when mixed with white snowdrops, *Galanthus*, which bloom about the same time. Since glory-of-the-snow tolerates a bit of shade, it can be planted under deciduous shrubs such as forsythia or spirea for early color. It also does well as a mat beneath the upright foliage of early daffodils. Glory-of-the-snow is an excellent choice for an open woodland-type setting where it can naturalize undisturbed.

Did You Know?

Glory-of-the-snow was discovered in 1842 in a mountain meadow in Turkey. The genus name *Chionodoxa* is Greek for "glory-of-the-snow." The plant was not introduced to England until 1877, making it a relatively new introduction to cultivation. There are less common white and pink varieties. Its close relative, *C. sardensis*, has darker blue flowers without the white center. This one is native to Asia Minor.

Glory-of-the-snow is a tiny plant treasured for its very early blooms. It pokes through frozen ground with gutsy determination, sometimes even through snow, which accounts for its common name. It makes a good partner for early crocus as it battles back Old Man Winter. It is extremely hardy and produces very blue flowers, about five to a cluster. Once it gets established, glory-of-the-snow will naturalize and settle in for the long haul. The sweet blue color is scarce at any time of the year and especially appreciated against a backdrop of snow. If undisturbed, they eventually provide a solid mat of blue. It is best not to disturb them when they get thick and wonderful looking.

Other Common Name
Snow Glories

Bloom Period and Seasonal Color
Blue flower with a white center, appearing in March.

Mature Height × Spread
3 to 6 in. × 2 to 4 in.

Grape Hyacinth

Muscari armeniacum

Grape hyacinths are free spirited flowers. The blooms are shaped like tiny bells and are slightly fragrant with a fine texture and thick density. The classic grape hyacinth is treasured for its rare true blue color. They require almost no attention once established and will come back year after year with good cheer. They make a fabulous combination with daffodils. Their color with the daffs' pristine white-and-bright yellow looks like something Van Gogh would have painted. A large batch of them naturalized together in a field is simply delightful. Be sure to allow the slender foliage to live life to the fullest if you want the plants to naturalize. Grape hyacinth attracts bees when in flower, but this may be desired for pollination of nearby plants.

Other Common Name
Bluebell

Bloom Period and Seasonal Color
Spikes of blue flowers in April and May.

Mature Height × Spread
6 to 12 in. × Variable spread

When, Where, and How to Plant

Plant bulbs in the fall as soon as you get them. Seed can be started as soon as they ripen (when the seed pods begin to drop seeds). Sow in flats outside. Germination takes up to sixty days. Transplant in the fall in a sunny or shady spot. Sandy loam soil is best. Avoid soggy sites and prepare the soil thoroughly (see chapter introduction). Loosen heavy clays with organic matter and sand if needed. Grape hyacinths are very small so plant in drifts or groups. Space 2 to 3 inches apart and 3 inches deep.

Growing Tips

Water at planting and if the soil becomes excessively dry in spring. They often do not need fertilizer, but an application of 5-10-5 in the spring, after bloom, will help strengthen the bulbs.

Care

Allow foliage to mature to keep the plants spreading. Divide in autumn if necessary and replant immediately. Remove spent flower stems. The flower stalks get unattractive as they fade. Resist cutting back the leafy patches when they get wild looking. Grape hyacinths have an unusual habit of producing foliage in the fall. This will overwinter and may need to be groomed as the flower buds appear. Grape hyacinth is generally pest free.

Companion Planting and Design

Plant in borders, nooks, or crannies. Grape hyacinths are well suited for rock gardens and for filling crevices and gaps well. Plant in open fields for naturalizing or mix with spring bulbs. There are several other worthwhile species and varieties.

Did You Know?

In Highland Park, there is a big old mansion that was converted to a Young Men–Young Women's Hebrew Association (YM-YWHA) years ago. It was a wonderful spot to visit with my dog. One day in spring we walked by the old tennis court. From under the gnarled old trees, out to the open grass for almost an acre, grape hyacinths were blooming. There were thousands, probably spread from when the site was a carefully tended garden. The next day I returned with a flower-loving friend to share the beauty, but the grass had been mowed.

Hyacinth
Hyacinthus orientalis

When, Where, and How to Plant
Plant in September or October. Choose a bright, sunny location with good drainage. Avoid western exposures. Like all bulbs, hyacinths require well-drained soil. They need a heavy layer of mulch to minimize the freezing and thawing that naturally occurs in winter and that will cause an eventual decrease in flowering. Plant hyacinth bulbs 5 to 6 inches deep and 5 to 6 inches apart. Work the soil deeply (at least 1 foot deep). Mix in fertilizer with manures and/or bonemeal, but don't allow fertilizer to come in direct contact with the bulb.

Growing Tips
Water at planting and if the ground becomes dry in the spring. Fertilize after they finish blooming in the spring and again in the fall (see chapter introduction).

Care
Remove flower stalks as blooms finish. Keep plants mulched, especially during the winter. Allow leaves to age naturally before removal. They generally need to be replaced every three to four years. Pests are rarely a problem, but when planting choose areas that have not grown bulbs for a few years.

Companion Planting and Design
Clusters of hyacinths around shrubbery provide early spring color. Avoid planting large expanses of hyacinth alone. Patches mixed in with early tulips or daffodils can be quite pretty. Plant by entranceways, mailboxes, or lampposts where you can see them from all angles. Create a border with a staggered row, perhaps even leaving skips here and there to avoid monotonous uniformity. The uneven terrain of a rock garden prevents the marching soldier look.

Did You Know?
Hyacinths were common as far back as 1596. At that time, they were not cultivated on a large scale because the flowers were not very pretty, even though they had good color and a nice scent. By 1734, they were one of the six most popular garden flowers. The Dutch government was extremely concerned that their popularity would result in a duplication of the tulip mania that occurred one hundred years earlier (see chapter introduction) and so published a history of the economic depression which resulted. Hyacinth mania was avoided.

Hyacinth flowers look a lot like cotton candy. The prolific blooms surround the stiff stem so that the inflorescence is perfectly uniform. This is a useful trait when you are arranging cut flowers or planting in an open area where flowers will be viewed from all angles. On the other hand, this uniformity and stiffness is extremely formal to the point of being rigid. Use them in mixed plantings to add definition to a more informal or naturalized area, or try them as part of a border. Hyacinth flowers are cherished for their sweet, powerful scent, whether planted at the backdoor or when forced indoors. It is only fair to warn you, however, that some people find the scent overpowering.

Other Common Names
Dutch Hyacinth, Common Hyacinth, Garden Hyacinth

Bloom Period and Seasonal Color
Flowers appear in March to April in many colors, including white, yellow, blue, purple, and pink.

Mature Height × Spread
Up to 18 in. × 6 to 12 in.

Lily
Lilium spp.

Lilies are gorgeous, with three- to ten-inch blooms that are trumpet to star shaped. They are regaining popularity, but it is amazing that they haven't always been at the top of the hit parade. The plants are care free, spread into robust patches without becoming invasive, and are the tallest herbaceous plants you are likely to have in your garden. Oriental hybrids have the biggest flowers; these appear in August. Asiatic hybrids are the earliest lilies to bloom (in June) and produce small star shaped flowers in many intense colors. Trumpet lilies, also known as Aurelian hybrids, bloom in July and are the tallest. Smaller, speckled tiger lilies have the longest bloom and are among the best for naturalizing. Martagon lilies have drooping flowers with curving petals and anthers that seem to be exploding out of the center.

Bloom Period and Seasonal Color
Blooms in a range of colors, appearing from June to September.

Mature Height × Spread
2 to 9 ft. × 12 to 18 in.

When, Where, and How to Plant
The best time to plant is early fall. Spring-planted bulbs may not give their best show until the second summer. Plant immediately. A sunny spot is acceptable, but flower color may fade there. Partial shade or protection from midday sun is ideal. Avoid wet ground. Prepare the ground deeply and add plenty of organic matter. Lilies prefer acidic soil, so do not add lime. Depth and spacing varies, but as a rule, plant the bulb 3 times as deep as it is tall. Never let bulbs dry out, and take care not to damage either stem or bulb roots.

Growing Tips
Water at planting and when the ground gets dry. Fertilize with bulb fertilizer or bone meal when planting or dividing. An application of 5-10-5 in the spring is beneficial. Use organic mulch.

Care
Taller varieties may need staking. Remove the flowering portion of the stalk when the flowers fade. Divide when overcrowded and less vigorous. Mulch heavily. Cut, do not pull, stalks when yellow. You can propagate by planting the bulblets that grow at the base of the stems. Lift the bulbs and plant individual bulb scales or plant "bulbils," the small bulb-like growths that appear in the leaf axils of some types. Lilies are usually pest free.

Companion Planting and Design
Plant lilies by themselves for cut flowers, but use their vertical habit to advantage wherever possible. The roots do best in shade or when protected by groundcover. Try tucking bulbs between low, spreading shrubs. Mix lilies in the back of a perennial border. Mums in the same bed will draw attention away from fading stems. A single stem in a vase makes an arrangement by itself.

Did You Know?
Many people are not aware that the Easter lily is fairly hardy. Plant out after danger of frost. Foliage will die back. These lilies may produce a second bloom in late summer. In the future, expect flowers in July or August, the Easter lily's natural season. (Greenhouse professionals must manipulate lilies with a complicated ritual to make them bloom at Easter.)

Magic Lily

Lycoris squamigera

When, Where, and How to Plant

Plant when the bulbs are available. This may be in the spring before the foliage comes out, in the summer before they bloom, or in the fall after they finish. Plant in sun or light shade. Provide a little protection from the worst of winter weather, especially in the northwestern part of the state. It might be best to plant magic lily against a south wall, especially if there are shrubs to protect the area from northern winds. Prepare the soil deeply to ensure good drainage. Plant 4 to 6 inches deep and 8 inches apart. In northwestern New Jersey, plant bulbs 6 inches deep. Mulch heavily.

Growing Tips

Fertilize with 5-10-5 fertilizer while the leaves are growing in the spring. Water during dry periods.

Care

Bulbs should be left in place for many years. Mark the areas where the bulbs are planted to avoid damaging them during their several dormant periods. Let the leaves mature fully before cutting them back. Cut the flower stalks when they finish blooming. Mulch heavily during the winter. Magic lily is generally pest free.

Companion Planting and Design

Plant magic lilies with sweet alyssum, annual baby's breath, petunias, or spring bulbs. Don't hide magic lily with the foliage or flowers of other plants. If they are too crowded, you won't be able to appreciate their magical appearance in late summer.

Did You Know?

Years ago I planted magic lilies in deep shade under an enormous old ailanthus tree. Every spring they sent up leaves. The leaves eventually got lost in daylilies. No flower ever appeared. Three or four years went by, and I completely forgot about the magic lilies. Early one spring, the ailanthus tree was pruned, letting in more light. Late that summer, something poked up in the shadiest part of the garden. It shot up like a rocket—a soldier-straight stem with a bulbous tip. Then it bloomed, and a single magic lily erupted into a cluster of pink flowers. It was the closest thing to a magic plant that ever appeared in my garden.

The magic lily deserves its common name. Once the flower stalk emerges, it seems to shoot up an inch or two every time you turn your back. Then poof, the flowers appear. No leaves—just an eruption of flower clusters on top of a very straight, naked stem. But plants cannot live on flowers alone. The leaves emerge in spring, grow long and strap-like, then disappear in midsummer. There is no trace of the plant until the sudden appearance of the flower stalk. Magic lily's flower stalks appear so suddenly that it is always a surprise. You'll think Jack traded his mother's cow for bulbs instead of beans. Plant low growing annuals such as petunias or dwarf marigolds in late May, and they will fill in the gaps as magic lily's foliage fades.

Other Common Names

Hardy Amaryllis, Resurrection Lily

Bloom Period and Seasonal Color

Deep pink lily-like flowers appearing in late August.

Mature Height × Spread

Up to 3 ft. × up to 2 ft.

Peruvian Daffodil

Hymenocallis narcissiflora

Peruvian daffodils are unique. They have petals and a central cup like the traditional daffodil, but the petals are long, almost threadlike, and curl back. These wispy petals are what has generated the common name "spider lily," which it shares with some of the Lycoris species. The center cup is larger than any daffodil and so resembles a small white lily. As its name suggests, this plant is from Peru. A patch in bloom looks like something right out of Munchkinland in Wizard of Oz. The bulbs are quite large and closely resemble an amaryllis bulb, which is a relative. If you to travel to the Caribbean for a winter vacation, you will see Peruvian daffodils blooming everywhere.

Other Common Names
Spider Lily, Basketflower

Bloom Period and Seasonal Color
Fragrant, unusual flowers in white or pale yellow appearing in summer.

Mature Height × Spread
2 ft. × 12 to 18 in.

When, Where, and How to Plant
Direct plant in spring in a sunny location, or you can start the bulbs in pots earlier. Transplant out after danger of frost. Prepare the soil deeply. Plant 6 inches deep and 12 to 18 inches apart. The bulbs need plenty of water until they bloom and should be well drained. Add organic matter at planting time. Plant at least six bulbs together to appreciate the singular blooms.

Growing Tips
Water deeply from the time the bulbs are planted until they bloom. Fertilize regularly; every two to three weeks is suggested, but it depends on the fertilizer you use, so follow directions. (See chapter introduction for more on fertilizer.)

Care
Remove spent blooms. Dig bulbs after the plants have been lightly frosted. Take extra care not to damage the roots while extricating them from the soil. Store bulbs where they will be cool and dry, but warmer than most bulbs. 50 to 59 degrees Fahrenheit is ideal. Japanese beetles may feed on the petals. Hand pick or check with your Cooperative Extension Agent for current pesticides.

Companion Planting and Design
Make sure Peruvian daffodil is in plain view to "wow" your visitors. If you plant with low-growing annuals such as ageratum, petunias, or verbena, Peruvian daffodil will take center stage while in bloom. Mixed with something taller, such as red zinnias, they will blend nicely but won't easily upstage everything else. Peruvian daffodils make excellent cut flowers. Their fragrance is lovely.

Did You Know?
Years ago an elderly gentleman approached me with a twinkle in his eye. He asked if I could identify the flower he held. I recognized it as the Peruvian daffodil. He was impressed that I knew the unusual flower. The bulbs had been handed down from his grandmother, and he did not expect me to know it. As a reward, he sent me a shoebox full of the bulbs. The large healthy bulbs bloomed with enthusiasm. I heard shortly after that the gentleman had passed away. He left me a treasure for which I will be forever grateful.

When, Where, and How to Plant

Plant from mid-September to mid-November. Planting in a sunny warm spot will result in the earliest blooms, but *I. reticulata* can put up with a little shade. As with all bulbs, avoid soggy ground. Dig deeply. These plants like sandy soil, so add a 2:1 mixture of organic matter and sand to loosen things up. Plant 3 to 4 inches deep and space 3 to 4 inches apart. If planting *I. reticulata* in containers, place bulbs 1 inch deep and 2 inches apart. Store in a cold basement or garage. Bring indoors in late winter to enjoy early flowers.

Growing Tips

Water in the fall so that the plants stay moist and again in the spring until they finish blooming. Use a 5-10-5 fertilizer in the spring.

Care

Keep the area well mulched in winter. Allow the foliage to mature fully before cutting it back. Because they spread so slowly, reticulated iris rarely need division. Potted bulbs can be planted out after the weather warms up. Pest problems are rare.

Companion Planting and Design

Tuck the bulbs into rock gardens or any nook where the early spring flowers will be appreciated. Plant by the front door, the path to the car, under the mailbox, or in some other place you visit often. You will want to be able to soak up its cheer when you need a winter boost. If you plant reticulated iris in the back forty, the flowers will be up and gone before you ever see them. The world of iris is extremely complicated. The large German bearded iris is by far the most common.

Did You Know?

Years ago I visited a greenhouse that specialized in containerized bulbs. They had a large pile of reticulated iris ready for the trash heap. The plants had bloomed and faded without being sold. The leaves were mostly yellow. I rescued a bagful of the unwanted plants and put them in my garden. They bloomed the following spring and for many years after that. They are sweet little flowers, but tough little plants.

Reticulated irises are early spring treasures that have the tough job of blooming while winter is still gleefully blowing a cold wind. Each flower is short lived, but an established patch will produce so many blooms that you will have color for several weeks. Iris reticulata spreads, though at a sleepy snail's pace. It will never naturalize over large areas but does create compact patches full of delightful, fragrant little flowers. In a sunny, protected nook, plants may bloom as early as January. If you can get close enough, poke your nose in for a pleasant surprise. They are sweetly fragrant. On a cold day the scent may be hidden, so if your nose is dissatisfied, try again when the winter sun is warming the earth.

Other Common Names

Dwarf Iris, Netted Iris

Bloom Period and Seasonal Color

Blooms in February to April in blue, red-violet, or deep purple.

Mature Height × Spread

4 to 6 in. × up to 12 in.

Snowdrop
Galanthus elwesii

A patch of dainty white snowdrops poking up in late winter creates gentle ripples of excitement like a small pebble in a pond. The pristine white flowers of snowdrop nod their heads shyly as their three petals droop gracefully toward the ground. The flowers of the giant snowdrop G. elwesii are 1¼ inches long and reach up to 10 inches in height. Plants closest to the house will bloom first and may be the very first flowers of spring. The giant species, G. elwesii, makes a bigger splash and actually looks coarse next to its diminutive relative, G. nivalis. The common snowdrop spreads more enthusiastically, so it may have the greatest impact over time. It is difficult to choose between the two species.

Other Common Names
Milk Flower, Giant Snowdrop

Bloom Period and Seasonal Color
White blooms appear in February to March.

Mature Height × Spread
8 to 10 in. × 3 to 4 in.

When, Where, and How to Plant
Plant in early fall as soon as you get the bulbs. Snowdrops are a woodland plant and prefer partial shade or full shade. They will grow in full sun if they must. If you locate them close to the house, they will bloom earlier. Plant quickly when you receive the bulbs so that they don't dry out. Because snowdrops are a woodland plant, they prefer a moist, humusy soil. Add plenty of organic matter to the soil. Plant 3 inches deep and 3 inches apart.

Growing Tips
Water and incorporate bulb fertilizer or bone meal into the soil at planting. They are dormant during the heat of summer, but a deep watering in early fall, if the ground is still dry, will help root growth.

Care
Do not disturb these plants if at all possible. They do not like to be moved. Allow the foliage to fully mature before cutting it back. Snowdrops are one of the earliest flowers to bloom, and if you plant them in a shady part of the lawn, they will usually have finished before it is time to mow the grass. A little winter mulch is beneficial for snowdrops planted in beds. They are virtually pest free.

Companion Planting and Design
Naturalize snowdrops under evergreen trees, along a wooded path, or in a rock garden. Plant in large patches or these little flowers will be lost. They make a stunning purple and white combination with dwarf iris. Its close cousin, the common snowdrop, *G. nivalis*, has flowers that may reach 1 inch wide but grow only 6 inches tall. Both prefer a bit of shade.

Did You Know?
The name Galanthus is Greek for "milk flower." This is a fairly well established fact. The origin of the name "snowdrop" is lesser known. According to the Farmer's Almanac's *Flower Gardening Secrets*, it comes from the German word "schneetropfen." "Schnee" means "snow," but "schneetropfen" actually refers to a popular earring from the 1600s.

Tulip
Tulipa spp.

When, Where, and How to Plant
Plant tulips in the fall, from mid-September until Thanksgiving. Choose a sunny spot. Prepare the soil deeply and thoroughly, digging down at least 12 inches. Add a 2:1 mixture of organic matter and sand as well as some bone meal. Provide plenty of moisture and excellent drainage. The general recommendations are to plant 4 to 8 inches deep and 4 to 8 inches apart. Larger bulbs go deeper and require more space. To encourage tulips to perennialize, or to last more than two to three years, plant 8 to 10 inches deep.

Growing Tips
Water at planting. Fertilize in the fall or spring when new leaves emerge (see chapter introduction). Tulips need plenty of water in the spring. If they don't get 1 inch of rain a week while they are growing, they will require supplemental watering.

Care and Maintenance
Remove dead flowers immediately since seed production can take up to 30 percent of the bulb's energy. Allow the foliage to completely yellow before removal. Hide ripening foliage with colorful annuals. If you intend to add bulbs to the bed in the fall, take care to mark where it is safe to dig. It is easy to damage bulbs when you can't see the leaves. Replace when the flowers begin to decline. Bulbs may last three to five years. Insects and diseases don't usually cause problems as much as deer, rabbits, and squirrels.

Companion Planting and Design
Tuck clumps among shrubs, add to a perennial border for early color, plant along the road for drive-by impact, or grow in a rock garden for added zing. Species tulips work well for naturalizing. Early tulips overlap with late daffodils, but late tulips may share the spotlight with early iris.

Did You Know?
Tulips make splendid cut flowers, but they continue to grow after they are cut. A bunch in a vase with some greenery and baby's breath is no problem. When used in a centerpiece, however, the stems may elongate several more inches, ruining whatever balance you created.

Tulips are lovely flowers, but their claim to fame is intense, vivid, rich blasts of color. They are cup-shaped with six petals. There are late-season parrot tulips with ripply edged petals, fringed tulips with petals that are rimmed with soft "bristles," and even lily-flowered tulips with pointed petals. On a hot day, they open wide like a stargazer lily and have passionate colors. It is this captivating quality that has given rise to an incredible and somewhat mysterious history. Tulips appeared in Turkey in about 1554 where they were under cultivation in the Sultan's garden. How long they had been cultivated prior to that time is unknown, as there are no wild types that can be clearly traced. Today we enjoy the tulip for its spring cheer, ease of cultivation, and tremendous variety.

Bloom Period and Seasonal Color
Blooms in March through May in an enormous range of colors including red, white, yellow, orange, and deep purple.

Mature Height × Spread
2 to 36 in. × 12 in.

Wild Hyacinth
Camassia leichtlinii

The soft blue flower spikes of wild hyacinth resemble wood hyacinth, a species of Scilla, far more than they do the true garden hyacinth. The starlike flowers appear on tall, airy spikes. The blooms arrive when the big spring flush of color is fading. The late May flowers will take you right up to alliums and the rest of the garden display that explodes in June. All wild hyacinths are native Americans. This is one of the few garden bulbs that can make that claim. Wild hyacinth prefers a touch of shade and heavy, moist soils, another unusual characteristic for bulb flowers. The loose spikes of blossoms have an unrefined elegance like handspun yarn.

Other Common Names
Camass, Indian Hyacinth, Zuamach, Quamash

Bloom Period and Seasonal Color
Blossoms in white or blue, appearing in May.

Mature Height × Spread
Up to 4 ft. × 10 in.

When, Where, and How to Plant
Plant in the fall after the weather cools to prevent sprouting. Mid-October should be fine. A site with partial shade is preferred, but these adaptable plants will endure full sun. Choose a site with heavy, moist soils but no standing water. Add organic matter to sandy soils to help retain soil moisture. Plant bulbs 3 to 4 inches deep and 6 inches apart. Plants can also be grown from seed but it will be four to five years before they bloom. Sow seed as soon as it is ripe. Germination will take anywhere from 30 to 180 days.

Growing Tips
Keep wild hyacinth well watered during the growing season. An application of 5-10-5 after bloom or the use of a water-soluble fertilizer will help to replenish the bulbs for the following year.

Care
Allow foliage to fully mature before removal. For the best display, do not disturb the plants. Divide in September only after clumps become overcrowded. Replant bulbs immediately. Use an organic mulch to prevent soil from drying out.

Companion Planting and Design
Wild hyacinth does not like to be disturbed, so plant the bulbs where they can stay awhile. It will naturalize if given room to spread and can be used in mixed beds, as borders, or at the water's edge. Wild hyacinth makes excellent cut flowers.

Did You Know?
Camassia were valued as food in many Indian cultures where they were roasted, cooked in soups, or pounded and made into loaves. The flavor is supposed to be quite sweet and has been described as licorice-like. In her wonderful book *Who Named the Daisy*, Mary Durant quotes Mary Elizabeth Parsons: "Grizzly bears, when more plentiful in the early days, were particularly fond of the bulbs. Indians today (1900), value them very highly as an article of diet . . . Indeed, the Nez Perce Indian war in Idaho (1877) was caused by encroachments upon territory which was especially rich in these bulbs."

Winter Aconite
Eranthis hyemalis

When, Where, and How to Plant

Plant in late summer or early fall. Late August is best. Potted plants are sometimes available for sale after they have finished blooming in later winter. Plant these immediately. Winter aconite prefers sun while in flower but shade later on (see Care below). Plant as soon as possible after obtaining the corms. Soak for twenty-four hours prior to planting. Winter aconite prefers moist, well-drained soil. It is adaptable but prefers an alkaline pH. An application of lime would be helpful since most New Jersey soils are somewhat acidic. Plant large patches of this tiny flower. Space the corms 3 inches apart and plant 3 inches deep.

Growing Tips

Water at planting, especially if transplanting from an established bed. Water deeply during unusually hot, dry springs. Lime occasionally, even in established beds. Fertilize in fall or very early spring (see chapter introduction).

Care

The most important thing you can do for winter aconite is leave it alone. There is a twist, however. More than one reference suggests that for best results you should transplant the plants while in bloom. If you try this, get as large a clump as possible to avoid damaging the tubers. Allow the foliage to fully mature before you cut it back. Mice and chipmunks can be a problem.

Companion Planting and Design

Winter aconite is ideal for planting under shade trees. If you can be patient, plant many corms at a slight distance from your favorite window where they will eventually spread into a golden sea. A patch outside the front door will bring cheer until a green tide of leaves comes in on the sea of gold.

Did You Know?

Winter aconite is native to Europe and has been under cultivation since at least the 1500s. In 1948's *Bulbs for Home Gardens*, John Wister quotes John Gerard's circa 1500s description of the "power" of winter aconite to protect against scorpions: "It is of such force, that if the scorpion passe by where it groweth and touche the same, presently he becometh dull, heavy and senseless."

This plant needs a new common name, one that expresses its intense good cheer. The name winter aconite doesn't even give a hint of its charms. (I suggest "sunspots" or "yellow zingers.") While the world is still cold and barren, winter aconite cries out to awaken a silent world. It bursts forth with 1 1/2 in. buttercup-like flowers as if the sun were melting and drops of sunshine landed in your yard. This plant spreads with a slow determination. It is part of the army that fights back winter while gardeners fuss over houseplants and mark catalog pages with sticky notes. Each honey-scented bloom has five to nine petal-like sepals and a pincushion center full of anthers and filaments. In a cool spring, the flowers will last for weeks, maybe even months.

Bloom Period and Seasonal Color

Bright yellow flowers appearing February to March.

Mature Height × Spread

3 to 4 in. × 2 to 3 in.

Down the Shore Plants
for New Jersey

Those of us who grew up with the Jersey shore know it is one of the greatest places in the world, from the wide beaches of Wildwood to the rocky outcroppings of Sandy Hook back to the well preserved Island Beach State Park and the Victorian wonders of Cape May. There are mansions and tiny bungalows, quiet nooks and the outrageous boardwalk at Seaside Heights. On Friday evenings in the summer, a large percentage of the state mobilizes and heads "down the shore" to indulge in the sun, sand, and surf. There is no other place quite like it.

Plan for Unique Conditions

It wasn't long ago when much of the shore area was fairly deserted outside the summer months, but that is no longer the case. Year-round populations have grown, and new developments continue to spring up all along the coast. Landscaping these properties is a challenge; the strong winds and salt air make life difficult for growing green things. Some plants mentioned elsewhere in this book are very tolerant of these conditions. American holly is one of the best, and the rugosa rose is a hardy flowering beauty. Hydrangeas do well, and so does the purple leaf sand cherry. Butterfly bushes add color all summer and attract droves of butterflies.

Bayberry

Maintenance of the grounds is an important consideration. If you have a summer home, you probably do not want to spend your time pruning and spraying the shrubbery while you are there. You can tell how common this feeling is by the predominance of "pebble lawns" at summer homes instead of grass. While a little weed control is usually necessary, pebbles eliminate the need for mowing. Zoysiagrass is another alternative. It tolerates drought and prefers the sandy soils usually encountered at the beach. Zoysiagrass turns brown at the first sign of cold weather, but if you only see it in the summer, it doesn't really matter. Seasonal use also affects your choice of flowering shrubs. Early spring bloom doesn't count for much if the homeowners don't arrive until the middle of June.

Having a more traditional landscape to meet the needs of the established (and growing) year-

The White Flowers of Beach Plum

round population requires some special consideration. Adding organic matter to the soil will help the soil hold onto moisture. This is important under most growing conditions, but the need for organic matter in sand is even more crucial. It's like telling someone to dress warmly—it has a more intense meaning at the North Pole.

As you move inland, the salt becomes less of a problem, but sandy soils persist in many areas. Inland plantings may still have to be tolerant of dry conditions, otherwise you may spend a lot of time supplying water.

There are a few tips for getting plants established. Starting with young trees in pockets of improved soil may be easier than trying to establish larger trees that have been grown under more advantageous circumstances. This is particularly useful on rocky ridges where there is not enough space to set a larger rootball. If the roots are allowed to find their own way, they may establish themselves in spite of the limitations. While deep planting can be a disaster under normal soil conditions and sure death in wet soils, it may protect the roots from rapid drying in sand.

Helping Your Plants Grow

Carefully check the preferred growing conditions of the plants you choose. Some plants that have evolved in beachy conditions may prefer the natural sandy soil to amended soil. On the other hand, many many common garden plants require a great deal of soil amendments to get established. Always remove strings, tags, wires, and plastic burlaps. Always dig a hole two or three times as big as you think you need. Backfill with amended soil if that is recommended for the specific plant, and plant at the same height it was in the ground or container. Tamp down the soil gently but firmly after planting and absolutely always water thoroughly after planting.

It is often necessary to stake or support newly planted ornamentals that are planted in sandy soil. The loose soil may not hold them up in the wind. Very deep stakes are required to do the job effectively, or you can use buried logs with guy wires attached. (Your local garden center can tell you how to do this.)

It is a good idea to do a major pruning at the time of planting. This will help take the pressure off the newly installed root system that is trying to settle in without the benefit of much moisture. It is also helpful for cutting wind pressure and so reducing damage to plants not yet ready to handle heavy off-the-water wind. The closer to the water and the sandier the soil, the more these extra precautions are necessary.

Bayberry
Myrica pensylvanica

This seaside favorite is native from Newfoundland to Maryland, mostly along the coast. It can be found growing right in the path of direct salt spray and is extremely tolerant of sandy soil conditions. This combination of qualities makes it irreplaceable in the shore landscape. Bayberry usually stays between five and ten feet but is sometimes taller. The thick, dark-green, almost leathery leaves are considered semi-evergreen. They may turn a little purple before they drop (if they drop), but fall color is not a major asset. The berries, which are an important attribute, can form in large numbers on female plants. They have a waxy quality and are the source of the scent in bayberry candles. As an added bonus, bayberry fixes nitrogen in the soil.

Other Common Name
Northern Bayberry

Bloom Period and Seasonal Color
Small gray berries persist all winter.

Mature Height × Spread
12 ft. × 12 ft.

When, Where, and How to Plant
Plant in late March or early April. Transplanting seedlings is not always successful. Take along a large hunk of the original soil to give the plant a better chance for survival. If you are planting in early fall, stick with container-grown plants. Bayberry grows in sun or partial shade. Acidic soil conditions are a must—and rarely a problem in New Jersey. Bayberry will tolerate very sandy soil, but it is better to mix an abundance of organic matter into the soil prior to planting. Roots will take a while to get established. Organic matter helps retain moisture while roots are settling in. (See chapter introduction for more about planting.)

Growing Tips
Water thoroughly at planting and whenever soil gets dry. Once established, bayberry is tolerant of dry conditions, but sandy soil can get too dry very quickly. These are sturdy plants and will likely thrive without additional fertilizer.

Care
Bayberry has no serious insect or disease problems. It can be trained as a standard (an upright plant with a single stalk). New shoots grow quickly, but older wood has a slower growth rate. Prune away new shoots if you want to keep the plant confined.

Companion Planting and Design
Bayberry can be mass planted or used as a border planting. It has been planted successfully on highways where winter salt spray overwhelms most plants. Its spreading root system anchors it in windy conditions, though it may be stunted or "'sculpted" in heavy wind.

Did You Know?
It takes $1^1/2$ quarts of berries to make one 8-inch bayberry candle. Gather berries in October or early November. Boil in water for about five minutes and skim off the wax or let the wax harden when cooled. It can be used by itself or mixed with tallow. Pure bayberry does not burn as brightly as regular candles, but it does give off a lovely scent. The wax may also be substituted for animal fat in the making of soap. Store bayberry products in plastic bags or sealed containers to preserve the scent.

Beach Plum

Prunus maritima

When, Where, and How to Plant

Plant in late March or early April, in sandy, acidic soils in full sun. Beach plums appear on "secondary dunes" where the salt spray is not as intense and the variation of vegetation is greater. You can propagate beach plums from seed, but for particular habit or fruit quality, use a container-grown plant. Add organic matter to help retain soil moisture. Since this plant suckers, you may be able to propagate an existing plant by division in the early spring. (See chapter introduction for more about planting.)

Growing Tips

Water thoroughly at planting and whenever soil gets excessively dry. A light application of 5-10-5 fertilizer in early spring may be beneficial, but beach plum thrives in the wild without any help.

Care

The plant stays small but suckers from the base. If this is a problem, prune out the branches in early spring. No particular insects or diseases are known for beach plum, but all *Prunus* are prone to scale and leaf spots. Your Cooperative Extension Office can help you with control recommendations.

Companion Planting and Design

Beach Plum can be found growing with bayberry, shadbush, and highbush blueberry. It will also thrive in inland locations with heavier soils, but there are many more popular, choices for those circumstances.

Did You Know?

To make beach plum jelly, take two and one-half pounds of fully ripe plums and one pound of slightly green plums. Crush in the bottom of an enameled kettle (leaving in the pits and the skin) and cook in one and one-half cups of water. Bring to a boil and simmer for twenty minutes while stirring. Strain in a jelly bag to get four cups of juice. Put the juice back into the kettle with three cups of sugar. Boil until the mixture reaches 220 degrees Fahrenheit or until jelly sheets from the spoon. Remove from heat, skim, and pour into sterilized half-pint jars. Leave one-eighth inch of room at the top of each jar. Cap with two-piece screwband lids.

It is difficult to say whether the little beach plum is prized more for its lovely white flowers in the spring, its tasty fruits for jams and jellies, or its ability to tolerate sand, salt, and wind. It is native along the coast from Maine to Virginia. The plant spreads from suckers but also reproduces from seed; there is, therefore, tremendous variation in the size and habit of the plant and in the size and color of the fruit. The fruits range in color from red to purple to yellow, and in size up to two inches in diameter. The fruit is almost always round. Its taste is tart, but the jelly produced from this plant is served as a side dressing for meats and is treasured by its devotees. The fruit is harvested in August when it reaches its full color.

Other Common Names
Shore Plum, Black Plum

Bloom Period and Seasonal Color
Showy white half-inch flowers in groups of two or three, appearing in May; fruits in August.

Mature Height × Spread
6 to 12 ft. × 6 ft., but highly variable

Butterfly Bush
Buddleia davidii

This summer-blooming shrub is a great choice for down the shore since it blooms its heart out during much of the summer season. The flowers are fabulous when cut, and a single bush will draw butterflies almost continually. A single plant may be a bit open and gangly to be an ideal specimen plant, but three together are dramatic and provide an opportunity to enjoy the many color choices. Butterfly bush may die to the ground in Zone 5, the coldest part of New Jersey, but the warmer shore areas are just fine. The many varieties offer a wide range of colors and different sizes. If all you plant is a collection of butterfly bushes, you will have flowers and butterflies all summer.

Other Common Name
Summer Lilac

Bloom Period and Seasonal Color
Spikes of tiny flowers in white, pink, lavender, deep purple, wine, or yellow from July until frost.

Mature Height × Spread
10 to 15 ft. × variable spread, usually taller than wide.

When, Where, and How to Plant
Plant in early spring or early fall. Choose a sunny location but not directly in the salt spray. Butterfly bush prefers well-drained, fertile soils but will tolerate a range of soil conditions. In the sandy soils at the shore, be sure to add copious amounts of organic matter, such as leaf compost, to the soil when preparing the hole. An organic mulch will help retain soil moisture. (See chapter introduction for more about planting.)

Growing Tips
Water thoroughly at planting and whenever the soil gets dry. Fertilize every spring with 5-10-5 fertilizer to compensate for the poorer soil.

Care
Butterfly bush can be cut way back in spring before new growth has commenced. This helps keep it in check for small gardens. Prune off dead branches every spring and then shape. Shrubs large from the previous year may need more severe pruning to keep them in bounds, but a harsh winter may do quite a bit of the pruning for you. The more frequently you remove dead flowers in the summer, the more flowers you will get. Butterfly bush is generally pest free.

Companion Planting and Design
Locate butterfly bushes at the back of a perennial border or on the sunny side of a row of evergreens. Their somewhat coarse habit doesn't stand alone well, but different varieties clustered together offset the open nature of the shrub. Masses together can get thick enough to provide privacy in summer. If you cut them back in late fall, they will let the sun in over the winter. To enjoy blooms and butterflies, plant off the deck or patio. Cut flowers for bouquets in the morning, preferably after a good rain or deep watering.

Did You Know?
This delightful summer shrub has a spring blooming cousin, *B. alternifolia*. This species has similar spikes of lavender flowers in late May on pendulous branches. It is distinguished by having alternate leaves and producing flowers on the previous year's growth. It has the same wonderful capacity for drawing butterflies.

Common Sea Buckthorn

Hippophae rhamnoides

When, Where, and How to Plant

This plant is a little uncooperative about getting established. Plant in late March or early April with container-grown material for the best results. Choose a sunny location in infertile, sandy soil. (Sounds like the beach to me!) Sea buckthorn will tolerate salt spray. It establishes more rapidly in poor soils than it does in fertile soils, and it prefers a damp subsoil. You may be able to transplant plants from suckers if you are particularly careful. You can also layer branches or grow from seed if you are willing to be patient. Rooting cuttings is extremely difficult. (See chapter introduction for more about planting.)

Growing Tips

Water at planting and when soil gets dry until it gets established. Since sea buckthorn prefers infertile soils, there is no need to fertilize. Besides, sea buckthorn fixes nitrogen.

Care

Staking may be beneficial in windy locations, at least until it gets established. Prune suckers if desired. Sea buckthorn also benefits from occasional pruning to shape. It has no serious insects or diseases.

Companion Planting and Design

Plant size is usually around 10 feet, so you can use it as a foundation plant if you remove its suckers to contain its spread. Planting sea buckthorn en masse or as a border may be more appropriate. Due to its salt tolerance and stabilizing capability, this plant may be a good choice along highways where salt is a winter problem. You can plant up to six female plants for every male plant and still have sufficient pollination for fruit set. The plants are pollinated by wind, so the male should be in close proximity.

Did You Know?

Sea buckthorn is native to Europe as well as western and northern China. It is used extensively in Europe along roads and highways. One reference mentions that the fruits, which are very acidic, can be used for making jams or sauce. It is supposed to be very high in vitamin C.

The limitations of salt and sand make the bright orange fruits of common sea buckthorn quite precious. Fruit arrives on female shrubs but requires a male in close proximity. The berries are hard but edible; tastiness is debatable. The foliage is grayish green, three inches long, and narrow, similar to a willow leaf. There is not much in the way of fall color, but the berries ripen by September and are striking against the attractive foliage. Common sea buckthorn can form its own thicket of thorny branches if left unpruned. This may have something to do with roots evolving in search of water. This tendency is helpful along a border or in a mass, but in restricted space it can be annoying.

Other Common Name
Swallow Thorn

Bloom Period and Seasonal Color
Small yellow inconspicuous flowers in April followed by orange berries in September.

Mature Height × Spread
10 to 40 ft. × 10 to 40 ft.

Crapemyrtle
Lagerstroemia indica

The wonderful summer flowering crapemyrtle is of questionable hardiness in much of New Jersey, yet it thrives at the beach. There is a thin band of the warmer Zone 7 that runs from Monmouth County down to the tip of Cape May. That lovely Victorian resort town has a crapemyrtle at every turn. Crapemyrtle blooms on new wood, so a severe winter or enthusiastic spring pruning will not prevent the abundant spikes of summer flowers. The large panicles of tiny flowers come in white, pink, purple, and dark red. When properly pruned, the trees attain a graceful vase-like shape, and mature trees have attractive exfoliating bark. Crapemyrtles are common in the south, where seedlings can pop up in the sidewalks like weeds. In New Jersey they are treasured, as they are far less common.

Bloom Period and Seasonal Color
Spikes of tiny white, pink, purple or red flowers from July to September; fall foliage of yellow, orange, and red; colorful exfoliating bark all year.

Mature Height × Spread
15 to 25 ft. × variable spread

When, Where, and How to Plant
Plant in late March or early April. Container material is more common, but balled trees should do fine. Look for varieties that indicate increased hardiness, especially the twenty-nine varieties released by the National Arboretum. Check their website (www.usna.usda.gov) for a list of names. Choose a sunny location with a bit of protection from winter wind. Avoid the direct salt spray of beachfront property and wet ground. When preparing the hole, add copious amounts of organic matter to the soil, such as leaf compost. (See chapter introduction for more about planting.)

Growing Tips
Water thoroughly at planting and whenever the soil gets excessively dry. Avoid excessive watering as can happen with automatic sprinkler systems. After severe winter kill or heavy pruning, fertilize in early spring with 5-10-5 or a water-soluble fertilizer according to directions. Do not fertilize in summer or fall.

Care
The newer varieties are less susceptible to mildew and so are generally pest free. The biggest chore is spring pruning which will vary based on the severity of the previous winter, the space limitations and the variety. At the northern beaches, consider winter protection such as a burlap screen, at least until crapemyrtle is well established.

Companion Planting and Design
Locate in a place where you can see the summer flowers, such as the deck, flanking the front door, or outside the kitchen window. The trunks stay bare a significant way up so they are ideal for planting groundcover or summer annuals underneath. The further north or inland your location, consider planting on the south side of an evergreen border. This provides both protection from winter wind and a perfect backdrop for summer flowers.

Did You Know?
A mature crapemyrtle can be spotted from the Garden State Parkway in the Newark area. It is located in front of one of those lovely older city homes. The enormous crapemyrtle blooms in vivid pink for much of every summer. It must have received much TLC in its early years to get established so far north, but it is magnificent now.

When, Where, and How to Plant

Plant in early spring or early fall. Japanese black pine is so salt tolerant that it can be found within a few feet of the high water mark. Find it a sunny location on moist but well-drained soil. As a border plant, it is somewhat unpredictable in habit. It will sprout from seed and fill in, but its shape is irregular at best. Japanese black pine is not difficult to get established. Move seedlings in early spring. If the soil is particularly dry, add organic matter to retain moisture. New plants growing in windy situations should be staked. (See chapter introduction for more about planting.)

Growing Tips

Water newly planted trees and pay close attention to watering until the plant is established. Fertilizer is rarely needed.

Care

Snipping the candles in early spring will help keep this unconventional pine more compact and full. Japanese black pine tolerates shearing better than most pines. A type of oyster-shell scale known as *Lepidosaphes pini* has recently been found to infest pine needles in the center of needle clusters. Spread by wind, it is more a problem along the shore than anywhere else in our state. Applying dormant oil in April will be helpful, though it is difficult to penetrate the clusters. To control *Lepidosaphes pini* in the young stage, spray in mid-June and again in August with one percent horticultural oil, or check with your Cooperative Extension Service for recommendations.

Companion Planting and Design

Japanese black pine makes an invaluable landscape ornamental for residential settings at the shore and is extremely functional in dune stabilization and land reclamation. As the tree ages, the trunk can take on a very crooked appearance. While not a traditional choice for a specimen plant, the crooked habit may be interesting in the right spot. Hydrangeas seem to thrive in their shadows. For summer color, underplant impatiens or caladiums.

Did You Know?

Japanese black pine is native to Japan. It is considered a good choice for bonsai and an absolute must in Japanese-style gardens.

The irregular shape of Japanese black pine is not well suited for a formal setting, but most seaside plantings are far from formal. The tree's habit is open and spreading but somewhat pyramidal. Whether Japanese black pine is hardy to Zone 5 is questionable, but the shore areas in New Jersey are all Zone 6 or 7. The bark becomes fissured in irregular plates as the tree ages. Cones are up to three inches long. The dark-green needles are in bundles of two and last up to five years. Often, a large number of seedlings can be found beneath a mature tree. Japanese black pine does not do well in rich soils and so does not generally thrive inland.

Bloom Period and Seasonal Color
Evergreen

Mature Height × Spread
20 to 90 ft. × 20 to 40 ft.

Summersweet
Clethra alnifolia

Summersweet's fragrant summer blooms are appreciated wherever it puts down roots, but its tolerance of seaside conditions is an important asset. This shrub will spread by suckers. In most situations this is really not a problem. It can be pruned hard in the spring since its lovely flower spikes are produced on new growth. Summersweet leafs out rather late. The two- to four-inch long leaves are bright green all summer, turn yellow in October, then fade to brown before dropping. Flowers appear at the uppermost tips of the branches, which makes them easy to appreciate with your eyes or your nose. The flowers are deliciously fragrant but not overpowering. Bees love them. Summersweet tends to stay in the small end of its height range unless planted in moist soil under shady conditions.

Other Common Names
Sweet Pepperbush, Sweet Alder

Bloom Period and Seasonal Color
Spikes of tiny pink or white flowers in July or August; yellow fall color.

Mature Height × Spread
4 to 10 ft. × 4 to 12 ft.

When, Where, and How to Plant
Planting in early spring is preferred. You can plant summersweet almost anywhere. The ideal site will have a little shade and moist, acidic soil that is high in organic matter. However, summersweet will take full sun to heavy shade and gravel soil to wet spots. It is tolerant of seaside conditions and is native from Maine to Florida. Summersweet is generally available in containers, but you may come across a large balled specimen on occasion. Suckers can be divided in early spring. Add plenty of organic matter such as leaf compost when you are planting in sandy soil. This helps conserve and maintain soil moisture, giving the plant its best shot at getting established. An organic mulch will help replenish the organic matter in the soil and will also help keep the soil moist in hot weather. (See chapter introduction for more about planting.)

Growing Tips
Water thoroughly at planting and whenever soil gets dry until it is established. A light application of 5-10-5 in early spring after a heavy pruning will help summersweet to fill in.

Care
Little maintenance is required unless you want to keep summersweet from spreading. If this is the case, prune in early spring. Summersweet has no insect or disease problems. Snip off the flower skeletons to keep the bush tidy if desired. Keeping the mulch thick will reduce moisture evaporation from the soil. This native plant is well adapted to the New Jersey climate.

Companion Planting and Design
There are dwarf forms of summersweet that make good foundation plants, but the species is useful as a border plant, for mass planting, and even as a specimen in small yards.

Did You Know?
We have a summersweet planted by the path to the front door. It established easily and produces pink flowers for much of the summer. The sweet fragrance and delicate flowers make me smile every time I walk by. It is surprising that summersweet is not more commonly used.

Tamarix
Tamarix ramosissima

When, Where, and How to Plant
Plant in late March or early April. Tamarix' summer flowers, small size, and salt tolerance is an ideal combination for small yards at the beach. It does not do well in highly fertile soils but adapts to most other conditions. The ideal location would be in full sun in acidic, well-drained soil. Avoid water and sewer pipes. The roots are somewhat "minimalistic," so take care to protect what roots are there. A container-grown plant will disturb the roots as little as possible. This plant thrives in sandy soil and does not require extensive soil preparation to get established. (See chapter introduction for more about planting.)

Growing Tips
Water thoroughly at planting and until it becomes established. Then water whenever soil becomes excessively dry. Go easy on fertilizer to avoid too many scraggly shoots.

Care
The unruly habit of tamarix makes spring pruning desirable. If cut to the ground every year, it sends up a flush of green growth in spring. This is not necessary but may make the appearance more acceptable. It grows quickly and will fill in by summer. Do not expect serious pest or disease difficulties, but as with all plants, keep your eyes open for problems before they become severe.

Companion Planting and Design
The dramatic lines created by the long flowering branches give tamarix a touch of elegance. They look lovely as they wave in the wind. Its odd look makes it tricky to mix with other plants. The midsummer flowers come at the right time to enjoy them when you are in sun and surf. Treating it as a specimen plant with sun-loving annuals around the bottom may be your best bet, but an entire hedge could be outrageous.

Did You Know?
There is often confusion between tamarack *Larix decidua* and tamarisk. Tamarack looks much like a needled evergreen but is in fact a very large deciduous tree that can reach 100 feet. Tamarack and tamarisk do not have the same site preferences, so be sure to ask for and purchase the right one.

Tamarix is extremely salt tolerant and makes a great choice for the shore area. The leaves resemble scales, so even when the plant is in full leaf it maintains a unique appearance. The overall image is "fluffy." This is even more true when tamarix is covered in its delicate pink blossoms. The flowers appear in midsummer and can last for up to six weeks. The plant blooms on new growth, so the flowers blossom at the branch tips where they are most conspicuous. Each long flowering branch can be up to three feet long. In winter, tamarix takes on a rather loose, weedy appearance. Severe spring pruning will rejuvenate scraggly plants and keeps the minuscule foliage as lush as possible. Since it blooms on new growth, tamarix will still bloom come summer.

Other Common Names
Tamarisk, Salt Cedar, Five-Stamen Tamarisk

Bloom Period and Seasonal Color
Masses of feathery pink flowers on the ends of long branches in June and July.

Mature Height × Spread
10 to 15 ft. × variable width

Evergreen Trees *for New Jersey*

Evergreen trees play another important role in the landscape. They define spaces and set the tone for either a formal or more natural setting. In summer they provide the backdrop for seasonal display, but they must be interesting enough to carry the focus in winter.

Traditionally, landscape designers have frowned upon mixing deciduous material with evergreens. Perhaps it is time to break some of these rules and make your yard a personal statement. What could be lovelier than dogwood flowers peeking out from under a cluster of spruce and pines? The dogwood enjoys the shade, and the dark-green needles will make the flowers jump out like a Van Gogh painting. Shade-loving oak leaf hydrangeas thrive beneath mature white pines, bringing midsummer color to shadowy nooks.

Plan Ahead

One must avoid certain problems when dealing with evergreens, however. A common problem is planting young evergreens in places without sufficient room to grow. Many a blue spruce has outgrown the spot outside the front door. It can't be pruned down to size, so the only option is to cut it down and start over.

A second problem is the tendency to plant monocultures. A long, straight row of a single evergreen creates a very formal look, like a row of marching soldiers. That is great if you like marching soldiers, but you have a problem if one or two trees should die. New, short trees used as replacements will draw the eye to the irregularity instead of the original line. In general, it looks patched and incongruous.

American Holly 'Canary'

A staggered planting of different-sized trees eliminates the soldier look and the replacement problem. A staggered row fills in quickly and so establishes privacy in short order. Use different species to eliminate the risk of losing everything with a single blow. In tight spaces work with narrow "columnar" varieties. 'Skyrocket' juniper and 'Flushing' yew are two. There are many others. Think beyond a row of boring arborvitae. A mixed planting will not only be softer on the eye, it will perform better in the long run.

A more serious problem with monocultures occurs with the appearance of insects or disease. Once a pest has a foothold, it will spread through a monoculture like wildfire. It can wipe out, or severely damage, the entire planting before you notice. For example, bagworms on arborvitae will take out a border planting in no time.

Choosing locations for evergreens requires serious thought. You will have to live with them for a long time. While they create privacy year-round, they can also block your view, which may be desirable or not.

Time to Plant

Planting techniques for evergreen trees are similar to planting shade tree. Match the plant requirements for light, moisture, and soil types to the location. Dig a hole much larger than the root ball; two to three times as wide and twice as deep is a good rule of thumb. Amend the removed soil according to the existing soil type and the plant's soil preferences. Backfill so the plant is at the same height it had been in the ground or the top of the soil level in the pot. Remove all tags, wires, strings, and ropes. These sometimes hide in the dense

White Fir

foliage. Untie any burlap but only remove plastic burlaps. The natural burlap will decompose. Fill around the roots with the amended soil. Tamp down firmly, but more gently, right on top of the roots. Water deeply. A thick layer of organic mulch is always a good idea. Evergreens are more likely to need staking since they catch the wind all year, and if they shift over the winter it is especially difficult to correct.

When planted on the north side of a house, evergreens will block the wind and protect the house during winter weather. They can make a remarkable difference in heat loss. Planted on the south side, they are great for summer shade, but deciduous trees will let in winter rays.

Don't plant evergreens too close to the house, or too close together. You need room to get around plantings to do routine maintenance. Whatever species you choose, find out their rate of growth as well as their anticipated height at maturity and plan accordingly.

There are a few species to avoid. Norway spruce gets spruce canker badly; this is a disease that is ultimately fatal. Austrian pine has struggled with tip blight for the last twenty years and no longer should be planted. Hemlocks are beautiful, but the woolly adelgid has become a plague in recent years and chemical control is difficult.

If your deciduous shade trees form the foundation of your yard, the evergreens build the walls. Later you will get to decorate.

American Holly

Ilex opaca
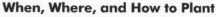

The American holly is native to New Jersey and so can be expected to do well throughout most of the state. In the wild it is more often found in the south, in both the Pine Barrens and the shore area where it tolerates sandy soil and salty conditions. In the woods it tends to be an open, almost spindly tree. When planted in full sun, American holly is much more full and rich looking. A little protection from wind and afternoon sun in the winter is beneficial. The holidays would seem incomplete without holly's brightly colored berries. It is important to know that berries appear only on female trees. This can be a problem when you are attempting to grow seedlings. There is no way to know a seedling's sex until it matures.

Bloom Period and Seasonal Color
White flowers in late May to early June; red berries in winter on female plants.

Mature Height × Spread
40 to 50 ft. × 18 to 40 ft.

When, Where, and How to Plant
Plant American holly in late March or early April. It can be planted in early fall if you provide winter protection. (See chapter introduction for more on planting.) American holly prefers acidic soil, hates wet feet and prefers sandy soil, though any well-drained soil will do. Choose a site that is out of the winter wind. Avoid western exposures. If planting American holly in the northern part of the state, add both organic matter and sand to heavy clay soils to improve drainage; water settled around the base during the winter is deadly. Pruning at planting is beneficial. Containerized material is less likely to wilt and may not need pruning. You can take off as much as one-third if wilting occurs.

Growing Tips
Water at planting and when the ground becomes dry. Fertilize in March or early April with $1/2$ cup per plant of 10-10-10 fertilizer. Never fertilize after early July.

Care
Flowers and fruit both appear on the current year's growth. This means that trees can be pruned in December, making the prunings available for indoor use without preventing the following year's fruit set. Wait until your holly has reached 6 to 7 feet before doing any holiday pruning. Leaf miners can do damage by burrowing between leaf layers; control these pests in mid-May. Check with your county extension service for current pesticide recommendations. Leaf spines may sometimes puncture other leaves, causing the holly to appear spotted. There is no control for this.

Companion Planting and Design
The rich-green or variegated leaves do much for the winter landscape. For specimen plants or groupings in key locations, it is especially important to grow named varieties. This will ensure berries where you want them. American holly is a good choice for planting at the shore, but watch where you walk—holly leaves can hurt.

Did You Know?
Hollies propagate readily from cuttings taken in December. They grow slowly. Expect to see older leaves yellow and drop in April and May. Hollies are so much a part of New Jersey history that Millville was once known as "Holly City of America."

Arborvitae
Thuja occidentalis

When, Where, and How to Plant
Plant in early spring or early fall. (See chapter introduction for more information on planting.) In a sunny location it will be quite full and dense. Although arborvitae tolerates some shade, it will be more open and leggy. It requires abundant soil moisture, so avoid excessively sandy soil. Arborvitae tolerates limestone soils. Add copious amounts of organic matter to sandy soil and to the entire bed before planting if possible. Make sure the rootball is moist prior to planting since drying out can be a major problem. Arborvitae is usually easily established if you don't let it dry out; a thick layer of organic mulch will help.

Growing Tips
Since arborvitae thrives under moist soil conditions, water deeply, especially during hot, dry summers. Keep the mulch in good condition to reduce water evaporation from the soil. Fertilize in early spring with 5-10-5.

Care
Arborvitae can be sheared lightly in April and again in June if necessary. Use a pair of hand pruners to maintain a natural shape. Overgrown trees cannot be severely pruned. If the bottom branches die back, they will not fill in. The biggest problem may be winter damage. Branches have a tendency to bend or snap under the weight of ice and snow. Try to shake off the snow while it is still light and fluffy or before it accumulates. Bagworms can be serious. The pointed "bags" are made of bits of twigs and leaves, so they look like part of the tree. The hungry critters within are very destructive. Remove bags when you see them and spray in mid-June and late June with *Bacillus thuringiensis* (Bt).

Companion Planting and Design
From a design perspective, the narrow pyramidal habit is very useful in smaller residential properties and for foundation plantings. As a border planting, arborvitae makes a formal straight row without taking up an excessive amount of room. While they have only a moderate rate of growth, the dense branches quickly create privacy. In a staggered row, they get the job done even faster.

Did You Know?
The leaves smell like apples when crushed. Early settlers made a tea from the twigs.

The arborvitae is native to the east and can be found wild in many areas of New Jersey. This fact alone has appeal for those that stress the environmental advantages of planting material which evolved under local conditions. In addition, arborvitae is far more tolerant of marshy soil conditions than are many landscape plants. While it is effective and attractively green in summer, there is nothing very exciting about this plant; however, it is still in demand. It does work well as a backdrop for more colorful plantings. On the down side, most varieties turn a rather pitiful brown in winter. They are however, workhorses in the landscape, and especially appreciated in wet ground.

Other Common Names
Eastern Arborvitae, American Arborvitae, White Cedar

Bloom Period and Seasonal Color
Green most of the year, brownish in winter.

Mature Height × Spread
25 to 60 ft. × 10 to 15 ft.

Colorado Blue Spruce

Picea pungens

The Colorado blue spruce is a beautiful tree. Its color stands out whether it is planted as part of a group or as a single specimen tree. It is magnificent with a dusting of snow and provides a haven for birds in the winter as well as a place to nest in the summer. Its biggest drawback is its overuse in the landscape. In a small yard, it can be an overwhelming focal point year-round that overshadows the rest of the yard. Blue spruce is popular as a Christmas tree. If you purchase a balled tree for the holidays, it will usually do well when planted outside. These trees have sharply pointed needles, but their color and scent make up for it.

Bloom Period and Seasonal Color
Dusty blue needles all year.

Mature Height × Spread
In cultivation: 30 to 60 ft. × 10 to 20 ft.
In wild: 135 ft. × 30 ft.

When, Where, and How to Plant
Evergreens will tolerate spring or fall planting. (See chapter introduction for more information on planting evergreens.) A balled tree purchased for the holidays will do better planted immediately after the holidays rather than waiting until spring. Choose a location with plenty of sun. Spruce prefers a moist soil type, but blues will tolerate drier conditions than most. Blue spruce is adaptable. Good planting practices generally result in healthy growth. Shake off excessive snow to make it less vulnerable to winter damage.

Growing Tips
Water thoroughly at planting. Stake when newly planted to keep them upright until establishment. Fertilizer is often not needed in better soils, but an application of 5-10-5 or the use of a water-soluble fertilizer in early spring may be beneficial.

Care
Prune slightly each spring by snipping the new growth (called "candles") back halfway. This will force side shoots to grow and maintain a fuller, more compact tree. Spruce can suffer from severe mite infestations. Control in May and again in September. Check with your Cooperative Extension Agent for current pesticide recommendations. Do not use oil sprays, which remove the needles' blue color. Spruce gall aphids cause damage that looks like miniature pineapples on the tips of the branches. Spray in April or early May and repeat in early fall. Remove the galls by August.

Companion Planting and Design
Do not plant blue spruce by the front door. It will soon outgrow that space. Mixed in with other evergreens for a border planting or privacy screen, blue spruce adds color and character. Tuck in deciduous shrubs such as crapemyrtle or vitex for summer color.

Did You Know?
In its native Rocky Mountains, this tree can live for 800 years. It grows very slowly but produces large crops of seeds every two to three years. Blue spruce readily reproduces from seeds, which require no pretreatment. Seedlings vary in the degree of blue color.

Cryptomeria
Cryptomeria japonica

When, Where, and How to Plant
Plant cryptomeria in early spring or early fall. It is not a difficult tree to grow. (See chapter introduction for more information on planting evergreens.) Choose a sunny location where it will be protected from high winds. Because cryptomeria is so sensitive to wind, trees planted in fall may require winter protection for at least the first year. Do not overcrowd this tree; it needs room to grow. Cryptomeria prefers rich, moist soil that is not heavy or wet, with a slightly acidic pH. Add organic matter, such as compost, at time of planting to help hold soil moisture.

Growing Tips
Water thoroughly at planting and whenever the soil gets dry. Cryptomeria does need a bit more water than many other evergreens. Fertilizer is often not necessary, but an application of 5-10-5 or a water-soluble fertilizer in the early spring will encourage new growth.

Care
Cryptomeria is an easy-care tree. It should need little or no pruning. Leaf diseases show up on occasion but are seldom significant.

Companion Planting and Design
Its upright but relatively narrow habit makes it a good choice for smaller yards and urban settings. The closeness of buildings in these areas makes it relatively easy to find a spot where the wind is blocked. When protected from wind, cryptomeria makes an attractive, interesting evergreen specimen. Some distinctive cultivars exist with different growth habits. 'Knaptonensis' is a mounded dwarf propagated from a "witches'-broom" discovered in Italy in 1930.

Did You Know?
There are several examples of Cryptomeria in the New Brunswick area. They were once a favorite of landscape designers at Rutgers University. A mature cryptomeria specimen is striking. The bark peels in long strips. It is particularly lovely and provides interest for the winter landscape.

Cryptomeria is an evergreen that has an unusual but graceful appearance. Its reddish brown bark is its greatest claim to beauty. The rich color is particularly evident during winter, and is enhanced by the bark's habit of peeling away in long, thin strips. Cryptomeria's tiny needles are only one-quarter inch long. They persist for four or five years and turn bronze in the winter, or brown if the tree is subject to winter wind. The round cones appear at the branch tips and grow about one inch in diameter. They are attractive both on the tree and in wreaths and dried arrangements.

Other Common Name
Japanese Cedar

Bloom Period and Seasonal Color
Reddish-brown bark; needles turn bronze in winter.

Mature Height × Spread
60 to 180 ft. (rarely) × 20 to 30 ft. in Japan

Douglas Fir
Pseudotsuga menziesii

The Douglas fir is native to the Pacific Northwest and the Rocky Mountains. Be sure to purchase a locally grown tree, especially as a Christmas tree. This will prevent problems with regional variations. Western specimens subjected to cold in transit often experience a drastic needle drop when exposed to room temperatures. Locally grown trees can be purchased balled and can be planted out after the holidays. Douglas fir trees are slow growing when young, but they grow more quickly as they age. Seeds are produced in interesting cones with "bracts" resembling feathery wings; the cones can be used decoratively. Seed production does not begin until the tree is twenty-five to thirty years old. Maximum production is not reached for two hundred to three hundred years. Individual trees can live one thousand years if not cut down for their valuable lumber.

Bloom Period and Seasonal Color
Dark green all year.

Mature Height × Spread
40 to 80 ft. × 12 to 20 ft. (taller in its native Northwest)

When, Where, and How to Plant
Plant Douglas fir in early spring or fall. (See chapter introduction for more information on planting evergreens.) Keep holiday trees indoors for no more than ten days. Acclimate your Douglas fir on an unheated porch or breezeway for a few days before planting. Choose a location that is sunny but not windy, in well drained but moist soil. The soil pH can be neutral to slightly acidic. Add organic matter to sandy soils and a 2:1 mixture of organic matter and sand to heavy clay soils. Douglas fir trees are often sold balled and burlapped. Remove plastic burlap on balled trees prior to planting; natural fiber can be left on. Be sure to remove wire, string, and tags.

Growing Tips
Water thoroughly at planting and whenever soil gets dry, especially while getting established. A deep watering before soils become excessively dry is recommended. Fertilizer is seldom necessary on better soils, but an application of 5-10-5 or a water-soluble fertilizer in early spring will increase the rate of growth.

Care
When the tree is young, pinch the new growth back halfway to maintain a bushier, more compact shape. Remove dead or damaged branches as needed. Douglas fir is subject to some needle diseases. The most common in New Jersey is needle cast, which can be controlled in the spring when new growth is $1/2$ inch long. Check with your Cooperative Extension Service for current control recommendations.

Companion Planting and Design
Careful selection of your Douglas fir is well worth the effort. It is an elegant tree that works well in groups or as a specimen. Give it plenty of room to grow. Douglas fir dislikes windy sites and is inappropriate for use as a windbreak.

Did You Know?
Despite its common name, Douglas fir is not a true fir. In their native temperate rain forest, these trees are spectacular, reaching a height of 300 feet. Without the high atmospheric and soil moisture of that region, trees do not come close to that size or stature. The lumber is exceptionally valuable for both its strength and beauty.

Fraser Fir

Abies fraseri

When, Where, and How to Plant

Plant Fraser fir in early spring or early fall. (See chapter introduction for more information on planting evergreens.) It does well as a balled-and-burlapped Christmas tree. Plant immediately after the holiday; do not wait until spring to plant. Fraser fir prefers sun but will tolerate a little shade. It may even benefit from some protection in dry, sandy soil. This tree is an excellent choice for the smaller yard. If you are transplanting a specimen, root pruning in advance will make the transition easier. Fraser fir prefers moist soil conditions, and the addition of organic matter to sandy soils will be beneficial. Water thoroughly at planting.

Growing Tips

Do not ever let soil conditions become excessively dry. Water often after planting until the tree becomes established. In hot, dry, summer weather, occasional deep watering is recommended. Fertilizer is often not necessary on better soils, but an application of 5-10-5 or a water-soluble fertilizer according to directions in early spring will increase the rate of growth.

Care

Fraser fir is a low maintenance tree that requires little pruning or shaping. Summer stress is one of its few problems. Proper site selection, thorough soil preparation, and water when needed is the best way to protect it. It has no significant insect or disease problems.

Companion Planting and Design

Fraser fir makes a perfect specimen tree. Its pyramidal shape looks like it came from a Currier and Ives engraving. It mixes well with other evergreens and will benefit from the shade of its taller relatives. When used for privacy or as a border planting, evergreens look best in a staggered row with different species all together. In this situation, locate the Fraser in front. This will be the most effective placement since it is one of the smaller trees and you will want to enjoy its appearance.

Did You Know?

In its native environment, Fraser fir can be found at elevations as high as 6,900 ft. There it is mixed with red spruce and a few yellow birch. These deep, shady woods are acclaimed for their beauty. Red squirrels are the primary consumers of the seeds.

Fraser fir is an absolutely beautiful tree with a terrific scent. Its almost perfect pyramid shape requires little pruning to maintain. The dark-green color is rich and lustrous. Fraser fir is very popular as a Christmas tree and gains in popularity every year. The horizontal branches are perfect for hanging ornaments. This tree is native to the Appalachian Mountains in Virginia, West Virginia, North Carolina, and Tennessee. It is slow growing and smaller than many other evergreens, so it is a good choice for suburban yards. It struggles in hot, dry weather. This tree has all the appearances of the "perfect" evergreen and is a personal favorite.

Other Common Names
Southern Balsam Fir, Southern Fir, She Balsam

Bloom Period and Seasonal Color
Rich dark green all year.

Mature Height × Spread
30 to 40 ft. × 20 to 25 ft.

Himalayan Pine

Pinus wallichiana

If you have the room to grow a Himalayan pine, this is a magical tree. The secret space under a mature tree has a quality well worth experiencing. A Himalayan pine needs plenty of room to spread out. It can eventually reach fifty feet across, although growing is a slow process. Its enormous bulk is softened by the five- to eight-inches long needles that droop down, creating a delicate, feathery appearance. The needles are clustered together in groups of five and are so soft looking that you will want to stroke them. The light brown cones are up to twelve inches in length. There is a wonderful old specimen of Himalayan pine at the Rutgers Gardens in New Brunswick.

Other Common Name
Bhutan Pine

Bloom Period and Seasonal Color
Dark green all year.

Mature Height × Spread
50 to 150 ft. × 1/3 of the height

When, Where, and How to Plant

Plant Himalayan pine in early spring or early fall. (See chapter introduction for more information on planting evergreens.) Choose a location with plenty of room in full sun that provides some protection from winter wind. In a windy setting the top of the tree may thin out and become weak. Himalayan pine tolerates air pollution better than most pines, but it is too large for most urban settings. Acidic sandy loam soil, which is easy to find in New Jersey, is best for this tree. Be sure to plant a young tree, placing it in its permanent location. A container-grown tree will suffer very little root disruption in the planting process and may be preferred to a balled-and-burlapped specimen. In heavy soils, add a 2:1 mixture of organic matter and sand to ensure good drainage. Prepare a big area since Himalayan pine is a large, spreading tree. Water thoroughly at planting.

Growing Tips

Water as necessary to avoid excessively dry soil conditions. Fertilizer is seldom necessary on better soils, but an application of 5-10-5 or the use of a water-soluble fertilizer according to directions in the early spring will increase the rate of growth.

Care

Himalayan pine does not suffer any particular problems. Its needles will brown if temperatures drop to -15 degrees Fahrenheit. Keep pruning to a minimum since its natural shape and habit is one of its main attractions.

Companion Planting and Design

Although its size prohibits its use in most urban settings, its tolerance for air pollution makes it a great choice for parks or the grounds of some industrial sites. This potentially enormous tree is a great specimen but not well suited for mixing with other plantings. It will work beautifully with a scattering of daffodils around its edges or even daylilies for summer color.

Did You Know?

This tree is native to the Himalayan mountains where it is found at elevations of up to 12,500 feet. In its place of origin, the lumber is used for construction. 'Zebrina' is a variety with variegated needles with yellow bands. There is a breathtaking specimen at the National Arboretum.

Serbian Spruce
Picea omorika

When, Where, and How to Plant

Plant Serbian spruce in early spring or early fall. (See chapter introduction for more information on planting evergreens.) This tree prefers a bit of shade and does best in a moist location. The combination of narrow habit, its shade requirements, and its tolerance of air pollution makes the Serbian spruce one of the best choices for an urban environment. Protect specimens from severe winter winds (more easily done in a city setting). This tree requires well-drained soil; both heavy clay and sandy soils will benefit from the addition of organic matter.

Growing Tips

Water at planting and keep the soil moist thereafter. This is especially important while getting your Serbian spruce established. Fertilizer is often not necessary, especially since you want to keep this plant compact for growing in tight spaces. The use of 5-10-5 or a water-soluble fertilizer in early spring may be beneficial in poorer soils.

Care

Serbian spruce is a low maintenance tree. Its narrow habit eliminates the need for pruning. It can have trouble with pests such as aphids, spruce budworm, and borers, but there is no indication that such problems are pervasive.

Companion Planting and Design

Open rolling lawns may not be the best place to plant Serbian spruce, but it is a great choice for urban spots where buildings block the wind and space is limited. When planting in a border for privacy, make sure you mix Serbian spruce with more wind tolerant evergreens. Some examples are the hardy white pine, the Colorado blue spruce (native to the Rocky Mountains), or even the Swiss stone pine (native to the Alps of Europe). Then place the Serbian spruce on the more protected side of the staggered row.

Did You Know?

Serbian spruce is native to Yugoslavia, but before the Ice Age it could be found throughout Europe. A unique characteristic of this tree is that its needles are flat (like the hemlock's), not four-sided as are the needles of most spruces. There are several named varieties. 'Pendula' is the most common and has drooping and slightly twisted branches.

The Serbian spruce is one of the best ornamental spruces. Its narrow growth habit makes it a good choice for smaller yards or for border plantings where space is a problem. It is even considered tolerant of city air and is worth considering as an evergreen street tree. The leaves are dark green on the surface but have white stripes underneath. Since the Norway spruce has been overused—why not try something a little different? This tree has an exceptionally narrow trunk and grows into a slender pyramid with gracefully cascading branches. Some references report Serbian spruce is difficult to locate, but it is carried wholesale by Princeton Nursery, in Allentown, New Jersey, and should be readily available at the retail level.

Bloom Period and Seasonal Color
Dark green all year.

Mature Height × Spread
100 ft. × 25 ft.

Swiss Stone Pine

Pinus cembra

Swiss stone pine is a narrow columnar species. Its shape and its slow rate of growth make it ideal for suburban and urban yards. If you use one of these trees to frame your home, you will not have to worry about cutting it down in ten years. There are five needles per cluster, usually two to three inches long, though they can reach up to five inches. Needles persist for four to five years. The habit of the Swiss stone pine opens up as it matures, though not as much as most other pines. They tend toward being flat-topped with drooping branches as they age. Because they grow slowly, they may be a bit more costly than other pines of similar size. Its beauty and growth habit make it worth the extra expense.

Other Common Name
Arolla Pine

Bloom Period and Seasonal Color
Green all year.

Mature Height × Spread
30 to 100 ft. × 15 to 25 ft.

When, Where, and How to Plant

Plant Swiss stone pine in early spring or early fall. (See chapter introduction for more information on planting evergreens.) Choose a sunny, open area in well-drained, slightly acidic soil. Swiss stone pine is considered very hardy and tolerates windy, exposed conditions better than the Serbian spruce does, although both work well in smaller yards. Swiss stone pine transplants relatively easily. It prefers well-drained soil, so heavy clay soils will benefit from the addition of a 2:1 mixture of organic matter and sand.

Growing Tips

Water thoroughly at planting and whenever the soil gets excessively dry. A 5-10-5 fertilizer can be applied in early spring after the tree becomes established.

Care

A variety of insects and diseases can affect pines, but none is of particular danger to the Swiss stone pine. Its narrow growth habit generally makes pruning unnecessary. Where a particularly compact plant is desirable, the candles can be pinched back halfway to force lateral bud formation. When more pruning is necessary, take care to prune back to a side branch or shoot and not beyond. If you cut all the way to bare wood, the needles will not re-sprout.

Companion Planting and Design

The narrow growth habit and slow rate of growth makes this pine an excellent choice for smaller yards. Its tolerance of windy conditions makes it a good choice for windbreaks and privacy plantings. Mixed in a staggered row, its appearance offers a bit of diversity among other evergreens, but be sure to plant it in front of faster growing trees. A white pine will soon hide a Swiss stone pine, and you do not want to miss its beauty.

Did You Know?

Swiss stone pine is native to the Alps and grows at an elevation of 10,000 feet. Very old trees become open and flat at the top. The large seeds are edible. *P. pumila* or dwarf Siberian pine is a shrubby species that can reach 9 feet. Native to Siberia and Japan, it is sometimes considered a regional variation of the Swiss stone pine.

Umbrella Pine

Sciadopitys verticillata

When, Where, and How to Plant

Plant umbrella pine in early spring or early fall. (See chapter introduction for more planting information.) Choose a sunny spot with a bit of protection from blazing summer sun and winter wind. Umbrella pine is not particularly fussy about getting established. (We transplanted a five-foot tree in late spring without difficulty.) It requires good drainage, so amend clay soils with a mixture of 2 parts organic matter and 1 part sand. Dig a very large hole for the rootball. Stake this tree, especially during the first winter, since umbrella pine's full shape and thick branches will catch the wind.

Growing Tips

Water thoroughly at planting and when soil gets dry. Since it is such a slow grower, an application of 5-10-5 in early spring may speed things up.

Care

Umbrella pine's slow rate of growth makes major pruning unwarranted if the tree is located properly. Winter damage may require the removal of a dead branch or two, and occasional pruning to shape may also be necessary. Those few branches you do remove can be used as greens in flower arrangements. They last for weeks and provide an exotic look. The umbrella pine has no serious pest problems.

Companion Planting and Design

Umbrella pine makes a great specimen tree. It can also add interest to a border planting. Since it does best with a little protection from hot afternoon sun and winter wind, planting this tree in a staggered row with other pines may create the perfect spot. Its slow growth rate makes it one of the evergreens more suitable for use as a foundation planting. It may be the ideal tree for the corner of the house.

Did You Know?

The umbrella pine is not really a pine at all. It is in the family Taxodiaceae, which makes it a closer relative of yews and the giant redwood of California. Propagation is difficult. This is a major reason there are not more umbrella pines in the trade. Even so, they can be found without an extensive search.

At first glance, umbrella pine looks like just another evergreen. Then you realize it's different, and you want to touch it to see why. The needles are arranged in whorls that resemble umbrellas with their fabric blown away. Umbrella pine has long needles up to five inches in length, as well as scale-like needles on the branches. The texture is mesmerizing. The dark-green needles are thick, almost succulent in appearance. They retain their color year-round. Though the habit is described as "broadly pyramidal," the term "chubby" probably gives a better visual image. This tree opens as it ages but grows so slowly that the person who plants it may never get to see it open up.

Other Common Name
Japanese Umbrella Pine

Bloom Period and Seasonal Color
Dark green all year.

Mature Height × Spread
30 to 70 ft. (Up to 120 ft. in Japan) × variable spread

White Fir
Abies concolor

White fir's fullness and color soften the appearance of its stiff shape. Bluer specimens provide strong competition for the Colorado blue spruce. The white fir is not planted nearly as often as one would expect. The two-inch-long needles have a blue tint, though the degree of blueness varies among seedlings. The needle texture is slightly flattened but pudgy. White fir is accepting of an urban environment and will grow in spite of heat, drought, and rocky, barren soil. It does not like heavy clay soil and does best in deep, sandy loam soils. The white fir tree grows fairly rapidly when young but slows down as it ages. It takes about forty years before a tree is mature enough to produce cones, and the average life span is about three hundred-fifty years.

Other Common Names
Concolor Fir, Colorado Fir

Bloom Period and Seasonal Color
Bluish needles all year.

Mature Height × Spread
30 to 100 ft. × 15 to 30 ft.

When, Where, and How to Plant
Balled-and-burlapped trees do best when planted in late March or early April. Container material can be planted in early fall. (See chapter introduction for more planting information.) Choose a sunny or mostly sunny location. White fir will tolerate less than ideal locations better than many other evergreens. While considered very cooperative, transplanting white fir is not always easy. It should do well if good soil preparation is practiced and if it is not planted in heavy clay soil. Make sure the location is well drained. Add a 2:1 ratio of organic matter and sand to clay soils. Stake newly planted white firs since they so easily catch the wind.

Growing Tips
Water thoroughly at planting. White fir is somewhat drought tolerant, but water deeply when the ground gets dry. Unless you are in a rush for this plant to get big, fertilizer is rarely needed.

Care
White fir should not be significantly pruned—severely pruned limbs will probably not re-sprout. Insects and diseases pose no major problems. Stake a white fir until you are certain it is established. You may be better off keeping the stakes in place for two or three years, but check frequently to make sure ties do not cut into the bark.

Companion Planting and Design
Do not plant this tree in a tight spot. White fir is an excellent choice for the not-too-small suburban yard or city location. The combination of the color and texture of the needles gives white fir a unique appearance. Use it to create interest in a mixed planting or for use as a year-round focal point.

Did You Know?
White fir is occasionally used as a Christmas tree. It has a very pleasant citrus odor. While the blue spruce's sharp points make it less desirable for indoor use, white fir gives a comparable look without the tendency to stab the decorators. It was at one time the wood of choice for making butter tubs because it imparted no additional flavor to the butter.

White Pine

Pinus strobus

When, Where, and How to Plant

Plant white pine in early spring or early fall, or immediately after the holidays if used as a balled Christmas tree. (See chapter introduction for more information on planting evergreens.) White pine prefers well-drained, moist, fertile soils, but it is one of the most adaptable evergreens. It does not tolerate salt, pollutants, or severe wind. It is easily established. Thorough soil preparation gives the best chance for success. Stake fall or winter planted trees to keep them upright until their roots take hold.

Growing Tips

Water thoroughly at planting. To minimize yellow needles over the winter, provide deep watering when temperatures soar and soils tend to dry. A 5-10-5 fertilizer in early spring will encourage new growth, especially if trees are heavily pruned.

Care

Snipping the candles in spring will keep white pine full and compact. Light pruning consistently every spring will allow white pines to make an effective hedge. Keep the top rounded to shed snow, since the weight on a flat-topped hedge may break branches. A mature hedge can be sheared very lightly. White pine weevil can be a problem; remove any dead branches in early summer. Spray in early to mid-April to prevent this injury. Contact your Cooperative Extension Service for control options.

Companion Planting and Design

White pine can be used as a hedge if not over-pruned. It is not a good choice for down the shore or even as a city tree. However it is a great tree to mix with other evergreens in a mixed border or even as a specimen tree. Plant on the north side of the house (if it is not too windy). Its fullness will provide winter protection.

Did You Know?

The wood of white pine was at one time claimed by the British throne to be used for ship masts. This royal greed was one of the factors that contributed to the Colonial rebellion and, ultimately, the American Revolution. It is still an important species for lumber, but there are few giant white pines left in the east.

The white pine is an extremely important native tree. Its adaptability, tolerance for pruning, ease of transplanting, and graceful appearance has made it one of the most popular landscaping trees. White pine has the natural ability to reseed itself in abandoned fields and so is useful in land reclamation projects. Following a dry summer, the needles on some trees may yellow, but in most years white pine retains its bluish green color. The five-inch-long needles grow five to a bundle. Young trees are considered pyramidal in shape, but they are another of the "chubby" pyramids. They are commonly used as Christmas trees and treasured for their "poofy" appearance, but watch out! Ornaments tend to slide off its long, slippery needles.

Other Common Name
Eastern White Pine

Bloom Period and Seasonal Color
Bluish green all year.

Mature Height × Spread
80 to 100 ft. × 20 to 40 ft.

Ground Covers *for New Jersey*

Ground covers are extremely useful for covering the ground. This may sound like an oversimplification, but it is the practical truth. If you don't cover the ground with something, nature takes over. Wait long enough and you will have a mature forest.

The most popular ground cover is grass. This ubiquitous green carpet holds up under foot traffic, is pleasing to the eye, and creates an environment conducive to family life. Unfortunately, forcing grass to grow where it doesn't feel comfortable can be a constant battle, and good quality grass is rather high maintenance. There are also places where grass is inappropriate. You wouldn't want grass under shrubs, and no one wants to mow grass in a rock garden. Steep slopes can be dangerous, and you may not want to spend your time mowing at a weekend getaway house. Determine how much grass you need to satisfy the demands of your family's activities, then find the areas where you can use other ground covers.

Ground covers add interest to the landscape with texture and color and sometimes even flowers. Ground covers help grass be at its best by eliminating places where grass is less than ideal. For example, a great place for ground covers is beneath shade trees. The shade, along with the tree roots, can make growing grass almost impossible. In addition, mowing under trees is a problem since surface roots interfere, and an occasional nick in the bark is not good for the tree. Use ground covers to connect beds and to provide definition of space. They can help direct the flow of foot traffic. Once established, they are invaluable in controlling weeds.

Ground Covers Have Needs

Planting ground covers is a bit different than planting either grass or shrubs. Some ground covers can be planted from seed, but most are from potted material, and many are propagated from rooted cuttings, often in a flat. Planting container material at the same depth it was in the pot is standard operating procedure, but transplanting cuttings that have a bit of a root, or separating rooted cuttings from a flat requires a bit more attention. You need to get enough root and stem underground without burying it so deeply that the stem rots. If the stem is completely green, it is more likely to rot. Try to find the spot on the stem where it stops looking like a root and looks more like a green stem. Keep the green stem above ground. Separating plants in a flat requires a gentle but firm hand to pull apart the tangle of roots while breaking as few as possible.

Ground covers usually are planted to cover an expanse, so soil preparation is done more like the preparation for grass than individual plants. Amend the soil based on the soil type and the specific needs of the chosen ground cover. Spacing of the plants depends on the species as well as the speed at which you need the plants to fill in. An organic mulch between the plants will help control weeds until the ground is completely covered. How often you need to water is species dependent, but try not to let any plants get overly dry until you are sure they are firmly established. Care of ground covers is species

Sloped Landscape with Creeping Juniper

specific. Some will spread too aggressively with regular fertilization while others will benefit. In most cases you will not want to prune or shear ground covers since the general idea of their use is to reduce maintenance chores. Read about the individual plants included in this chapter for your options with each species.

Most ground covers hug the ground and stay under eighteen inches tall. Up to three feet may be acceptable, but the size of the ground cover needs to be in proportion to its surroundings. The amount of sunlight available will also affect your choice. If a townhouse rock garden is in blazing sun, try one of the sedums.

Try Something Different

Any of the "big three" (pachysandra, ivy, and myrtle) are ground cover choices that work well, but you may want to try something a little different. Bunchberry is related to our native dogwood; it is a beautiful ground cover that thrives in shade, but only in the coldest part of the state. Liriope is an evergreen with strappy leaves and late-summer flowers. Pink-flowered lily-of-the-valley is dusty pink.

The popular switch grass, *Panicum virgatum*, reaches seven feet and historically did a fine job of covering the vast grass prairies. It is a good choice for erosion control and taming open fields in a hurry. The tiny leafed, six-inch saxifrage London Pride (*Saxifraga* × *urbium*) is perfect in a rock garden outside a townhouse, but it isn't going to keep three acres of soil in place.

Grass doesn't stand a chance in wet ground, but you can try *Houttuynia cordata* 'Chameleon'. It prefers very moist soil and tolerates soil that is constantly wet. It grows vigorously in full sun and gives a blast of color with leaves showing yellow, green, bronze, and scarlet.

Grass is a basic component of landscape design. While ground covers will never replace perennials and woody ornamentals for interest, they do offer a bit of zing to the otherwise mundane. If grass were a loaf of sandwich bread, then ground covers are English muffins, and bagels, and crusty Italian bread, and maybe even corn muffins. Indulge a little!

Bugleweed
Ajuga reptans

Bugleweed forms a solid mat of leaves that are interesting both in texture and color. The species is dark green, but the varieties get outrageous with purple and even multi-colored variegation. In partial shade, the leaves reach four inches. Full sun keeps them slightly smaller, but the colors are more vivid. Ajuga is in the mint family and has mint's enthusiasm for spreading. The plants send out runners up to ten inches long, which put down roots along the way. The flower spikes are held above the foliage. For such a small plant, it puts on a significant display. It will eventually reseed, but the seedlings tend to revert to the green species type.

Other Common Name
Carpet Bugle

Bloom Period and Seasonal Color
Early May to mid-June in white, pink, blue, or violet. Dark green, purple, or variegated almost evergreen foliage.

Mature Height × Spread
6 to 12 in. × variable width

When, Where, and How to Plant
Planting in early spring is best. It will do well in both sun and shade, but its colors are brighter in sun. Avoid very hot and dry locations. Bugleweed can be started from seed, but that usually results in species type plants. Container-grown plants are generally available, and you can sometimes purchase them by the flat. Plant bugleweed 6 to 12 inches apart in moist, well-drained soil. The addition of organic matter is beneficial. (See chapter introduction for more on planting.)

Growing Tips
Water at planting and during hot weather. A light application of 5-10-5 fertilizer in early spring will give the plants a growth spurt. Take care not to be overly generous, as heavy feeding encourages root diseases, especially in poorly drained soils.

Care
In the spring, divide the established plants. Watch for creepers that invade the space of other plants, including your lawn. Direct runners to fill in bare spots by pinning them to the soil in the direction you wish them to grow. Once they root, remove the pins. Remove escapees and give them away or plant them elsewhere. Don't throw them on the compost pile or they will probably root there, too. To control seedling volunteers, remove seedheads before they shatter. Mowing the flowers as they fade, but before the seeds mature, will reduce seed dispersal. If you have planted a particular variety and you wish to maintain it, weeding out the volunteer seedlings is a must. You can also replant the bed if it gets jumbled together. Ajuga is a sturdy plant and has few, if any, pest problems.

Companion Planting and Design
Bugleweed is an excellent choice for under trees or along borders. The use of substantial edging such as railroad ties or larger rocks will help prevent it from creeping to unwanted places.

Did You Know?
Bugleweed is considered evergreen in most of New Jersey but may get a little ratty by spring. A nip and tuck here and there will tidy things up. Its big blast of flowers is in early spring, but it may surprise you by throwing up an occasional spike throughout the summer.

Creeping Juniper
Juniperus horizontalis

When, Where, and How to Plant
Plant in early spring or early fall. Container-grown material can be planted any time the ground can be worked. Plant in a sunny location since it tends to become open and scraggly in the shade. Dry rocky soil or heavy clay is acceptable. Adding organic matter for junipers is not required. Creeping junipers don't require a higher pH but will tolerate it. They are easily established.

Growing Tips
Water at planting and whenever the ground becomes excessively dry. A light application of 5-10-5 fertilizer in early spring will give them a boost.

Care
Occasionally prune dead or straying branches. Wear gloves to avoid irritation. Always prune back to a side shoot, or you will lose the branch entirely. Bagworms can completely defoliate a juniper if left unattended. Juniper blight usually affects the twigs, but it can kill an entire plant. Most of the time however, Junipers are tough.

Companion Planting and Design
Creeping junipers are useful for rock gardens, on steep slopes, and for mass planting. They even tolerate container culture. In urban conditions, they hold up under pollution and city grime but can be a little boring when planted in large numbers. Daffodils planted directly beneath the branches will come up through the foliage. Consider mixing in a few interesting rocks with an assortment of creeping junipers. Try shades of green or blue junipers, a few mat types, and some that are on the shrubby side. For variety, throw in one with some leaf variegation. They are effective in preventing erosion on a slope and can take the heat of a south- or west-facing exposure.

Did You Know?
Juniper berries can be used to make gin, and four berries can be substituted for a bay leaf in cooking. Try putting a few juniper branches on the outside grill, where it is thought to add an interesting smoky flavor to cooking meats.

Creeping junipers are workhorses and are among the easiest plants to grow. These plants can be green, blue green, or metallic blue. Many have a purple tint in fall and winter that can vary from plum to silvery purple or bronze purple. The number of varieties is endless. They are native to the northeastern United States and are particularly tolerant of rocky, sandy soil conditions and hot, dry locations. They are very adaptable for use in the landscape (they can be found in the wild in swamps as well as on sea cliffs). The leaves of all varieties are "glaucous," which means the needles are covered in a grayish, bluish, or whitish waxy coating that can be easily wiped off.

Other Common Names
Creeping Savin Juniper, Creeping Cedar

Bloom Period and Seasonal Color
Evergreen with a possible hint of blue green or metallic blue, possibly a touch of purple in winter.

Mature Height × Spread
1 to 2 ft. × 4 to 8 ft., but variable

Dwarf Japanese Juniper

Juniperus procumbens 'Nana'

Of all the groundhugging junipers, this is the most beautiful, possibly because it doesn't look much like a juniper. Its small needles and layered branches are far more exotic than most, and it is the perfect choice for a Japanese garden or even for bonsai. J. procumbens 'Nana' is tolerant of shore planting conditions. Mature needles have a bluish cast but emerge a bright green that turns slightly purple in winter. The needles are small, densely packed together—and sharp! The effect is more like moss than a juniper. I once had a tiered garden in an urban setting. 'Nana' was planted in one corner of the uppermost tier. It draped down four railroad ties and spread out on the lowest tier, two levels below. It was stunning!

Bloom Period and Seasonal Color
Evergreen with a slight bluish cast and a touch of purple in winter.

Mature Height × Spread
1 ft. × 4 to 12 ft.

When, Where, and How to Plant
Plant in early spring or early fall. 'Nana' needs full sun but is flexible regarding soils and moisture. Use a location where it has room to spread. Its detail is best viewed close up. It is an excellent choice for a specimen plant in small yards, but tumbling over a structure best shows off its character. It is a slow grower at about 6 to 8 inches each year. While some gardeners believe it is difficult to establish, I have planted several over the years in very different environments with no difficulty.

Growing Tips
Water at planting and when it is excessively dry. A light application of 5-10-5 in early spring will give 'Nana' a boost but is often not necessary.

Care
'Nana' is tolerant of pruning, including the pruning required for bonsai. Take care to prune back to a side shoot. The *Phomopsis* twig blight that affects other junipers affects 'Nana' severely, so you may not want to overindulge in this species. The disease can be controlled by spraying an appropriate fungicide at budbreak and at fourteen-day intervals. Prune out infected twigs; when pruning an infected plant, dip the pruners in a solution of household bleach between cuts. This will reduce the spread of the disease.

Companion Planting and Design
'Nana' makes an impenetrable barrier to weeds. Try using it on slopes, terraces, or embankments. A single plant is often enough, even for design uses. J. procumbens 'Nana' is a must for draping over a wall. A rock wall is best, but any wall will show off the many layers of branches as they cascade over and down. It is interesting enough to be a focal point all year but blends beautifully with spring bulbs or summer annuals. Down the shore, the contrast with the "pebble lawns" is stunning. It is also suitable for container culture.

Did You Know?
There are some absolutely magnificent old plants in the Dwarf Conifer Garden at the National Arboretum in Washington, D.C. If you are in that area, even a drive-through visit is worthwhile.

English Ivy
Hedera helix

When, Where, and How to Plant

English ivy can be purchased by the pot, bare root, or in flats. If transplanting, try to get pieces that have some roots already started. If needed, cuttings put in water will usually root. A rooting hormone and sterile potting medium increase the chance of success. Since English ivy prefers deep, rich, humusy soil, double-dig the soil and add copious amounts of organic matter. Plant in early spring or early fall. Since it can grow in sun or shade, you can plant it almost anywhere, but it will stay the most attractive out of winter sun and wind. Ivy tolerates a wide range of soil pH. It adapts well to containers and shows some tolerance for shore growing conditions.

Growing Tips

Water at planting. Pay extra attention to the watering needs of newly planted cuttings until they are established. While somewhat drought tolerant, plants in full sun may need water in extreme heat. A 5-10-5 fertilizer in early spring will help in the first two to three years. Once growth takes off, fertilizer is probably not needed.

Care

Established patches can grow with enthusiasm, requiring the occasional significant haircut. Ivy is subject to mites, which can be particularly bad on potted plants indoors in the winter but will show up outdoors as well. Leaf spots can be a problem and require treatment with an appropriate fungicide at budbreak, ten days later, and then twenty days later. Control mites whenever they appear. A strong spray of water will wash away most mites, but if the infestation persists, check with your Cooperative Extension Service for current insecticide recommendations.

Companion Planting and Design

Plant in beds under shade trees, along slopes that may be difficult to mow, on steep banks for erosion control, or up a wall. Ivy will cover a chain-link fence but must be woven into the fence for the clinging air roots to hold. On the ground, you can use it to spread over an old broken black-topped area or concrete patio or even an ugly old shed.

Did You Know?

There is an old saying about ivy: "The first year it sleeps. The second year it creeps. The third year it leaps!" After planting, be patient.

What would ivy covered halls be without this dependable old favorite? English ivy is native to many parts of Europe and was one of the earliest plants brought by settlers. English ivy will produce small clusters of flowers in "umbels" in October. The branches with the ability to bloom have a more simple foliage considered the "adult" leaves. The adult branches grow more like a woody plant and less vigorously than the juvenile foliage most people recognize. The flowers develop into black berrylike fruits that are poisonous. Because it is a vine, it tends to climb things in its path. Take care not to let it encircle the trunk of a woody ornamental, or even a mature shade tree. The vine will eventually strangle the branch or trunk.

Other Common Name
Evergreen Ivy

Bloom Period and Seasonal Color
Mature plants produce small greenish white flowers in October.

Mature Height × Spread
Ground cover: 6 to 8 in. × variable width
Climbing: 90 ft. × variable width

Lamb's Ears
Stachys byzantina

The common name of this plant is quite appropriate. Its silvery leaves are shaped much like the ear of a lamb and are incredibly soft. Because of this seductive attribute, lamb's ears have been featured in gardens for the blind. These are tough, fuzzy little plants. The plants form a thick mat relatively quickly. They are almost evergreen but require some cleanup in the spring. The flowers receive mixed reviews. The very straight spikes produce "interrupted" blooms that are spaced out along the stem. As cut flowers, they look lovely with iris that bloom at the same time, or the flowers can be left on the spikes to dry for use later on. Some gardeners remove them immediately to keep the focus on the foliage.

Other Common Names
Woolly Betony, Woundwort

Bloom Period and Seasonal Color
Purple flowers from late June through July and occasionally afterward.

Mature Height × Spread
6 to 18 in. in bloom × 18 to 24 in.

When, Where, and How to Plant
Start from seed indoors in the spring. Divide established plants or start from potted plants in spring or fall. These plants will do best with mostly sun, although light shade is not devastating. Well-drained average soil is adequate for them. Space the plants 12 to 18 inches apart. If you plant from seed, you will get plants typical of the species. There are not many varieties readily available, but if they have characteristics that interest you, stick to potted plants or divisions. Lamb's ears are easy to establish with little fuss and even endure shore conditions.

Growing Tips
Water at planting and whenever the soil becomes excessively dry. Fertilize with 5-10-5 after spring pruning.

Care
Spring tidying is the biggest chore. Dead centers of a mass planting require division and replanting of the young shoots. Sometimes they will volunteer from seed, but not aggressively. When the center is only mildly deteriorated, they can often be rejuvenated with a significant pruning. Pull unwanted seedlings, especially if you want uniformity of a particular variety. Cut flower stalks before they get ugly. Lamb ears have fungus problems in hot humid weather but can be protected with well-drained soils in full sun.

Companion Planting and Design
Use lamb's ears by itself or mixed with darker ground covers. It works well with spring bulbs followed by summer annuals, remaining as a link between the two seasons. The velvety texture provides terrific contrast in a rock garden. The color contrasts beautifully with other foliage and forms a wonderful background for colorful blooms. Pale pinks and soft blues may benefit the most from this type of background, although brilliant red or deep purple splashed against the silver looks wonderful, too.

Did You Know?
Known as betony in the herb world, lamb's ear has a long, interesting history. According to *Rodale's Illustrated Encyclopedia of Herbs*, in the Middle Ages lamb's ear was used to ward off evil spirits. The English volume *Demonology and Witchcraft* states: "The house where Herba betonica is sown is free from all mischief."

Moss Pink
Phlox subulata

When, Where, and How to Plant
Install potted plants in early spring or early fall. Divide established plants in the fall. Plant moss pinks in full sun with loose, well-drained soil. In heavy soil conditions, add a 2:1 mixture of organic matter and sand to loosen up the soil. You may try planting in raised beds or on a slope. Plant 12 inches apart for a quick cover. Moss pinks spread quickly and are not difficult to get established.

Growing Tips
Water at planting and whenever the soil gets excessively dry. Shearing can be done after bloom time. Fertilize after shearing in the spring with 5-10-5 fertilizer.

Care
Moss pinks must be divided every few years to keep them full and healthy. It's best to divide in the fall. Shearing or mowing in the spring when they finish blooming will promote new growth and keep them thick enough to control most weeds. If you have a large area, you can use the lawn mower set high. Spider mites can be a problem, but moss pinks are not as susceptible to powdery mildew as their upright cousins, garden phlox. A heavy spray of water will wash away many of the spider mites. A heavy infestation will require an appropriate insecticide.

Companion Planting and Design
Rock gardens display this plant to perfection, but mixed borders and any sunny open area will be suitable. When mass planted, the drive-by impact is spectacular. Moss pinks are tolerant of shore planting conditions.

Did You Know?
Something as simple as a bank of flowers can have an amazing impact. When I was a child, my family had no garden. Someone mowed our grass and that was about it. Then one day my father asked the landscaper to put in a few "pinks" where the yard sloped down to the driveway. They were so beautiful I could hardly believe my eyes. Years later, I saw Phlox subulata blooming at a nursery and instantly recognized it as my childhood favorite. After all the flowers I have grown, I can still picture those "pinks" as clearly as if they were planted yesterday.

Moss pinks are native to the Northeast. They can be found from New York to North Carolina. Moss pinks produce an amazing number of flowers for an extended season of bloom. They create a sea of brilliant color that looks best in a rock garden or draped over a wall. At the peak of flowering, it is difficult to see the foliage through the flowers. After bloom, the half-inch leaves form a dense mat. They are dark green, needlelike, and densely packed. The flowers fade to a green carpet forming a perfect background for summer flowers. The leaves are almost evergreen but look a bit tattered by spring. A single plant can cover a large expanse. Its stems are almost woody. Eventually the center dies, and the plant must be divided.

Other Common Names
Ground Pink, Mountain Pink, Moss Phlox

Bloom Period and Seasonal Color
Flowers in white, pink, lilac, magenta, purple, or variegated, appearing in March through May.

Mature Height × Spread
6 in. × 1 to 3 ft.

Pachysandra
Pachysandra terminalis

It would not be possible to write about ground covers and exclude pachysandra. It is one of the "big three" (the other two being ivy and myrtle). The dark green leaves are up to four inches long and one and one-half inches wide. They are dentate (they have indentations along their edges) and are arranged alternately along the stem but form a rosette at the tip. While not exciting, pachysandra is dependable, evergreen, non-invasive, and competes effectively with tree roots. Pachysandra spreads by "stolons" or stems that run along the ground sending out new roots and shoots. It grows at a moderate rate and transplants easily. The flowers are not dramatic, but they add a little interest in early spring.

Other Common Name
Japanese Spurge

Bloom Period and Seasonal Color
Glossy green, with spikes of white flowers in early May.

Mature Height × Spread
6 to 12 in. × variable spread

When, Where, and How to Plant
Plant in early spring or early fall in shade and acid soil conditions. Avoid exposed locations in sun and wind, or the foliage will suffer. Pachysandra needs an abundance of organic matter in moist but well-drained soil. When preparing soil, pile on the leaf compost and till it in. Transplant cuttings with roots already started. Plants are sold by the flat or possibly bare root. Plant 6 inches apart for quick cover. Apply an organic mulch to help control weeds. This also adds needed organic matter as the mulch decomposes.

Growing Tips
Water thoroughly after planting, but don't keep the soil waterlogged. Water in times of drought. Fertilizer is usually not needed unless the soil conditions are very poor.

Care
Trim back at the edges if it creeps beyond its bounds. Once established, it is an effective weed barrier. Pachysandra canker can be a major problem. You can recognize it by circular areas where the plants are brown and flopped over from the base. If not controlled, it can take out the entire planting. An appropriate fungicide applied three times at ten- to fourteen-day intervals should solve the problem. Add a "spreader sticker" to the solution for more effective application. This will help the fungicide stick to the shiny, slippery leaves.

Companion Planting and Design
Pachysandra is excellent for use under shade trees, small trees, mature evergreens, shrubs, and in any shady nook. It can be effective in tight, semi-urban settings, provided there is adequate soil preparation.

Did You Know?
In *The Complete Shade Gardener*, author George Schenk observes that in Japan, he never found a planting of this native plant, even though the Japanese use ground covers extensively. It is unfortunate they do not appreciate it. Meanwhile, it tends to be overused in the United States. Save it for truly deep shade where not much else will grow, and elsewhere use something with a little more spunk.

Periwinkle
Vinca minor

When, Where, and How to Plant
Plant in early spring or early fall. Light shade is best; in full sun it may have winter leaf discoloration; in deep shade it may not bloom. It does best in moist soil that is high in organic matter; it will endure poor soils but grows much more slowly. It can be planted from divisions and roots easily from cuttings. Plant rooted cuttings 6 inches apart for quick cover the first year, or 12 inches apart if you don't mind waiting for it to fill in.

Growing Tips
Water thoroughly at planting. It is particularly important to keep the bed moist the first year. Periwinkle will fill in more rapidly and look better if watered when very dry. In poorer soils, use a 5-10-5 fertilizer in early spring.

Care
Established plantings can endure drought, but newly planted beds need extra attention to soil moisture. You can shear or prune long runners to force branching. An annual shearing is suggested to keep the plant vigorous but is not always necessary. Propagate by layering. Periwinkle may be subject to a few diseases, but they have little impact, and it usually thrives without incident. Once established, beds are very long lived, requiring no particular care.

Companion Planting and Design
Periwinkle is a great choice for planting under shade trees and can successfully grow among surface roots. It is useful on banks and slopes for preventing erosion. It can substitute for a traditional lawn but will not withstand heavy foot traffic. This is not a plant that can be appreciated from afar. Keep it close to enjoy its foliage and delicate flowers.

Did You Know?
Annual vinca, or *Catharanthus roseus*, is similar to periwinkle but has white or pink flowers and is often incorrectly referred to as *Vinca rosea* or *V. major*. The real *V. major* is a perennial ground cover, but it is hardy only to Zone 7. The variegated form of *V. major* is commonly used for container gardens. Make sure you get the one you really want!

This is the last member of the "big three" (myrtle, ivy, pachysandra) and my personal favorite. It gets delightful blue flowers! The plant stays low and compact. The dark-green leaves are in pairs, two inches long and richly glossy. (As if elves come out at night and polish each one with a soft cloth.) It spreads by rooting as it moves along the ground. Periwinkle is evergreen and often holds its color through the winter. In winter sun, the foliage may turn purple bronze. There can be many pinwheel-shaped blooms, and they last for several weeks. More sun promotes more flowers, sometimes even a few over the summer. Unfortunately, periwinkle seldom flowers in very deep shade. Periwinkle is native to Europe and western Asia but has naturalized in parts of the eastern United States.

Other Common Names
Vinca, Myrtle, Dwarf Periwinkle, Lesser Periwinkle

Bloom Period and Seasonal Color
Lilac blue flowers appear in late April.

Mature Height × Spread
3 to 6 in. × variable spread

Sweet Woodruff
Galium odoratum

Sweet woodruff has many fine qualities, including its ability to grow in deep shade. It has unusual leaves, delicate spring flowers, and a lovely aroma used in perfumes as well as wine. It is listed as evergreen or semi-evergreen, but that is a stretch in New Jersey. The leaves are wonderful! They are arranged in whorls of six to eight slender, inch-long leaves around a thin square stem. The whorls repeat every inch. It is more the leaves that have the delicious scent. The fragrance has been compared to fresh-cut hay, which may account for its other common name "bedstraw." The tiny white flowers are not showy but very sweet. Small cymes (branched clusters that bloom from the center) are held above the leaves and last for four to six weeks.

Other Common Name
Bedstraw

Bloom Period and Seasonal Color
White flowers from early May to mid-June.

Mature Height × Spread
6 to 12 in. × variable but enthusiastic spread.

When, Where, and How to Plant
Plant in early spring or early fall in partial to deep shade. Choose a place where you can let it naturalize instead of locating it in a formal setting. It thrives in deep soil containing humus and needs generous moisture. Abundant organic matter in the soil will help retain water. Sweet woodruff will volunteer from seed, and potted plants are generally available locally. Spring plantings of small divisions spaced 7 inches apart will fill in by autumn if grown in ideal soil conditions. An organic mulch will be beneficial as well, at least until the plants fill in. Sweet woodruff prefers an acid soil, so do not add lime.

Growing Tips
Water at planting and continue to keep moist. Fertilizer is seldom needed.

Care
The biggest problem is keeping this plant from creeping beyond its bounds. It can spread from its roots as well as seeds. The beds may need a little tidying up in the spring when the previous year's foliage dies down. I know of no diseases or insects for sweet woodruff. Overall, it is an easy-care ground cover.

Companion Planting and Design
Sweet woodruff has a deep woods aura. It looks perfectly at home with trilliums poking up through its foliage or a few interesting ferns scattered through its domain. It can be used under shade trees or lower growing shade loving shrubs such as rhododendron and mountain laurel. It is lovely under a stretching dogwood. The flowers and leaves are best appreciated by viewing up close. They are lovely both to see and to smell.

Did You Know?
The folklore and herbal history of sweet woodruff is extensive. During the Victorian era, the leaves and flowers were mixed with other herbs in sachets as a protection against moths. It has been used in wreath making to provide aroma and even to stuff mattresses. During medieval times, it was used to decorate churches for religious holidays.

Wintergreen
Gaultheria procumbens

When, Where, and How to Plant
Plant in early spring or early fall in a shaded or partially shaded location. This is not a good choice for a large expanse since it grows so slowly. It is best in a naturalized woodland setting where the rich humusy soil is deep and moist. Do not add lime, but do add lots of organic matter, especially leaf compost. Transplanting from the wild is difficult, so it is best to use container-grown plants. It is possible to divide established plants, but it is probably not worth the effort since they grow so slowly. Pine needles make a good mulch, but any organic mulch will be beneficial. Plant 12 inches apart.

Growing Tips
Water at planting. Wintergreen prefers moist soils, so do not let the ground dry out, especially the first year. It is native to the pine barrens where the soil is pretty barren of nutrients. No fertilizer is necessary.

Care
Wintergreen is low maintenance. It grows slowly and is not invasive. It rarely, if ever, needs to be pruned. Insects and diseases are not mentioned in the literature so are probably not serious. You may have to weed around the plants since they will not fill in quickly; mulch will help with that.

Companion Planting and Design
Wintergreen is excellent for shaded rock gardens and can be wonderful around azaleas and rhododendrons or along a woodland path. Mix with woodland wildflowers such as trillium, Jack-in-the-pulpit, and bloodroot for an especially pretty early spring display.

Did You Know?
Do you remember the "Teaberry Shuffle"? Teaberry chewing gum has been around forever, and you were supposed to do the shuffle when you chewed. The flavor originated in wintergreen ground cover. Oil of wintergreen is in many products that are used to treat sore, aching muscles. For a cup of wintergreen tea (in the tradition of native Americans and early colonists), use a teaspoon of chopped leaves in a cup of water. Steep to taste.

Wintergreen is native to the woods of the northeast. The shiny, inch long, dark green leaves and bright red berries are easy to recognize. The scent of a crushed leaf is unmistakable any time of year. Wintergreen is the original source of oil of wintergreen. It was once harvested in large quantities and shipped to distilleries. (It is now almost exclusively laboratory synthesized.) Wintergreen is very slow growing. The stems creep along the ground half buried. The mostly white flowers appear in spring but continue to open until July. Red berries first appear in July and continue ripening through the fall. Sometimes delicate fresh flowers open in the presence of the previous year's fruit! The berries have an unusual refreshing taste.

Other Common Names
Checkerberry, Teaberry, Mountain Tea

Bloom Period and Seasonal Color
Early spring flowers are white with a hint of pink; red berries appear and evergreen foliage turns a rich burgundy in fall.

Mature Height × Spread
3 to 6 in. × variable spread

Lawns *for New Jersey*

According to The Lawn Institute, located in Rolling Meadows, Illinois, there are six grass plants in every square inch of lawn, over 850 in every square foot, and about 8.5 million in every 10,000 square feet (one-quarter acre) of lawn. That's a lot of grass. There is a tremendous range in attitudes toward lawns. Some people don't care what is growing as long as it is mostly green and not poisonous. Others want a rich, uniform, dark-green, perfectly manicured work of art. Most people fall somewhere in between.

There is no doubt that having some green grass where we can wiggle our toes is one of Nature's great gifts. The work of mowing, fertilizing, liming, seeding, and controlling pests is not, however, a joy. The degree of commitment homeowners have to their turf is very individual. If having a picture-perfect lawn is your idea of heaven, then go for it. If not, try to find the balance between effort and pleasure that best fits you and your family's needs.

It is impossible to cover lawn care in great detail in the context of this book. There have been volumes written on this subject alone. The following points are presented in a way to help you evaluate the different aspects of lawn care so that you, the homeowner, can make an informed decision about the kind of lawn you want.

Kentucky Bluegrass

Instant Gratification with Sod

Sod is nothing more than transplanted grass. Sodding is not an excuse for poor soil preparation, and it does not mean that once you put down sod you will have a perfect lawn forever. What it does mean is that you can have an instant lawn of thick, virtually weed-free grass. It means you will have a protective cover that will prevent many weed seeds from getting started. It means you will be able to wiggle your toes in cool green grass in a matter of days.

The use of sod gives you tremendous flexibility in lawn establishment. As long as the ground can be prepared properly, you can install sod. You don't have to wait for the right weather as you do when using seed.

Sod needs to have a high percentage of Kentucky bluegrass to hold it together. Bluegrass spreads by rhizomes and effectively holds the sod together by its network of roots. It is a sun-loving grass, and it will not last long in a shady area. Sod containing fescue, a more shade-tolerant grass, does exist, but it has to be mixed with bluegrass to keep the cut sod from falling apart. If you decide to use a primarily bluegrass sod in a shady area, you can overseed with fescue in the spring, or even better, in early fall. The fescue will fill in as the bluegrass thins out. Understand your needs and make sure you purchase sod that is "New Jersey certified."

Using Seed

The best time to do a major seeding is early September. The ground will still be warm from summer, and that will encourage germination. By the time the grass is up, the air temperature will have cooled off, and the tiny grasses will enjoy growing in the absence of heat stress. In general, rye grass will germinate first, then fescue. It can take up to twenty-eight days for the bluegrass to germinate. (More information on specific grasses is included later in this chapter.)

The type of seed you choose is dependent on the growing conditions. Use only high-quality seed. This is very important. Bargain seed mixes are no bargain; in fact, they can be a disaster. It is always good to have different types of grass in the mix, which aids in insect and disease prevention. In a sunny area, use at least sixty percent Kentucky bluegrass, but make sure you have at least two different kinds of bluegrass to make up that sixty percent. The other forty percent should be evenly divided between fine fescues and fine turf-type perennial rye. In the shade, use sixty percent fine fescues and split the other forty percent between Kentucky bluegrass and perennial rye.

Preparing to Plant

Whether using seed or installing sod, the steps for preparing your yard are the same. It doesn't pay to skimp on soil preparation. First, strip the old grass and weeds. This can be done in several ways, including mechanically by digging or hoeing, or chemically with herbicides (depending on your gardening philosophy). The fertility of your soil will greatly effect the success of your lawn. I recommend having your soil tested to find out what its needs are regarding the use of organic matter, lime, and fertilizer. Your County Cooperative Extension Office can test the soil for a small fee. (See book introduction for more information.) After adding the materials as recommended by your test results, till everything into the soil at a depth of six to eight inches. Till the soil only when it is moist, not wet or dusty-dry. After tilling, level the dirt, smooth it out, then lay your sod or seed.

Choosing Your Grass

Grass is green. Even bluegrass is green. The question is: "How green does it need to be?" A rich, dark green lawn that comes up in the spring is a beauty, no doubt about it. Different species and even different varieties vary in color slightly, but to push grass to be as dark as possible can cause difficulties.

Nitrogen is the substance that greens up a lawn. It develops that deep emerald color that glistens in the sun. A dark-green lawn also grows faster and so has to be mowed more often; then you will have to deal with more clippings. It is also very tender and extremely susceptible to many insects and diseases that thrive on the tender growth. Learn the consequences of a dark-green lawn and be prepared to deal with insects and diseases in a timely manner, or the dark green can become dead brown in no time.

You may want to develop an appreciation for medium green. Medium green can be a very good thing. It is sturdier and slower growing. It is good to practice moderation in all things, including green.

Feeding Your Lawn

For grass, fertilizer is food. The sun provides part of the food, but fertilizer provides the rest. The numbers on the bag refer to nitrogen (N), phosphorus (P), and potassium (K), always in that order. Some "organic" fertilizers need explanation since this term has more than one meaning. A very common lawn fertilizer is 10-6-4, 50 percent organic. In this fertilizer, half the nitrogen is in a chemical form that is released quickly and available to the grass plants immediately, like a quick shot in the arm. The other 50 percent is the "organic" component, which is in a chemical form that is released slowly over time to continually supply the grass with what it needs. You see the term "organic" used less frequently now in this context, as the more appropriate term "slow-release" is becoming the norm.

The other type of organic fertilizer is like cow or chicken manure. Such fertilizers are generally not as high in N-P-K, but they may have more of the minor elements, and they also supply "organic matter," an important component of soil structure. It is, however, very difficult to be sure that what comes out of a cow is consistent. Sometimes the nutrient level is not even included on the package, so you cannot be sure how much of the essential elements you are adding. If you feel more comfortable using natural products, this is a very good approach, but it may be more difficult to achieve a perfect lawn. The grass itself doesn't really care whether the nitrogen came out of a cow or out of a fertilizer manufacturing plant as long as it is in a form the plant can use.

The best way to know how much fertilizer you need is to have your soil tested. Any other approach is nothing but a guess. If you prefer to guess, 10-6-4, 50 percent organic (slow release) applied at a rate of 10 pounds per 1,000 square feet is reasonable. Apply in early spring and again in late fall. Sometimes you can skip a spring application or at least delay it until late spring. Never fertilize in the heat of summer.

The truth is, even if you never fertilize your lawn, you will still have grass, or at least something green. Frequent mowing puts some pressure on broadleaf weeds to keep them from taking over, with the secondary benefit of leaving smaller clippings that can be left on the lawn to decompose. The grass types that can tolerate lower soil fertility will dominate. Crabgrass and some broadleaf weeds will fill in any open spaces.

Zoysiagrass

If you choose to fertilize only when the urge grabs you, it is better done in the fall. That is when you get root development, which is more important for making a sturdy lawn than the delicate green topgrowth in the spring. If you have to decide between fertilizing heavily and never fertilizing, go with never. An excess of fertilizer will kill grass, and most other things, in the blink of an eye. Whatever the plants can't use just runs off into the environment, causing more problems than it is worth. Your lawn will never win any awards if you don't fertilize, and you will have to settle for yellowish green color, but don't think you will get out of mowing. If there is a lawn, you have to mow.

Understanding pH Levels

Lime is used to alter the pH of the soil. It also supplies calcium. New Jersey soils tend to be on the acidic side, and the addition of lime brings the pH up to a point where the grass will be happy. The only way to know for sure how much lime you need is to have your soil tested. The amount needed is dependent on the existing pH as well as on your soil type. Once you get your soil pH adjusted properly, a maintenance

Perennial Ryegrass

application is twenty to twenty-five pounds of pulverized or granular limestone per thousand square feet once a year. Test again every three or four years to be sure your pH level is where it should be.

What Is Thatch?

There are tremendous misconceptions about thatch. It is not made of grass clippings. The top of the grass, the part that gets cut off when you mow, is so tender and delicate that it breaks down in no time. Three or four days after you mow, you will have a hard time finding the clippings you left behind.

Thatch is dead grass plants. As the new grass emerges from the growing tip, the oldest part of the plant dies. As it ages and matures, it gets thicker, tougher, and almost woody. It develops a texture like coarse straw. This is thatch. The faster you push your lawn to grow and the more nitrogen you apply to get it to "green up," the more rapidly you will develop thatch. Thatch creates a barrier to the roots. Water, pesticides, and fertilizer get trapped in the layer of thatch and never get down to the roots where they are needed. Seed will not germinate if it sits on top of a layer of thatch.

Thatching and dethatching are terms sometimes used interchangeably to mean thatch removal. Whatever you call it, when thatch gets one-half inch thick, it is time to get rid of it. Remove thatch in early fall. Small areas can be worked by hand with a special rake designed for thatch removal. This is difficult work, so larger areas may require the use of a mechanized de-thatching machine (they can be rented), or you can hire a professional to do the job for you.

How to Mow

The frequency of mowing required is dependent on a number of factors, but grass height is the most important. Never mow shorter than to $1^1/2$ inches; two to $2^1/2$ inches is better, especially during the summer. As a rule, mow the grass when it gets twice as tall as the desired mowed height. For example, if you want to mow the grass to two inches, mow when it reaches four inches. You can allow the clippings to stay on the lawn as long as they do not form a mat on the surface. If they do, they will smother what is underneath. Keep your mower sharp. Get the blades sharpened early before the grass needs to be cut the first time in spring. Otherwise you will be behind a long line of other procrastinators, and the lawn will be up to your knees before you get your blades back.

Weed Control

A thick, healthy lawn is the best weed control, but sometimes weeds will pop up with even the best lawn care. Never use a chemical weed control the same season you seed. Do not apply weedkillers in hot weather. You can apply a single broadleaf weedkiller or a commercially prepared mix of weedkillers in the spring or early fall. The only way to effectively control crabgrass is to use a pre-emergence material (one that will prevent crabgrass from germinating) in the early spring, but most pre-emergence materials prevent desirable grass from germinating as well.

Weed identification is the key to effective weed control. One simple way to reduce the need for weed control is tolerance! Some weeds are really undesirable, but a little clover or a few violets may not be so bad. After all, a weed is only a weed in the eye of the beholder.

Water Correctly

This is important: If you cannot water correctly, do not water at all. It is a simple but important concept that is often disregarded. Simply put, you need one inch of water a week, put down all at once, in the early morning. The truth is, most New Jersey lawns would rather go dormant in hot weather. Giving a lawn a little water, or a lot in small doses, keeps it going but not thriving. If it gets brown from going dormant, it will recover. If it gets stressed from trying to grow when it should be dormant, you are in much worse trouble. It is definitely better not to water than to do it incorrectly.

Here is a little secret. Dr. Henry Indyk was the Rutgers Cooperative Extension Specialist in lawns for many years. Dr. Indyk was so well recognized as an authority that he once consulted for the Olympics in setting up their athletic fields. He never watered his lawn.

Tackling Pests and Diseases

Lawn diseases are extremely weather dependent. By the time you get it identified, chances are the disease will have run its course. Often the grass will recover, or you can overseed to fill in any bare spots. It is more important to get the disease identified so you can treat preventively the following year. This is especially beneficial if the same disease shows up repeatedly, year after year. Fairy ring is one disease that is easily recognized. In this case, the spores reproduce by dropping new spores to the outside edge of a circle. The outside edge is where healthy grass is available to the disease. The circle continues to get large while the inner part of the circle recovers. The ever expanding circle can get broken as the circle

Tall Fescue

encounters trees or buildings. Then all that is visible is part of a circle, maybe even just a arch. Dollar spot appears in warm, wet weather more commonly in late spring or early fall. The spots start out as small straw-colored patches that may run together forming larger spots. Most lawns recover on their own after a few weeks. A summer disease is *Fusarium* blight. This is a larger brown patch, and these spots may merge into dead areas covering large expanses. Sometimes weeds fill in the center of the spots creating a "frog's eye" look. There are many other diseases, and they are often difficult to identify with certainty without experience and a microscope.

The most common insect pests are grubs, sod webworms, and chinch bugs. Grubs are the larval stage of beetles, usually but not always Japanese beetles. They feed on roots, causing the grass to pull up like a carpet. The white grubs become C-shaped when disturbed. Sod webworm adults are moths that close up their wings like a cigarette. They fly away as you walk across the lawn. It is the larvae of these moths that actually damage turf, but they are most easily identified and located by the presence of adult moths. Chinch bugs are the smallest, about one-fifth of an inch long. They are black, but their wings fold over their backs making them look whitish. If you have an insect or disease problem, contact your local Cooperative Extension Agent to find out the current recommendations for control. They can change frequently.

Grass Species and Varieties

When it comes to grass varieties, you may have no idea how lucky you are to live in New Jersey. Rutgers University has one of the finest turfgrass-breeding programs in the country, if not the world. Dr. Reed Funk has evaluated, developed, and patented many varieties of grass here in the Garden State. That provides New Jersey homeowners with some of the best and most well-suited turf grasses that can be found. The lawngrasses presented in this book include the most current recommended types. They are taken from the New Jersey breeding program and from variety trials done around the country. The following list has kindly been provided by Dr. William A. Meyer, Professor of Turfgrass Breeding at Cook College, Rutgers University, and the New Jersey Agricultural Experiment Station.

Bentgrass (*Agrostis* species)

I am including information on bentgrass as a cautionary tale. Homeowners see it looking great on the golf course and want it in the front yard. No turfgrass professional recommends it for home use. It prefers cool temperatures, sunny conditions, and fertile soils. Don't even think about putting it in shade. It is extremely high maintenance and mowing is needed frequently, sometimes every other day. It is subject to a wide variety of insects and diseases. When bentgrasses are mixed with other lawngrasses, they can become patches that stand out and look more like weeds, or even patches of disease.

Colonial bentgrass is sometimes used for home lawns but is more often found on fairways; creeping bentgrass is finer and is used on greens; velvet bentgrass is the finest textured of the three and has the best shade tolerance. Penn Cross is the old standard variety and is still sold in quantity, but it is not as good as the new releases. If you absolutely must have it, be sure to get the new, better varieties.

Recommended varieties of bentgrass include: South Shore, L9, Pennlink, Providence, Penn A4, Penn G2, Penn A1, Penneagle.

Hard Fescue (*Festuca longifolia*)

Hard fescues are one of the fine fescues, but they deserve a little attention on their own. Fescues will not tolerate wet sites but are the best grasses for shady locations. Avoid close mowing and excessive fertilization. Hard fescues are non-spreading, so bare spots are not likely to fill in. The hard fescue has a fine texture and is low growing. It may do the best in shade of all the fescues and may have better disease resistance as well.

Recommended varieties of hard fescue include: Discovery, SR3100, Reliant II, Warwick, Ecostar, Brigade, Nordic, Spartan, Aurora, Aurora II, Oxford.

Kentucky Bluegrass (*Poa pratensis*)

There is no doubt that Kentucky bluegrass is the workhorse of the grass industry. It prefers cool temperatures, adequate soil moisture combined with good drainage, and lots of sunshine. To thrive, bluegrass requires lime and fertilizer. It is not tolerant of even moderate shade and deteriorates with close mowing and poor drainage. Bluegrass can go dormant during hot weather, but it has very good recovery when weather patterns change in late summer and early fall. There is no single type that is resistant to all the problems that can plague grass, so it is always a good idea to use a blend of several good quality grasses in your seed mix. There are many good varieties from which to choose.

Recommended varieties of Kentucky bluegrass include: Midnight, America, Princeton 105, Blacksburg, SR2,000, Eclipse, Unique, Shamrock, Washington, Preakness, Suffolk, Ram I, Adelphi, Livingston, Glade, Cheri, Lofts 1757, Julia, Liberty, Challenger, Moonlight, Bedazzled, Sonoma, Cabernet, Jefferson, Liberator, Total Eclipse, Award, Moonshadow, Langara, and Lakeshore.

Perennial Ryegrass (*Lolium perenne*)

One of the advantages of growing perennial ryegrass is its ability to germinate in five to ten days. This provides quick cover to keep weeds down while other grasses take their time coming up. Ryegrasses are more tolerant of shade than bluegrass and will grow in a wide range of soil conditions. Newer varieties are greatly improved with regards to color, persistence, texture, density, and lower-growing habit. The fine turf-type ryegrasses will blend well with other grasses, but the mixture will need frequent mowing to stay attractive.

Recommended varieties of perennial ryegrass include: Brightstar II, Palmer III, Premier II, Calypso II, Panther, Monterey, Secretariat, Catalina, Prelude III, Repell III, Divine, Laredo, Citation III, Manhattan III, Prizm, Elf, Accent, Top Hat, Omega III, Manhattan IV, Pinnacle II, Amazing, Applaud, Jet, Elfkin, and Citation Fore.

Red Fescue (*Festuca rubra*)

The red fescues include the chewings and creeping fescues. Chewings fescues are fine leafed and low growing, and they spread very little. Creeping fescue is also fine leafed but will spread a little due to small underground rhizomes. Chewings, creeping, and the hard fescues addressed earlier make up the fine fescues. They are extremely important, as fine fescues can tolerate moderate shade better than any of the other lawngrasses suited for New Jersey. Fine fescues will also tolerate poor, dry soils. Avoid wet locations, excessive fertilization, and close mowing. They mix well with bluegrass. Even in a sunny area, it is recommended that you have approximately 20 percent fine fescue in the mix. Be aware that Boreal, a variety of creeping fescue, is sold in large quantity and is very inexpensive. It is, however, considered a very poor selection. Avoid it if possible and choose an alternative from the following list.

Recommended varieties of chewings fescue include: Shadow II, Magic, Victory II, SR5100, Brittany, Tiffany, Brideport, Treazure, Jamestown II, Banner II, Ambassador, and Intrigue.

Recommended varieties of creeping fescue include: Jasper, Flyer II, Shademaster II, Jasper II, Cindy Lou, Aberdeen, Navigator, and Salem.

Rough-Stalked Bluegrass (*Poa trivialis*)

This is another grass you may come across that is not good for home lawns. You need to know about its characteristics when making choices. Rough-stalked bluegrass gets its name from the rough sheaths on the individual grass plants. It is very intolerant of hot, dry situations but does well in shade where it is cool and moist. Its light-green color and its tendency to spread along the ground when mowed makes it appear out of place in a well tended lawn. If mixed with other, more desirable grasses in a sunny situation, rough-stalked bluegrass can be considered a weed. Think carefully before including it anywhere, but be sure to use the better varieties if you use it at all. There are not a lot of named varietiess from which to choose.

Recommended varieties of rough-stalked bluegrass include: Saber, Laser, and Winter Play.

Tall Fescue (*Festuca arundinacea*)

Tall fescue has undergone significant improvements in recent years. It is primarily a bunch-type, cool-season grass, but it spreads ever so slowly from short rhizomes. It also tolerates heat and drought better than the other cool-season grasses and so will hold up in some places where Kentucky bluegrass gives up. Tall fescue is tough and can take foot traffic; it has been used in playgrounds and parks where durability is more important than looks. Definitely more coarse than the fine-leafed bluegrass, it can still be used to mix with bluegrass if mowed regularly. The newer turf-type varieties have been selected for finer texture and better color; objections to their use are dwindling. The new varieties maintain durability but are prettier to look at. The old standby, Kentucky 31, has been around since 1940. It is better than the species but is still a terrible lawngrass. Stick with the many new and improved varieties.

Recommended varieties of tall fescue include: Crossfire II, Houndog V, Falcon II, Jaguar III, Coyote, Coronado, Southern Choice, Genesis, Pixie, Tomahawk, Barlexas, Lancer, Marksman, Fine Lawn Petite, Virtue, Tulsa, Safari, Rebel Junior, Duster, Cochise, Apache II, Falcon III, Rembrandt, Millenium, Plantation, Olympic Gold, Silver Star, Tarheel, Wolfpack, and Prospect.

Zoysiagrass (*Zoysia japonica*)

People either love zoysiagrass or hate it. There are always as many inquiries regarding wiping it out as there are how to get it established. It is a warm-season grass that will thrive in hot summer weather on dry sandy soils. If you have a shore home that is used primarily in the summer months, it may be a good choice. Once the weather turns cold, zoysiagrass turns brown. It can stay brown for six months each year or sometimes even longer. If you aren't there, it doesn't matter, but it is a decided disadvantage for year-round living.

Zoysiagrass is planted from plugs, usually on a grid pattern, and it can take two or more years to completely cover an area. Once established, it spreads with enthusiasm and can creep into your neighbor's lawn whether they want it or not. There are not many varieties in the trade and only one recommended for New Jersey.

The recommended variety of zoysiagrass is Meyer.

Ornamental Grasses *for New Jersey*

Fifteen years ago, ornamental grasses were almost unheard of. The only grass people thought about was that which had to be mowed every Saturday whether they liked it or not. No one ever gave much thought to grasses blooming or being graceful or providing wildlife habitat. Grass formed a lovely green background for everything else.

How things have changed! Ornamental grasses are now front and center. There are grasses for just about every planting need and to suit every environmental possibility. It may come as a big surprise, but many of these grasses are absolutely stunning.

Show-Stopping Splendor

The first time I was impressed with the beauty of grasses was at a large property in Morris County. The landscape was designed by a landscape architect. He wanted to cut down on maintenance and also get the property to blend in with the surrounding rough fields and immature woodland. His suggestion was to simply stop mowing most of the lawn. A half-acre close to the house was still to be tended religiously, but the rest was allowed to do what it wanted. It was mowed once every two years or so, and woody material was pulled.

I arrived in late spring. The gently sloping field was a sea of delicate seed stalks proudly waving in the breeze on top of thin green stems. It was so lovely it was breathtaking. What had once been a thick traditional lawn was now something else entirely. The plants were the same, but the effect was dramatically different.

If this can happen with regular lawngrasses, plants selected for their natural beauty have an incredible untapped potential for show-stopping splendor.

Just about every garden center now carries a selection of ornamental grasses, so getting started is not difficult. Unfortunately, grasses in pots can look like a whole lot of nothing. The nature of ornamental grasses is such that many need a mass effect to be seen to their best

Grasses in Autumn, including Japanese Blood Grass and Miscanthus

Chinese Silver Grass and Hostas

advantage. Many others can play an important role in the landscape by offering winter interest with their long-lasting plumes. They often will not produce these features in a container. Don't let scruffy plants in pots discourage you, and don't base your design on what you see at the garden center. Many garden catalogs have pictures of a selection of ornamental grasses. These may offer a better idea of the qualities and attributes than you can get from looking at potted plants in a nursery. One of the most complete selections is from Kurt Bluemel, Inc., located in Baldwin, Maryland. Kurt Bluemel is one of the driving forces behind the explosive ornamental grass industry and has introduced several exceptional new varieties. A computer search will provide almost limitless options.

Great Selections for New Jersey

The ornamental grasses selected for this book are hardy throughout New Jersey. Great care has been taken to include basic, dependable varieties that are relatively easy-care. The home gardener may enter the world of ornamental grasses with every possible expectation of success. A few less-common grasses have been included to keep things interesting, but none is difficult to grow. All of these are available by mail, and many can be found at your local garden center.

Planting grasses is very basic. Match the plant's needs to the location and amend the soil accordingly. Grasses are almost always in containers, so dig a roomy hole and refill with amended soil so that the plant sits at the same height it was in the pot. Finish filling around plant, and tamp down firmly but gently. Water thoroughly. In general, they get established with little fuss.

Ornamental grasses should be an interesting and fun new dimension to your gardening efforts. Don't be afraid to try a plant that is out of the ordinary. These are not oak trees. If you like the results, you will be quite pleased with yourself. If you do not, yank the plants and try something else.

A garden is not something you plant and finish. It is not like laying bricks or pouring concrete. Gardening is an adventure in taming the wilds of nature. It is never really finished, and it is never quite tame. It is the perfect place to try something conventional.

Blue Fescue
Festuca glauca

Ornamental fescues are closely related to the lawngrasses but are far more interesting. They are characterized by a blue-gray color and a rounded habit. The botanical name of this species is often confused with other incorrect names, so it's best to stick with named varieties. Most of the blue fescues are evergreen clump grasses. Their blue color comes from a glaucous coating on the leaves similar to that on a blue spruce. There are four- to six-inch miniature varieties as well as some that may reach 18 inches. Most blue fescue are in the ten- to twelve-inch range. The close relative F. gigantea can reach two to three feet. Some produce very thin, delicate flowers, but blue fescue is cultivated more for its rolled blue-gray foliage.

Other Common Names
Sheep's Fescue, Blue Sheep's Fescue, Gray Fescue

Bloom Period and Seasonal Color
Flower spikes in summer; blue foliage all season.

Mature Height × Spread
18 in. × to 1 ft.

When, Where, and How to Plant
Plant or divide in early spring or early fall. Locate in full sun for the best color. Blue fescue survives in light shade, but expect less blue. Choose a well-drained site. Fescue is drought tolerant, but in really sandy conditions incorporate organic matter into the soil to hold moisture. It establishes easily but may need replanting every two to three years. You can propagate by seed, but expect variation in height and color. To maintain the characteristics of a named variety, propagate only by division. Set plants 6 to 15 inches apart depending on the variety and the look you desire. (See chapter introduction for more planting information.)

Growing Tips
Water at planting and when the ground gets dry. Once established, blue fescue will tolerate moderate drought. In early spring apply 10-6-4, 50 percent slow-release fertilizer.

Care
Cut back fescue to about 3 inches in early spring. If the center has died out, lift the clump. Remove and replant the outer tufts of healthy fresh growth. Dispose of the older, dead growth from the center. Some varieties slow their growth in summer heat and may get a little ratty. Don't prune while it is hot. In general, they perk up as the weather cools. Prune in the fall if they look bad. An organic mulch will help control weeds around the plants. Insects and diseases are rarely a problem.

Companion Planting and Design
Blue fescues are excellent choices for winter interest, ground covers, rock gardens, and for edging paths. The attractive neutral color softens bright colors that may clash and looks particularly lovely with pastel pink or lavender. In a bed of mixed grasses, blue fescue provides variation in color, height, and habit. The mounds complement the vertical habit of many other popular grasses.

Did You Know?
Blue fescue is an excellent plant in containers. Its small size and clumping habit allow it to fit without taking over. The soft but interesting color mixes with others well, and its drought tolerance is conducive to life in a container.

Feather Reed Grass
Calamagrostis acutifolia

When, Where, and How to Plant

Spring planting is best in cold climates, but early fall is acceptable in the southern part of the state. A sunny location will encourage the sturdiest plants with the most decorative seedheads. The plant will tolerate light shade if you are just looking for cover. Feather reed grass prefers rich, moist soils, and it will do well in heavy clay. Avoid dry, sandy soils. Feather reed grass is not difficult to get established. It can be divided in early spring. The addition of organic matter will help it hold onto soil moisture. (See chapter introduction for more planting information.)

Growing Tips

Water thoroughly at planting and also deeply during hot weather. An application of 5-10-5 fertilizer in early spring, before the new growth comes out, will help it to fill in thickly.

Care

Cut feather reed grass back in the spring to see its fresh green growth. Divide in early spring if desired. Cut the seed stalks as needed for fresh or dried arrangements. The seeds are generally sterile, so there is little chance that this plant will become invasive. Feather reed grass has no known pest problems.

Companion Planting and Design

Planted as a border plant, feather reed grass will create a golden band of color for most of the summer and straight through winter. Scattered plants in a mixed border will provide winter interest. Even when used as a single specimen, it can add a dramatic touch. A single clump is particularly useful in a small space. It can create vertical interest year-round without having to use a space-hogging woody ornamental. Clumps flanking the front steps can be very interesting, and there is no need to worry that these plants will ever outgrow their allotted space.

Did You Know?

The botanical name is derived from the Greek word "kalamos," which means "reed." There are 250 species in the genus, mostly from Europe and Asia. Some species are used as forage grass.

Feather reed grass is a perennial grass that grows in clumps. It works well mixed with other grasses but is showy enough to plant by itself en masse. One of its strong points is its long season of interest. The flowers show up in June with a hint of red; the seedheads mature to a golden tan and last until the following spring. These plumes will tower three to four feet above the foliage. They are very useful in dried arrangements or even as filler for fresh flowers. The foliage itself stays at about two feet. Grown in full sun, the plumes will be densely packed together and sturdy enough to stay upright through most of the winter. Feather reed grass tolerates light shade but will not be as prolific in flower production, and its stalks will be floppier.

Other Common Name
Reed Grass

Bloom Period and Seasonal Color
Seedheads that turn golden, then golden brown, then silver; appearing in June and lasting through winter.

Mature Height × Spread
5 to 7 ft. × 2 ft.

Frost Grass
Spodiopogon sibiricus

Frost grass is a clump type that spreads slowly. Its attractive six-inch leaves attach to an upright central stalk. There is a white midrib, and the bright green leaves have a fuzzy quality. In fall, they turn brown streaked with shades of deep purple and purple red. The flowers are exceptionally light and airy. Each is covered with fine white hairs and held far above the foliage, adding to the appearance of lightness. The spikes appear to be floating above the leaves. At first they have hints of purple but mature to a fuzzy brown. The flowers and even the foliage are excellent filler for floral arrangements. The spikes can persist well into winter, but when the foliage deteriorates you may want to cut back the plants.

Other Common Names
Silver Spike, Graybeard Grass

Bloom Period and Seasonal Color
Panicles July through August, emerging with hints of purple and maturing to brown.

Mature Height × Spread
2 to 3 ft. (5 ft. in bloom) × 2 to 3 ft.

When, Where, and How to Plant
Plant in early spring or early fall. Frost grass prefers full sun but can take a little shade. Too much shade will cause the plant to flop over, requiring staking. It is moderately tolerant of shore planting conditions as long as it is not allowed to dry out. In general, it does better at the northern end of its range, so it should do well almost anywhere in New Jersey. It can be planted from seed or divisions in spring. Container-grown material can be planted in fall. Since it does not like to dry out, you may need to add significant amounts of organic matter to sandy soils. Plant at the same depth it was in the container or in the ground before dividing. Cover with a thick layer of organic mulch to help retain soil moisture. It is not difficult to get established. (See chapter introduction for more planting information.)

Growing Tips
Water thoroughly at planting and during hot dry summers. This is especially true down the shore, where it will tolerate the conditions only if not allowed to dry out. Apply 10-6-4, 50 percent slow-release fertilizer in early spring.

Care
Prune in late fall or early winter if it gets unattractive. It does not appear to have any insect or disease problems. Frost grass can be divided in the spring.

Companion Planting and Design
Frost grass is a good choice for small gardens as well as for massing in larger areas. It is not overpowering and provides interesting elements in all seasons exept the dead of winter. It is a good choice for use along the edge of woods. Its interesting reedlike leaves and stalks make it suitable for specimen planting or for using in groups.

Did You Know?
Frost grass is native to prairies in Siberia. It can also be found in northern China and Korea. Japan introduced it to the rest of the world. This plant gets its common name from its fall foliage sparkling with an early morning frost.

Hakonechloa

Hakonechloa macra

When, Where, and How to Plant

Plant in early spring from container stock. Hakonechloa needs some shade. Its leaves will burn in full sun, especially during summer. Plant under tall shade trees as a ground cover where lawn grass would have a hard time. It needs moist soil conditions, good drainage, and high fertility. It is possible to grow from seed or from divisions made in the spring. If you are starting with heavy clay soil, add a 2:1 mixture of organic matter and sand. In sandy soils, add organic matter to hold on to soil moisture. Apply a thick layer of organic mulch to retain soil moisture and keep the soil cool.

Growing Tips

Water thoroughly at planting. The most important aspect of care is to keep the plant well watered during hot weather, especially if rainfall has been scant. A light dose of 10-6-4, 50 percent slow-release fertilizer in early spring will give this plant a good start.

Care

Replenish the organic mulch as needed. Hakone will do best in a humusy soil, and the mulch will continue to improve the soil as it decomposes. Cut back in early spring if necessary. It has no known insect or disease problems.

Companion Planting and Design

Hakonechloa will do well on gentle slopes where its graceful arching habit can be best appreciated. Although it does spread, hakone is small enough and sufficiently restrained to be suitable for container culture. It may be perfect when potted on the front porch or under a pergola. It is somewhat exotic in appearance, almost like bamboo, so it makes an excellent choice for oriental gardens. A woodland setting can be lovely, and it will thrive at the edge of woods as well.

Did You Know?

There are not nearly as many ornamental grasses for shade as there are for sunny areas. The grasslike sedges (*Carex* species) are not true grasses, but they do well in light shade. They are generally grouped with true grasses because of their similar appearance.

This is one of the better ornamental grasses for growing in shade. It makes an excellent ground cover under tall shade trees (which makes sense because it is native to the forests of Japan). Hakone is an out-of-the-ordinary plant that mixes perfectly with ferns, hostas, and astilbe to add interest to a shady spot. The dark-green color is rich and elegant. Hakonechloa is a slow-growing deciduous perennial that spreads from rhizomes but is never invasive. Its habit is almost weeping. One of the most wonderful attributes of this plant is its fall color. At first it turns pinkish-red; the winter season ripens it to a rich bronze. It will stay attractive well into winter. Draw attention to its beauty by planting it among other plants that offer autumn interest.

Other Common Name
Hakone Grass

Bloom Period and Seasonal Color
Non-showy blooms in late summer.

Mature Height × Spread
30 in. × 24 in.

Little Bluestem
Schizachyrium scoparium

Little bluestem is neither little nor blue but is smaller than "big bluestem", which can reach six feet. This is a clump grass that is very effective in a mixed perennial border. Its fall color is dramatic as it can turn golden orange to bronze. It is particularly eye-catching after a rain. Its stems are mostly green with a blue cast near the base. The foliage starts a light shade of green and darkens with age. Each leaf is up to one-half inch wide, twelve to sixteen inches long, and slightly hairy. Little bluestem is native to North America from Canada to Florida and west to Utah, though it is more common in the east. Little bluestem endures wind and snow and holds some color into winter. It is extremely drought tolerant and will do well in all but soggy ground.

Other Common Names
Prairie Beard Grass, Broom Sedge

Bloom Period and Seasonal Color
Flower spikes appear July through September; fall color in golden orange to bronze.

Mature Height × Spread
2 to 5 ft. × 12 to 18 in.

When, Where, and How to Plant
Plant in early spring or early fall. Little bluestem does best in full sun but will tolerate light shade. It is ideal for dry, sandy soils but requires a little water during the hottest weather. It can be used in a mixed border or a mass planting. It is impressive as a specimen, perhaps in a small garden. Little bluestem is very effective for erosion control. It is popular in transitional zones between wild areas and those under cultivation. It may reseed and can persist over time. Little bluestem can be started from seed but is more commonly grown from container stock or divisions. This grass is flexible regarding soil types and requires no particular attention to become established. (See chapter introduction for more planting information.)

Growing Tips
Water at planting and during the heat of summer. An application of 10-6-4, 50 percent slow-release fertilizer in early spring will benefit this plant.

Care
Prune hard in the early spring and divide at that time if desired. The literature is mixed regarding this plant's ability to reseed. One source credits it with little or no reseeding, while others say it is a potential pest. Since it naturally covers a large area, it must have room. Monitor it to make sure it doesn't get out of control. It has no known insects or disease problems, so there is little maintenance required.

Companion Planting and Design
Little bluestem is an excellent choice for mixing with other plants that feature fall and winter interest (such as asters and mums). Down the shore, it blends beautifully with the orange berries of the sea buckthorn shrub, which is tolerant of sandy soil. In average soils, little bluestem's lovely fall color complements the cinnamon-colored exfoliating bark of the paper bark maple.

Did You Know?
The flowers and dried foliage of little bluestem have ornamental value. The bright fall color is a lovely addition to an arrangement, and the foliage is suitable for craft projects. The seeds are a natural attraction for small birds.

Maiden Grass

Miscanthus sinensis 'Gracillimus'

When, Where, and How to Plant

Miscanthus does best when planted in spring. Sunny locations are best. They will behave acceptably in light shade but may need support such as stakes or string. Tying to a fence can work also. They are generally available in containers, although very large clumps can be balled in burlap. They are so adaptable to different types of soil that soil amendments are usually not necessary. They will adapt to an acid or alkaline pH. It is probably best to avoid seeding since the cultivars will not breed true. (See chapter introduction for more planting information.)

Growing Tips

Water at planting and, if possible, during dry conditions. A light application of 10-6-4, 50 percent slow release fertilizer in early spring will be beneficial.

Care

Miscanthus should be cut back in early spring. That is when the plants can be divided, if desired, but the impenetrable root system requires an ax or saw to make the divisions. Be alert for unwanted seedlings. In general, they have no serious insects or diseases, but occasional rust and mealybugs do show up. The plants generally recover on their own from all but the most serious cases. Flopping can be a problem with some varieties, as can dying out in the center of the clump.

Companion Planting and Design

There are dwarf varieties of Miscanthus suitable for small gardens and tall ones that can make excellent hedges. Mix the varieties with other perennials in a border planting or bed. They are an excellent choice for planting near water, but they are also considered adaptable to shore locations in sandy soil.

Did You Know?

Some selections are reported to have been under cultivation in Asia for centuries. Here in the United States, maiden grass was very popular in Victorian times. Old clumps can still be spotted near old houses.

Maiden grass is a popular and versatile ornamental grass. It is prized for graceful foliage that can be variegated green-and-white, green-and-yellow, tipped in silver or streaked with red. Fall color can be spectacular. Most are tall and arching, but some are almost rigidly upright. They grow in clumps that get bigger over time but seldom become invasive. Maiden grass is not particular about soil. Many are commonly planted at the water's edge, some even in standing water. Established plants tolerate drought but look better if watered. Maiden grass has a long season of bloom with fluffy seedheads hanging on well into winter. Flower spikes emerge in a range of colors, a rare quality among grasses. Almost all fade to tan by winter, but the strong lines of the foliage and the skeletons of seedheads add interest.

Other Common Names
Eulalia Grass, Japanese Silver Grass, Chinese Silver Grass

Bloom Period and Seasonal Color
Silver, tan, reddish, pink, coppery, red, or white spikes appearing from July through September; matures to tan or silver over winter.

Mature Height × Spread
3 to 12 ft. × 3 ft. or more

Moor Grass
Molinia caerulea

Moor grass is compact, unusually slow growing, and forms tight mounds of slightly arching foliage. Some are variegated. In fall, most turn bright yellow with an occasional hint of orange. 'Moorflamme' turns orange red. The abundant flowers emerge in early summer and tower over the plants. Each panicle is long and open, adding the impression of height without blocking the view. It may take two or three years before flowering, but moor grass is worth the wait. The flowers last well into fall, after which moor grass completely sheds its old growth. For winter interest, this is not a good choice. Moor grass will eventually self-sow, but the plants grow so slowly this is rarely a problem.

Other Common Name
Purple Moor Grass

Bloom Period and Seasonal Color
Late June to early July panicles with a purple tint that quickly turns tan.

Mature Height × Spread
1 to 7 ft. × 2 to 3 ft.

When, Where, and How to Plant
Moor grass does best when planted in spring. It is happiest in full sun but will accept light shade. Moist, fertile ground is best; definitely avoid dry alkaline soils. It will do well in the shore area but perhaps not right on the beach. The addition of organic matter will help keep the soil moist. Do not add lime. To get flowers the first year, plant divisions the size of a softball. You can grow moor grass from seed, but it will be years before the plants bloom. (See chapter introduction for more planting information.)

Growing Tips
Water at planting and during hot, dry summers. An application of 10-6-4, 50 percent slow-release fertilizer before the new growth comes out in the spring will be beneficial.

Care
Moor grass requires little care since it self-cleans and grows slowly. In fall, the leaves and stems break off near ground level where the plant has bulblike structures. It has no known pest problems. You may want to cut the elegant flowers for both fresh and dried arrangements.

Companion Planting and Design
Mix moor grass with perennials or other grasses in a bed or border. In the right spot, the tight, slow-growing mound of moor grass can make a lovely specimen plant. Its self-pruning will cut down on maintenance chores, and there will be no loss of summer beauty. Its open, airy flowers are profuse but transparent. Planted with a contrasting background, they will show to perfection. Consider planting moor grass against a dark backdrop.

Did You Know?
Moor grass is native to the bogs and open moors of Europe and Asia. Take advantage of its self-pruning by planting near gazebos, ponds, swimming pools, and other places less frequently visited in winter.

Northern Sea Oats
Chasmanthium latifolium

When, Where, and How to Plant
Northern sea oats do best when planted in spring. It can grow in sun or shade, but in dry soil, the tips of the leaves will tend to dry in full sun. The foliage will be dark green in its preferred site of partial shade. In more sun it will be lighter. Northern sea oats is salt tolerant and recommended for shore plantings. Moist, fertile soil is preferred, so the addition of organic matter will be beneficial. Plants are usually available in containers. They can also be grown from seed, or established plants can be divided in the early spring. Recommended spacing for a mass planting is 2 feet. (See chapter introduction for more planting information.)

Growing Tips
Water thoroughly at planting. In full sun, it will appreciate an occasional deep watering during hot, dry weather, especially in sandy soil. An application of 10-6-4, 50 percent slow-release fertilizer in early spring, after pruning, will be beneficial.

Care
Northern sea oats must be cut back severely in late winter or early spring. Watch for seedlings and prevent them from spreading to undesirable places. Divide in early spring if clumps are overgrown and flowering has become disappointing. This plant has no known pest problems and is low maintenance.

Companion Planting and Design
The dangling seedheads of northern sea oats can be particularly lovely for use beside ponds and water gardens. They are coveted for use in dried arrangements, as they last for up to a year. Northern sea oats do well in containers or mass planted on slopes and open fields, making it a great choice for decks near the shore. The use of planters with "reservoirs" at the bottom will minimize watering issues. For summer color, plant trailing geraniums around the perimeter.

Did You Know?
Northern sea oats are native to North America. It can be found wild from Pennsylvania south to Florida and west to Texas. Donald Wyman, Horticulturist at Arnold Arboretum of Harvard University for over thirty years, considered it one of the best native ornamental grasses.

Northern sea oats' drooping clusters of seeds are irresistible. The upright habit can be weighed down by the two-inch-long seed clusters. They arch gracefully over the branches and dangle, bob, and sway in the tiniest whispers of breeze. Spikes emerge green but mature to tan and are ultimately tinged with copper. They look most dramatic against a snowy setting. The leaves are wide for grass, up to 3/4 inch, and set along a central stalk. This gives a bamboo-like appearance that accounts for one of its many common names. Unlike bamboo, they are (thankfully!) not aggressive from the roots. Northern sea oats will spread from seed, sometimes rapidly. This is a bigger problem in areas of high moisture; dry ground slows it down significantly.

Other Common Names
Wild Oats, Bamboo Grass, Spangle Grass, Northern Oats, Spike Grass

Bloom Period and Seasonal Color
Flower spikes appear in summer and persist into winter, emerging green, turning tan, maturing to copper.

Mature Height × Spread
2 to 5 ft. × 2 ft. or more

Plantain-Leaved Sedge
Carex plantaginea

Sedges are not true grasses but have grasslike foliage and are generally planted with grasses. The foliage is often evergreen, and the clumps are generally well behaved. The narrow leaves come in a range of colors including copper, gold, silver, white striped, pink new growth, blue green, and yellow borders. The leaves can be straight, curled, whorled, palmlike, or drooping. The largest leaves reach three feet, but many petite species stay under a foot (as tiny as four inches!). The smaller types are suitable for containers and for tucking into rock gardens. Many are hardy only to Zone 7, but there are plenty of hardier varieties for New Jersey gardens. Plantain-leaved sedge is presented due to its hardiness and easy care. The spring flowers are typical of sedges, although slightly showier. They are brown, almost black, and held above the newly emerging leaves.

Bloom Period and Seasonal Color
Almost-black flowers appear in early spring.

Mature Height × Spread
1 to 2 ft. × 12 to 18 in.

When, Where, and How to Plant
Plant in early spring or early fall. Plantain-leaved sedge is a good choice for planting near water if it receives some shade. It does best in moist, fertile soil, but it will tolerate drier conditions as long as it is out of the sun. This *Carex*, like many others, is not difficult to establish. It is wise to add a generous amount of organic matter to hold soil moisture in dry soils. The use of a thick organic mulch will help recreate the forest floor environment similar to its native habitat. It is generally available as a container-grown plant, but it can be started from divisions or seed. (See chapter introduction for more planting information.)

Growing Tips
Water at planting and whenever soil begins to dry, until well established. Watering in hot, dry weather is essential, especially in more sun. Once established, in better soils, no fertilizer is needed. In poorer soils apply 5-10-5 or a water-soluble fertilizer. Too much nitrogen will encourage weak floppy growth.

Care
Brown tips appearing on the leaves can be trimmed with sharp scissors. Keep plants thoroughly mulched. Divide in early spring if necessary or to increase stock. They may self-sow when grown under preferred conditions. Plantain-leaved sedge requires little maintenance.

Companion Planting and Design
The bright-green leaves of this sedge make an excellent ground cover in shady areas. It will spread without being invasive. It looks at home planted with ferns, hostas, and trilliums mixed into a bed of periwinkle for contrast. Use it to line paths or fill in around azaleas and rhododendrons. Its spring flowers are attractive in a vase.

Did You Know?
Plantain-leaved sedge is native to the eastern forests of North America. There are over 2,000 species of sedges found all around the world, most in cool, wet climates. Some do well in dry or sunny situations, while others will tolerate occasional submersion. Plantain-leaved sedge is an excellent example of a high-quality native plant that can be tamed in the garden.

Prairie Dropseed
Sporobolus heterolepsis

When, Where, and How to Plant

Prairie dropseed is best planted in spring, although some sources indicate fall planting is successful. It prefers full sun but will tolerate light shade. Sometimes flopping becomes a problem if there is too much shade. It is extremely heat- and drought-tolerant, even accepting dry, rocky soil. It will do just fine in a wide range of soil conditions but the soil needs to be well drained. It is generally available as a container plant. Try to find two year old plants, if possible, as it grows slowly and takes three years to bloom. It demands little soil preparation unless drainage is an issue. (See chapter introduction for more planting information.)

Growing Tips

Water at planting and whenever the soil gets dry until it gets established. After that it is extremely drought tolerant. Apply 10-6-4, 50 percent slow-release fertilizer in early spring after mowing.

Care

This plant should be cut back in the spring. When mowed, it will drop its seed and may be self-sowing, but it is not invasive. It can also be divided in spring, but make the division a large size to cut down on the time it takes to get established. Its slow growth rate eliminates the need for frequent division. It has no pest problems, so should be very easy to maintain.

Companion Planting and Design

Dropseed can be planted as a ground cover for large areas, but in most gardens it will be used to its best advantage when mixed with other grasses or perennials. The graceful mounds blend with other perennials in a border or bed or even as a foundation plant. It can make a smooth transition between wild and cultivated areas.

Did You Know?

The seeds of prairie dropseed are attractive to birds and other wildlife. There are about one hundred species from different parts of the world, but few are under cultivation. There are no varieties of prairie dropseed at this time.

Prairie dropseed is considered a good choice for beginners. This native American grass once filled the western prairies, and its seed was harvested for food by Native Americans. The common name "dropseed" comes from the plant's tendency to easily drop its seed from mature seedheads. Excessive grazing and modern agriculture have devastated its natural range. The delicate sweet scent of the flowers lasts through September. This fragrance is not typical of flowers, and it has been compared to buttered popcorn. The autumn foliage color is a uniform, rich orange-gold. As winter progresses, the color matures to creamy brown. It stays very attractive through the winter. Prairie dropseed will tolerate dry, rocky soil, a trait not common among ornamental grasses.

Other Common Name
Northern Dropseed

Bloom Period and Seasonal Color
Flowers in August through October; fall foliage is orange gold.

Mature Height × Spread
3 ft. × 2 ft.

Snowy Wood Rush
Luzula nivea

Snowy wood rush is not a true grass but has grass-like foliage. The diminutive clumps are pleasing both to see and touch. Tiny hairs on the gray-green leaves feel velvety. The species is considered evergreen but may not last until spring. The very early spring flowers of snowy wood rush are among the first to bloom. The flowers are ivory white and arranged in "umbels" (clusters that resemble an upside-down umbrella). The ivory color dries to a creamy beige, adding appeal after other spring blooms are gone. Some of the eighty Lazula species are native to North America, but most under cultivation are from Europe. L. nivea is found in the wild from Spain to Poland.

Bloom Period and Seasonal Color
Almost white flowers, appearing in very early spring.

Mature Height × Spread
2 ft. × 8 to 12 in.

When, Where, and How to Plant
Snowy wood rush can be planted in early spring or early fall. A woodland setting of rich, moist, humusy soil is ideal, but these are cooperative small plants. While they can burn in the hottest part of their range, they will likely survive full sun in most of New Jersey. It is always beneficial to try to copy the conditions of a plant's natural environment. Woodland soil is rich in organic matter from the annual leaf drop. Applying significant amounts of leaf compost will create a similar environment. The use of an organic mulch is also beneficial. Snowy wood rush is usually grown from container stock but can be propagated by seed. (See chapter introduction for more planting information.)

Growing Tips
Water at planting and keep soil moist but not soggy. Fertilize with a light application of 10-6-4, 50 percent slow-release fertilizer in early spring.

Care
Prune back flower stalks as needed and cut back foliage in late winter if it looks less than acceptable. Divide established plants in early spring. Replace the organic mulch regularly to control weeds and retain soil moisture. Snowy wood rush has no known pests or other problems.

Companion Planting and Design
In the shade they love, snowy wood rush can be planted with trilliums, bloodroot, and violets. They can be used under trees as a ground cover, mixed in a border with other perennials, or used as a specimen. Snowy wood rush is an excellent choice for shaded rock gardens. The slender stems are tall enough to make excellent cut flowers, fresh or dry.

Did You Know?
L. nivea is particularly lovely when the morning sun shines across its dew-laden leaves. One source credits the origin of its botanical name (*Luzula*) with this sight. *Luzula* is derived from the Latin "luciola," which means "glowworm." Another source says it comes from the Latin "lux," meaning "light."

Switch Grass

Panicum virgatum

When, Where, and How to Plant

Plant in early spring or early fall. Switch grass will do best in a sunny location, but it will tolerate light shade. Too much shade will cause it to flop over. Moist, fertile soil is ideal, but it will grow even under extreme conditions. Switch grass can be planted from seed, but take care with mixed prairie seedings, as switch grass can take over a seed mix. It is most commonly planted from container-grown stock. Propagation is by spring division, especially if they are named selections. It is not difficult to get established and usually requires no special soil preparation. (See chapter introduction for more planting information.)

Growing Tips

Water at planting and under extremely dry conditions. This native is drought tolerant, but it may look better with an occasional watering during a hot, dry summer. A light application of 10-6-4, 50 percent slow-release fertilizer in the spring will be beneficial.

Care

Switch grass can be cut back in the spring, but the new growth will grow up through the old without much fuss if you prefer not to bother. Switch grass has no known pest problems.

Companion Planting and Design

Use it as an untamed hedge or as part of a mixed planting of grasses and perennials. It works well as a screen, or place a pair of clumps as a focal point. Its toughness makes it tolerant of seashore conditions and gives it desirable properties for growing along highways and roadsides. It is used as ground cover for erosion control and in land reclamation projects. The bold shape and flower skeletons can be particularly interesting when covered in snow. In summer, use switch grass to hide a view, or even better, to carve out a private nook.

Did You Know?

There are over 600 species of *Panicum* grasses. "Panicum" is the Latin name for Italian millet. *P. miliaceum* is the true millet, cultivated for its small round white seeds commonly used in bird-seed mixtures.

This native American has long been cultivated in Europe but is only recently gaining popularity in the States. Perhaps it is difficult to appreciate what is in one's own backyard. The tall-grass prairies were once a sea of switch grass undulating in the breeze. Between the tall upright plants, the flowers towering above, and its vivid fall color, the image can boggle the mind. Today, new varieties are being regularly released. Switch grass is easy to grow and adaptable to a wide range of soil types and moisture conditions. It even tolerates wind and salt spray for shore plantings. The clump habit spreads slightly but does not usually become a problem. The flowers are beautiful fresh and are long lasting when dry.

Other Common Name
Panic Grass

Bloom Period and Seasonal Color
Pink, red or silver panicles, opening in July and persisting all winter; fall foliage is yellow, orange red, rusty red, or purple red.

Mature Height × Spread
3 to 7 ft. × 2 to 3 ft.

Perennials *for New Jersey*

Gardening is an art form that includes four dimensions. The fourth dimension is that it changes over time. What may be perfectly balanced today can be out of whack before too much time has passed. Trees grow, light conditions change, ground covers spread, vines climb. You can measure the passage of time by watching a shade tree stretch and grow over the years.

A World of Constant Change

When you work with perennials, you put that progression over time into high gear. Perennials will develop from year to year, but they also change the look of your garden dramatically from spring through fall. They are simple enough to move from spot to spot if the mood suits you. Virginia bluebells,

Mix of Coneflowers and Daylilies

primrose, columbine, and bleeding heart in spring look nothing like liatris, evening primrose, and monarda in summer, which are completely different from false dragonhead, asters, and chrysanthemums in the fall. You can have a similar progression with the right assortment of woody ornamentals, but you can have many perennials in the amount of space that would accommodate only a few trees or shrubs.

Annuals need to be replanted every spring. You can mix them up and change the scheme from year to year, but annual flowers will look the same for the entire season. Perennials stay in the same place for two or three years at least (some can stay fifty years), but your garden will appear to be many different gardens in the same year. Making room for some of each gives you the best of both worlds.

Make a Plan and Keep Trying

Determine whether you want the same species planted in a mass, or whether you want to collect different ones. An enormous planting of raspberry parfait peonies will stop traffic cold while in bloom, but when

Yellow Flag Irises

it's over, it's over. If you plant twenty varieties of peonies carefully selected for color and time of bloom, you will have a much longer peony season, but to appreciate the sometimes subtle differences, you need to be at sniffing distance. In a small yard, up close and personal is all you have, so make it work for you. In large sprawling grounds, a single plant is often lost. You need to plan the right amount of grouping with enough variety to suit the size of your yard and your own personal interests, with an overall pleasing effect.

Don't think you have to get it all right with the first planting. What really tickles your fancy can be divided and spread out. Plants that fall flat can be replaced. Annuals can provide big blasts of color that camouflage the lulls in the progression of the perennials. Fill in with something perennial when you find just the right plant. One of the wonderful things about perennials is that it only takes a shovel to change things around. If you don't like it, move it. If you love it, divide it and you will have more. If you really hate it, toss it on the compost pile and try something new. It's not like digging out an oak tree because you decided you prefer maples.

Preparing to Plant

Growing perennials from seed may get you the species that tickles your fancy but will certainly extend the time until you see your first flower. Also, starting plants from seed indoors requires better growing conditions than found in most homes. A greenhouse or greenhouse window will give the best results, but a large window with an unblocked southern exposure may do the trick. Check the individual plant listings in this chapter to see which are more conducive to starting from seed and then be sure to follow directions that come with the specific seeds you purchase (found on the packaging). The more

Perennial Border with Daylilies

information you can gather about the specific genus, species, and even variety you are attempting to grow from seed, the more likely you are to be successful.

In most cases, perennials are available in containers. Locally, many containerized perennials are only available while in bloom, which makes them easier to sell. Containerized material can be planted anytime the ground isn't frozen. When getting ready to plant, match the growing requirements to the growing conditions in your garden. The general rule for planting perennials is to dig a hole at a depth that allows you to plant the perennial at the same depth the plant was in the pot.

Once you are ready to plant outdoors, whether you grew the plants yourself from seed or purchased them, you want to pay attention to amending the soil with organic matter when needed, as well as mulching those perennials that will fail under excessive heat and drought. Most perennials are not fussy, however, and will do fine in average soils. Within the plant entries, I may indicate to add sand to heavy clay soil. Never do so without adding organic matter as well, even if the plants prefer sandy soil. Sand and clay make concrete, and no plant will grow in it.

Dividing perennials takes a tad more attention to detail since the roots are somewhat damaged no matter how carefully the division is made. This approach is best done in early spring as the plants first emerge or in early fall in the case of spring blooming perennials such as peony and iris.

Join the Club!

On occasion, a particular perennial will capture your heart and run away with it. That is when you become a specialist. It is not difficult to become totally devoted to daylilies. Once you see how fabulous they can be and how many colors and varieties there are to choose from, you may find yourself wanting many. The same can be said for iris, or peonies, or chrysanthemums. There are societies or clubs for

Poppy

many popular perennials. The American Hosta Society, The American Iris Society, The American Peony Society, The American Primrose Society, and The National Chrysanthemum Society are a few. These specialty organizations will often offer plant exchanges or opportunities to get unusual, new, or historic varieties that are not readily available in the trade.

It doesn't matter whether you have row upon row of perennials or just a few tucked into a corner. When their time to bloom is approaching, you will peek and check and anticipate their beauty. There are perennials for shade or sun and for spring, summer, or fall. They can be tall or short and come in every color imaginable. They will bring you joy. You may find that your absolute favorite is the one blooming right now.

Chrysanthemum

Aster
Aster spp.

Asters are fall blooming perennials. They can be found growing as wildflowers in almost every abandoned field. There are over 600 species as well as an enormous number of hybrids and varieties. Chrysanthemums usually dominate the fall garden, but asters offer an easy-to-grow alternative. These flowers belong to the composite or daisy family. "Ray" flowers or petals surround its flat disc in the center. Wild asters often produce small flowers— only 1/4 inch across—that grow in large clusters. Hybrid asters make up a significant number of the garden varieties available. To search for any particular aster may be difficult, but there are many offered locally and by mail-order. Be sure to get all the available information on the variety you select to use them to their best advantage.

Other Common Name
Michaelmas Daisy

Bloom Period and Seasonal Color
Fall-blooming flowers in many sizes and colors, including white, pink, violet, purple, red, and blue.

Mature Height × Spread
6 to 8 in. or higher × variable spread

When, Where, and How to Plant
Plant fall-blooming perennials in the spring. This allows them to establish a strong root system before winter. Once they begin to produce flowers, root growth slows significantly. Asters need full sun and room to spread. They usually prefer rich, moderately dry soil. Asters are often available as individual potted plants, or sometimes by the flat. Because they prefer drier soil, it is best to add a 2:1 mixture of organic matter and sand rather than organic matter alone. Fall planted asters may have to be treated as annuals. If they return in spring, consider it a bonus. (See chapter introduction for more about planting.)

Growing Tips
Water at planting and when soil becomes excessively dry. When watering, do so thoroughly, making sure to water the ground around the plants and not the plants themselves. Fertilize in early spring with 5-10-5 to get them off to a good start.

Care
Asters prefer dry soil, but overly dry soil causes stress and makes them more susceptible to powdery mildew. Use a fungicide at the first sign of white spots; keeping water off the leaves will slow down the spread of the disease. The centers of plantings can become less productive over time and need to be dug out every two or three years. Replace with young divisions from the outer edge of the planting. This prevents excessive spread and keeps the patch blooming. Asters also spread from seed, so keep an eye out for volunteers.

Companion Planting and Design
Asters can be mixed with other fall-blooming perennials for an autumn display or can add color to a multi-seasonal bed. They tend to pick up when summer annuals begin to fade. Asters make excellent cut flowers.

Did You Know?
Victorian literature contains many references to Michaelmas and the Michaelmas daisy. As a Bronte and Austin devotee, I often wondered what this meant. I discovered that Michaelmas is a religious day honoring the archangel Michael. It takes place September 29, which also happens to be around the time when most asters (or Michaelmas daisies) are in full bloom.

Astilbe

Astilbe × arendsii

When, Where, and How to Plant

Plant astilbe in early spring or early fall. Astilbe is treasured for its enthusiasm in the shade, but it will tolerate full sun as long as the spot is not excessively hot and the soil is kept adequately moist. Avoid a western exposure up against a dark house, but bright morning sun with good air movement should be fine. Astilbe needs soil that is high in organic matter, so incorporate copious quantities of it into the soil prior to planting. Leaf compost is best, but peat moss can also be used. Dig deeply to ensure good soil drainage. Remember that high soil moisture is not the same as soggy ground. (See chapter introduction for more planting information.)

Growing Tips

Water at planting and keep soil moist, especially during hot, dry summer weather. A light application of 5-10-5 in early spring will give astilbes a boost for the season.

Care

Astilbe has few problems, but it needs to be divided every four or five years to maintain vigor. Remove spent flowers to keep the plant looking attractive and to prevent seed formation. Apply an organic mulch to retain soil moisture and to moderate fluctuations in temperature.

Companion Planting and Design

Astilbes planted in open spaces in a wooded area can be spectacular. A mass planting of a single variety or large patches of complementing colors is stunning. Try growing them along a bank under tall trees or in patches right through myrtle or pachysandra for a little midsummer color. They mix beautifully with ferns, hostas, and lily-of-the-valley. Plant around azaleas and rhododendrons. Astilbes come into their season just as these shade-loving shrubs are finishing up.

Did You Know?

Astilbes can make very attractive cut flowers if you cut them when they are only partially open. They make beautiful bouquets when combined with roses. The individual flowers resemble the soft delicate blooms of baby's breath, but in bright colors. Try red astilbe with yellow roses for zing or soft pink astilbe with white roses for a more delicate look.

There are about fourteen species of astilbe, two of which are native to North America. The rest originate in eastern Asia. Most common varieties are hybrids of four or five species. Leaves are compound, shiny or dull, dark green or with hints of bronze or purple. Flowers can be white, various shades of pink, or subtle-to-bright shades of red. Astilbe is an easy care perennial and a great boon in the shade. Plant all one variety in a group to make a big impact in a small spot. It doesn't take many astilbes to add zing to a bed of hosta or soft ferns, but a single plant will be lost. A mass of astilbes in a woodland clearing can function as a ground cover but is brilliant enough to seem magical.

Other Common Names
False Spirea, Meadow Sweet

Bloom Period and Seasonal Color
Flowers in many colors including white, pinks, and reds, appearing in June through August.

Mature Height × Spread
1 to 4 ft. × 1 to 2 ft.

Beebalm
Monarda didyma

The tubular flowers of beebalm are otherworldly. They start out resembling a sputnik, then develop a central disc, sometimes sending out more tubes in a tiered effect. They make an unusual-looking addition to cut flowers and may be white, pink, red, or purple. You will appreciate the butterflies, bees, and hummingbirds this plant attracts. Beebalm spreads, so provide plenty of room. The bloom period is fairly long, especially if you remove dead flowers. The leaves resemble mint leaves (they belong to the same family) but are generally larger. They have a fragrance with just a hint of citrus and are commonly used for tea. Native to eastern North America from Canada to Tennessee, beebalm was substituted for the black tea irate colonists dumped in Boston Harbor.

Other Common Names
Bergamot, Oswego Tea, Horsemint, Monarda

Bloom Period and Seasonal Color
Flowers appear from June through August in many colors, including white, pink, red, and purple.

Mature Height × Spread
3 ft. × 2 ft. or more

When, Where, and How to Plant
Plant beebalm in spring. Fall plantings do not usually survive the winter. A location in partial shade with deep rich soil is best. Beebalm can take full sun if planted where the soil never dries out. A spot with air movement will help minimize powdery mildew. Maintain soil moisture by adding plenty of organic matter. Space plants 18 inches apart. (See chapter introduction for more planting information.)

Growing Tips
Water deeply at planting and keep soil moist, especially during hot, dry weather. A light application of 5-10-5 fertilizer in early spring will give plants a boost.

Care
A severe pruning after bloom often triggers a second bloom. Removal of dead flowers during the season can extend the first round of blooms for over two months. Powdery mildew, while unsightly, is seldom fatal; it can be controlled with fungicides by spraying as soon as you see white spots. If you want to dry the leaves for tea, harvest before spraying. Cut plants down to the ground in fall. Divide in spring every two or three years. An organic mulch will help keep soil moist.

Companion Planting and Design
Beebalm can be overpowering. Do not plant it next to anything small and delicate. It can become ragged and sad looking from mildew at season's end, so you may not want to plant it in a formal garden or outside the front door. Try to choose a location where you can see the blooms from indoors. You may see a hummingbird race from flower to flower.

Did You Know?
Oswego tea is named for the Oswego (or Otsego) Indians who first introduced early settlers to its pleasures. It has a pleasant taste, but is sometimes taken to treat coughs or a sore throat. John Bartram, an American botanist in the 1700s, sent seeds to England. It has been cultivated throughout Europe since that time, where it is known as golden melissa or Indian nettle.

When, Where, and How to Plant

It is best to plant or divide black-eyed Susan in early spring. It prefers full sun but will tolerate light shade. Black-eyed Susan will grow in a wide range of soils with almost any degree of moisture content, though it will not survive in soggy sites. Black-eyed Susans are not fussy and establish easily. Potted plants are usually available in spring. If you see them in bloom in containers in the summer, you can pop them right in your garden. (See chapter introduction for more about planting.)

Growing Tips

Water thoroughly at planting and be sure to keep newly planted black-eyed Susans watered well during summer's heat. They will do well in better soils without additional fertilizers, but an application of 5-10-5 or a water-soluble fertilizer in early spring will be beneficial.

Care

Leaf miners and powdery mildew can affect the plant, but they are rarely serious problems. Control with fungicide if necessary. Continual removal of dead flowers will encourage more flower production. Divide every three or four years. Mulch heavily in the fall.

Companion Planting and Design

Black-eyed Susan spreads and shows to its best advantage when planted en masse, so give it room. It also works well in an informal perennial bed or as the perennial in an annual cutflower garden. Plant in an iris bed, and the summer blooming black-eyed Susan will take over after the irises have finished. They are excellent for cutting and blend beautifully with zinnias and giant marigolds in a brilliant summer bouquet. The conelike seedpods that follow the flowers are useful in dried arrangements.

Did You Know?

R. hirta, commonly a roadside plant, includes among its named varieties the beautiful gloriosa daisy. These plants make wonderful additions to your garden, either as annuals or biennials grown as annuals. While they may self-sow, they are not truly perennial. To avoid disappointment, be sure to get the species you want. The flowers of these two species can be very similar and are easily confused.

The color of a black-eyed Susan is hard put into words. It is an intense golden orange, and a field in bloom is electric. The full, hairy plants can reach twelve feet tall in moist fertile soil, but garden varieties are usually smaller. The flowers have brown-to-black centers that mature to a raised cone shape. Black-eyed Susans spread by rhizomes, and clumps often get quite large. The plant branches and produces many flowers along its length. Named varieties are far more compact and floriferous than the species. Plants often volunteer, but they invariably revert to the species type and lack the productivity and uniformity of the varieties. Keep in mind that they grow rapidly and can be divided in spring. Black-eyed Susan is native from New Jersey to Florida and west to Michigan. It is generally found in open fields.

Other Common Names
Showy Coneflower, Orange Coneflower

Bloom Period and Seasonal Color
Golden orange flowers appear July through October.

Mature Height × Spread
1 1/2 to 12 ft. × 2 ft., but variable

Blanketflower
Gaillardia × grandiflora

Blanketflower creates a colorful, long-lasting display. Its tolerance of dry growing conditions makes it invaluable. The large showy blooms are very attractive and make excellent cut flowers. Flower petals are almost raggedy tipped. The biggest blast of color comes in spring, but blanketflower will continue to produce a significant number of blooms for the rest of the summer. If you regularly remove the dead flowers as they fade, flower production will be more generous. G. grandiflora is a cross between the perennial G. aristata (which has yellow flowers), a native of North Dakota, Colorado, and Oregon, and the painted gaillardia, G. pulchella, native from Virginia to Florida and west to New Mexico. According to Hortus III, *the hybrid has now naturalized in the west.*

Other Common Name
Indian Blanket

Bloom Period and Seasonal Color
Blooms in red and yellow with orange or maroon bands, appearing July until frost.

Mature Height × Spread
8 to 36 in. × 18 in., but varies.

When, Where, and How to Plant
Strains of blanketflower can be planted from seed in spring and will bloom the first year. Plant container-grown plants in spring or fall. It is best to plant from divisions. Blanketflower tolerates heat better than many other summer flowers. Grow blanketflower in full sun in loose, well-drained soil. Heavy soils, especially those that stay wet over the winter, are deadly to the blanketflower. Add a 2:1 mixture of organic matter and sand at planting time to loosen soil. Space plants about 18 inches apart. (See introduction for more planting information.)

Growing Tips
Water at planting and when soil gets excessively dry, although blanketflower is exceptionally tolerant of hot, dry growing conditions. Blanketflower will do well in better soils without additional fertilizers, but an application of 5-10-5 or the use of a water-soluble fertilizer in early spring will get them off to a good start.

Care
These plants are short-lived. Clumps sometimes die out in the center and require division every two or three years. A major pruning in late summer will encourage a late fall bloom. Removal of spent blooms keeps fresh flowers coming, but the seedheads are also attractive. They have few if any pests.

Companion Planting and Design
Blanketflower's colors combine beautifully with yellow and orange marigolds in the garden or in a vase. It works well in a cutflower garden, as part of a perennial border, in rock gardens, in containers, or even as a ground cover for small areas.

Did You Know?
The Department of Parks in New Brunswick planted blanketflower in the island bed in the middle of Albany Street (a main road in the downtown area). The plants were placed under very young shade trees, with black-topped road and busy car traffic on either side of the site. They bloomed late every spring and sporadically through the summer for three or four years with very little attention.

Bleeding Heart
Dicentra spectabilis

When, Where, and How to Plant
Plant in early spring for best results. Plant bleeding heart in deep woodland soils in sites with partial to deep shade. Double dig, if necessary, in hard compact soils. Add large amounts of organic matter and use an organic mulch. (See chapter introduction for more about planting.)

Growing Tips
Water at planting and try to keep soil moist. Keeping the plants well watered in hot weather will prolong the seasonal life of the foliage. In well prepared soil that is high in organic matter, bleeding heart will be fine without additional fertilizer; however, 5-10-5 or a water-soluble fertilizer in early spring may be beneficial.

Care
An organic mulch will help replenish the organic matter in the soil. Bleeding heart has no serious insect or disease problems. It can live for years with little or no attention. Be sure to mark the location of the plant in order to avoid inadvertently digging it up in the fall. Plants can be divided in early spring.

Companion Planting and Design
Bleeding heart is an excellent choice for a shaded rock garden, under shade trees, or in a romantic nook. The white variety 'Alba' is not quite as hardy, but very lovely. Fringed bleeding heart, *D. eximia*, has fernlike foliage and pink dangling hearts that appear throughout the summer. Mix bleeding heart with spring flowers such as trillium, bloodroot, and violet. This plant works well with ferns and hostas, which fill in easily when the bleeding heart has finished blooming. The plant dies back by midsummer, but summer annuals planted at the base of bleeding heart can take over and last until frost.

Did You Know?
The plant does not produce enough flowers to allow you to cut them often, but a few mixed in with a spring bouquet of tulips can be stunning. The contrast of flower sizes and shapes, as well as the horizontal carriage of the bleeding heart blooms, creates a special image. A few sprigs in a bridal bouquet would be very romantic.

There is no flower as romantic as the bleeding heart. Each heart-shaped blossom is pierced at the point with a white dagger. Each row of pierced blossoms dangles from horizontal stems like a necklace Cupid would wear. Their shape is the poet's perfect symbol for a broken heart. Bleeding hearts are dependable perennials that return year after year with very little fuss. The foliage of the bleeding heart has its own appeal. The leaves are compound and graceful. The stems grow up and arch over. The upper part has a hint of red that turns yellow in hot weather but does not become shabby looking. When bleeding hearts fade, cut them back and let your summer annuals fill in the gap.

Other Common Names
Common Bleeding Heart, Old Fashioned Bleeding Heart

Bloom Period and Seasonal Color
Flowers in May and June.

Mature Height × Spread
1 to 3 ft. × 1 to 3 ft.

Candytuft
Iberis sempervirens

The snowdrift effect of candytuft in bloom is a large part of this dainty but durable perennial's appeal. Its tiny white flowers appear in flat or rounded clusters about one and one-half inches wide, and completely cover the plant. The narrow, dark green, one- to two-inches-long leaves stay green year-round. They form a thick mat that can be used as a ground cover in small spaces. Once the long-lasting flowers fade, upright bright green seedpods take their place. These seedpods are interesting to see and can be enjoyed as well (before removing them). Candytuft looks its absolute best when draped over a coarse gray rock. Walls cloaked in the veil of white are also impressive. While you're at it, roll out the white carpet under azaleas and rhododendrons. This can create a stunning effect.

Other Common Name
Evergreen Candytuft

Bloom Period and Seasonal Color
White flowers appearing late May through June.

Mature Height × Spread
4 to 12 in. × 3 ft.

When, Where, and How to Plant
Plant candytuft in early spring or early fall in deep, rich, well-drained soil. Candytuft is prized for use in partially shaded environments but will do well in full sun if kept moist. It will tolerate deep shade, though you can't expect quite the same avalanche of flowers. Plants are usually available in pots but can sometimes be purchased by the flat if you have an aggressive planting plan needing a lot of specimens. Candytuft is easily divided in early spring. This plant does not do well in soggy soil, especially in winter, so pile on organic matter and till it in to insure good drainage. (See chapter introduction for more planting information.)

Growing Tips
Water at planting and then keep candytuft watered, especially while it is in bloom. Dry soil shortens the blooming season. An application of 5-10-5 in early spring will give plants a great start for the season.

Care
As fascinating as the round green seedpods are, you need to remove them before they fully mature. If the seedpods are not removed, the plants become stretched out and bare at the base of the stems. A heavy all-over shearing will keep them thick. With some varieties, this pruning will trigger a second bloom in the fall. Candytuft is virtually pest free.

Companion Planting and Design
Candytuft is ideal for a rock garden and is lovely tucked here, there, and everywhere. It is also ideal for borders, slopes, terraced gardens, and in front of evergreen shrubs. Mixed with columbine, the creeping habit of the candytuft complements the arching stems of the columbine, and the dramatically different flower forms mix well. In shady sites, blend in bleeding hearts and violets. In gardens that get full sun, late season tulips popping up through a carpet of candytuft is gorgeous.

Did You Know?
Though color in the garden is one of the major thrills of gardening, white candytuft combined with tall spurred white columbine and white tulips creates a place for angels to visit. Bees will come, too. They love candytuft.

Columbine

Aquilegia × hybrida

When, Where, and How to Plant

Plant columbine in early spring in partial shade to full sun, but avoid hot western exposures. Columbine is usually available in containers. Plants can be grown from seed sown in early spring but won't flower until their second year. Fall-sown seed will bloom the first spring if overwintered in a greenhouse. Seed collected from garden plants is not likely to grow plants identical to the parents. Amend the soil with lots of compost or other organic matter to ensure good drainage. Space plants about 18 inches apart (See chapter introduction for more planting information.)

Growing Tips

Water at planting and whenever the soil dries. This is especially true in hot, sunny locations. Columbines will thrive in soils rich in organic matter, but you may supplement with a spring application of 5-10-5 to give them a boost, especially in poorer soils.

Care

Watch out for leafminers. They disfigure the leaves with wavy whitish lines on the leaf surface and cause early deterioration of the plant. Hand pick the damaged leaves and destroy them. Spray with an appropriate insecticide. When the plants reseed, the flower quality deteriorates. Don't bother trying to rejuvenate an infested patch. Start over with fresh plants every three or four years.

Companion Planting and Design

Columbines are excellent for rock gardens. They are too free-spirited for a formal design but can be mixed with ferns or trilliums in a naturalized setting. Columbines look wonderful with candytuft, coral bells, later blooming daffodils, violets, ferns, and hostas. The ferny columbine leaves help camouflage fading daffodil foliage.

Did You Know?

Columbine sometimes seem to grow from magic. I once planted a patch of multicolored columbine that came up its second year with enormous pure white flowers. Perhaps the original plants reseeded themselves, but they appeared to be the same plants in the exact spots. They continued to produce enormous white flowers for years. There was no clear explanation. I concluded it must have been the hand of the wood elves.

Wood elves live among the columbine. No other flower has enough beauty and whimsy to keep the mythical creatures content. Columbine leaves are reminiscent of a maidenhair fern, though they are not quite as finely carved. The exquisite buds shyly nod their heads, pointing long threadlike spurs into the air. Some open to face the sun, at which time the long spurs point down. Columbines are so fragile they don't seem real. But they are real and a special gift to remind us of the wonders of nature. Most columbines have spurs, though the length varies. A species from Texas and Mexico, A. longissima, has spurs up to six inches long! (There are even some without spurs, but why bother?) Double-flowered types are interesting but lack the ethereal quality that makes the singles so unreal. Columbines are not difficult to grow.

Bloom Period and Seasonal Color
Flowers appear in May and June in a range of colors.

Mature Height × Spread
18 to 36 in. × 18 in.

Daylily
Hemerocallis hybrids

There are 35,000 registered varieties of daylily. Even if you are not an avid gardener, you are likely familiar with the "wild" daylilies that can be found growing along the road. These are sometimes referred to as "tiger lilies," though in truth that name is reserved for a species of true lily. Ancestors of the daylily were brought over by early colonists. Plants you see along the highway are escapees from the originals. This is amazing when you consider that "wild" daylilies are sterile and spread only from the roots. The botanical name Hemerocallis *comes from the Greek for "beautiful for a day" as each trumpet-shaped bloom lasts for only one day. Don't be discouraged! One day is enough. Each plant produces so many flowers during the season that there is never a shortage of color.*

Other Common Name
Tiger Lily

Bloom Period and Seasonal Color
Flowers appear throughout the summer, in a huge range of colors.

Mature Height × Spread
1 to 6 ft. × 2 to 3 ft.

When, Where, and How to Plant
Early spring is the best time to plant, but planting any time from spring until mid-October is acceptable. Plant in full sun for maximum flowers. Light shade in the late afternoon will prevent color from fading prematurely. Daylilies tolerate up to half a day of shade but won't produce as many blooms. They are not particular about soil type, though moist soil (not soggy) will encourage flowers. Spacing is variety dependent, but 12 to 24 inches is the range, and 16 inches is most common. Plants are usually shipped bare root. Plant so the roots are covered by $1/2$ inch of soil. Plant potted specimens at the same depth they were in their containers. Mulch to help control weeds and retain soil moisture.

Growing Tips
Water at planting and keep daylilies well watered in hot weather to prolong bloom time. Provide an application of 5-10-5 fertilizer in early spring.

Care
Divide clumps any time from spring until about a month before the first hard freeze. Unless you must, try not to divide in summer, as this will disturb the blooming cycle. Remove scapes (flower stalks) when all the buds have opened. You don't want energy going into making seeds when it can go into making more flowers. Daylilies have no serious pests.

Companion Planting and Design
Plant daylilies en masse for viewing from a distance. Up close stagger different varieties to extend the season. Plant daylilies in rock gardens, as borders, or to follow spring bulbs. The lush foliage is perfect for hiding the fading foliage from bulbs, especially daffodils.

Did You Know?
If you want to try something different, you can eat your daylilies. Leaves have the best flavor when they are 3 to 5 inches long. They are often stir-fried in oil or butter. Flower buds can be eaten raw in salads or cooked in a variety of ways. They are supposed to be particularly luscious when steamed with snow peas. You can even eat the day-old flowers dipped in batter and deep-fried.

Evening Primrose
Oenothera spp.

When, Where, and How to Plant
Plant potted plants or even seed in early spring. Evening primrose thrives in full sun but can withstand light shade. This plant does well in hot, dry locations in poorer soil. Don't plant them in a confined bed close to the house—their spread can be overly aggressive. Heavy clay soils that stay wet must be double dug. Add organic matter and sand (in a 2:1 ratio) to increase drainage. Space plants 1 to 2 feet apart. Water after planting. Evening primrose may spread from seed, which can be good or bad, depending on your needs. (See chapter introduction for more planting information.)

Growing Tips
Water at planting and during severe droughts. Feed in early spring with 5-10-5 fertilizer.

Care
Japanese beetles enjoy evening primrose. Hand pick or spray with an insecticide at the first sign. Prune off faded flower stalks to prevent reseeding and possibly promote additional bloom. Keeping it in bounds is challenging. By choosing the right site and giving it room to spread, you can eliminate or minimize this chore. Divide an established patch in spring.

Companion Planting and Design
All oenothera spread rapidly and with enthusiasm, so do not squeeze them into tight areas. They can be used successfully as a ground cover. If you plant evening primrose in a large clay pot, you can sink the pot in the bed to both enjoy the flowers and contain the roots. The large, delicate flowers bring cheer to the perennial border. The lush growth of the primrose will nicely camouflage the maturing leaves of daffodils.

Did You Know?
O. biennis is the common evening primrose. The "skeletons," of its flower stalks make outstanding additions to dried arrangements. Pods open and curve back to resemble a flower. Soak stalks first in a solution of household bleach to lighten their color then in a bucket of fabric dye in the color of your choice. The inside surface of the seedpods will be a different shade from the outside. The effect is lovely.

Oenothera is native to North America. There are over one hundred species, of which at least one or two can be found in every state. Evening primrose produces one- to four-inch blooms and in theory, opens in late afternoon as the sun sets. The flowers stay open all night, releasing an intoxicating fragrance to entice night pollinators, then close again at sunrise. Sundrops or suncups are supposed to open with the rising sun and stay open all day. They, too, are fragrant, though not quite as intense. Then there is O. missouriensis, equally well known as Ozark sundrop or Missouri primrose, which opens in the afternoon. Most of the species produce bright yellow flowers, but the blooms of showy primrose, O. speciosa, are white or a lovely shade of pink. Sundrops are particularly useful in hot, dry soils.

Other Common Names
Sundrop, Suncup

Bloom Period and Seasonal Color
Blooms usually in yellow but also white or pink, appearing from May through July.

Mature Height × Spread
Usually 2 to 10 ft. × variable spread

False Dragonhead

Physostegia virginiana

False dragonhead comes into bloom at a time when it is really needed. By August, summer annuals may be showing signs of wear, with powdery mildew, stretched out petunias, and pansies that are finished. Along comes false dragonhead like a seventh inning relief pitcher. Each flowering stalk on this plant can produce many eight- to ten-inch flower spikes, resembling snapdragons. One spike grows at the top, and several others (called 'axillary' spikes) grow along the sides. The entire bloom can last for six weeks. Its leaves are toothed, oblong, and grow up to five inches long. Physostegia is native to North America and can be found growing from New England west to Minnesota and south to the Carolinas and Texas. The plants spread rapidly, but usually not viciously.

Other Common Names
Obedient Plant, Lion's Heart

Bloom Period and Seasonal Color
White or pink blooms, appearing August through September.

Mature Height × Spread
3 to 5 ft. × 18 in. or more

When, Where, and How to Plant
Early spring is the best time to plant. False dragonhead does best in full sun but can tolerate slight shade. Well-drained soil is important. When growing this perennial in shade, the soil should be kept on the dry side to avoid problems. You can start false dragonhead from seed, but the better selections are grown from division. They require better-than-average drainage, so be sure to amend soil with a 2:1 mixture of organic matter and sand and/or plant in a raised bed. (See chapter introduction for more planting information.)

Growing Tips
Water at planting, but don't overdo it. A light application of 5-10-5 in early spring will get the plants off to a good start.

Care
Division every 2 to 3 years is recommended. You may also want to keep an eye out for volunteers since this plant can spread from seed. False dragonhead is an easy-care plant. Watch out for root problems when the ground stays wet (the plants will begin to die back, often from the ground up).

Companion Planting and Design
This is a tall plant, so place it toward the middle or back of borders. It can also work in a rock garden, though not a tiny one. The spreading roots are tenacious, making it a good choice for a mild slope. Physostegia is very attractive popping up through low growing evergreens. The sight of pink flowers against the dark green ground cover is particularly pleasing. Make the biggest splash by mixing false dragonhead with perennial hibiscus and purple coneflowers for a major onslaught of passionate pink. The spikes make excellent cut flowers, especially with large flowered zinnias or lots of cosmos.

Did You Know?
False dragonhead is a member of the mint family and has the classic square stems to prove it. The flowers will supposedly remain in place if twisted or jostled, which earns this plant its other common name, "obedient plant."

Hellebore

Helleborus spp.

When, Where, and How to Plant

Plant in early spring or early fall in partial to deep shade. Hellebores like deep, rich, moist soil that is high in lime. Divide established plants in early fall. These plants do not like to be disturbed, so be sure to plant them where they can stay a while. When planting, use potted plants to disturb the roots as little as possible. Dig deeply or double dig in hard-packed soil. Incorporate significant amounts of organic matter and be sure to lime thoroughly. Organic mulch will help retain soil moisture.

Growing Tips

Water at planting and keep moist during hot dry weather. An application of 5-10-5 after flowering in spring is beneficial.

Care

Always wear gloves when you work with hellebores; plant juices can cause a skin irritation. Hellebores are also poisonous if ingested. Hellebores are very long-lived and have no serious pest problems. They do not like to be disturbed, so divide these plants only if you must. If dividing, do so in August or September. It will take a while for the plants to reestablish. Lenten rose will sometimes spread from seed but is never invasive. Pot up unwanted seedlings and give them away. These plants are too wonderful to waste.

Companion Planting and Design

When hellebores bloom they are just about the only show in town. Place them where you will be sure to see them on gray wintery days. Consider planting at the base of witchhazel, a shade-loving small tree that also blooms in late fall or early winter.

Did You Know?

The Christmas rose was an integral part of a Victorian Christmas. The open flowers were floated in a bowl of water as a table centerpiece. To be sure they would be available, the Victorians often forced flowers in a greenhouse. English ivy, barberry, or holly may have been used as the greenery. It is quite curious that this flower went out of fashion, but we're glad they are back.

Hellebores bloom with enthusiasm when most of the outdoor world is down for a long winter's nap. Christmas rose, H. niger, blooms in December and lasts until spring. Lenten rose, H. orientalis, often opens in January. The nodding blooms are slightly camouflaged by the foliage, so they need to be appreciated up close. Plantings with giant zinnias or softball-sized peonies would make hellebores almost invisible, but in the bleakness of winter, hellebores have no competition. That is why the gutsy little plants are so striking. Even the palmately-divided leaves are pleasing. They are almost evergreen but get a little ratty over the winter. In recent years, these plants have skyrocketed in popularity. There are new varieties, hybrids, and unusual species everywhere.

Other Common Names

Christmas Rose, Lenten Rose, Stinking Hellebore, Bear's Foot Hellebore

Bloom Period and Seasonal Color

Blossoms in creamy white, greenish, purple (and purple speckled), appearing in late December through early spring.

Mature Height × Spread

1 to 2 ft. × 1 to 2 ft.

Hosta

Hosta spp.

Hostas are to shade gardeners what flour is to the baker. While usually not overly exciting, hostas are absolutely dependable in deep shade. There are over 800 registered varieties. Most bloom during the summer, some are quite showy, and others have a wonderful sweet fragrance. Leaves are the distinguishing feature for the large majority of hostas. They come in infinite shades of green, green and white, green and yellow, blue-green, and other color combinations. They can be as wide as they are long or long and narrow, heart shaped or almost round. The texture can be paper thin, thick and deeply veined, smooth, crinkled, or wavy edged. The leaves die down completely in the winter. Once established, hostas will last for years.

Other Common Names
Plantain Lily, Funkia

Bloom Period and Seasonal Color
White, violet, or lavender flowers in summer.

Mature Height × Spread
1 to 3 ft. × variable spread

When, Where, and How to Plant
Hostas can be planted in early spring or early fall. Hostas prefer partial shade or even deep shade. Some will tolerate sun, but there are many other planting options for those places. Dappled shade under trees is ideal. Plant from potted plants or divisions. Hostas need woodsy soil that is deep, fertile, high in organic matter, and well drained. Provide better than average soil preparation. Add a large quantity of organic matter such as leaf compost and double dig heavy soils. Hostas establish slowly and will do best when left where they were originally planted. (See chapter introduction for more planting information.)

Growing Tips
Water at planting and maintain moist, not soggy, soil. An annual application of 5-10-5 or the use of a water-soluble fertilizer will help produce an abundance of lush foliage.

Care
Hostas resent being moved, so don't divide them unless necessary. Remove spent flower stalks to keep the plant's energy going into leaf and root production. Clean up dead leaves in the fall to keep the garden tidy and to avoid harboring pests. Unfortunately, slugs love hostas and their moist shady environment. When slugs eat developing foliage, leaves open to reveal a series of chew marks all across the surface. Control with slug bait or diatomaceous earth. Hostas with thicker, waxy, textured, leaves are somewhat less susceptible than the more delicate varieties. Mulch will help keep soil moist but will also encourage slugs.

Companion Planting and Design
The ideal environment for hostas is also perfect for rhododendrons, azaleas, mountain laurels, drooping leucothoe, and skimmias. Mix hostas with bleeding hearts, ferns, trilliums, and violets. For summer color, add a mass planting of one color impatiens or begonias. The contrast can be very pleasing.

Did You Know?
Some people adore hostas. If you happen to be one of them, you might be interested in joining the American Hosta Society. Its headquarters is in Vancouver, Washington.

Iris

Iris spp.

When, Where, and How to Plant

Plant in early spring or early fall. Unless clearly marked "shade tolerant," plant iris in full sun. Bearded iris must have soil with excellent drainage. For wet sites use Japanese iris or yellow flag. The rhizomes should barely show at the surface, and the fans of leaves should point out so that the plants do not grow together. Do not mulch. (See chapter introduction for more planting information.)

Growing Tips

Keep iris well watered during drought, especially moisture loving types. Fertilize in early spring and again after bloom with 5-10-5 or use a water-soluble fertilizer.

Care

Remove dead foliage to minimize overwintering of insects and disease. Remove faded flower stalks to prevent seed production. Most iris need to be divided every three or four years. Ask your garden center about options regarding when to divide. Two big pest problems are the iris borer and a bacterium that causes the leaves and rhizomes to rot (*Erwinia carotovora*). Iris borer larvae can be crushed or sprayed with an appropriate insecticide when the leaves are 4 to 6 inches long, repeating in ten day intervals. Good sanitation is important as a control. Borer damage exposes iris to bacterial rot, recognized by a horrible stench in the deteriorating leaves. Eliminate infected portions of the rhizome; which will need exposure to air to fight the infection. Let the rizomes dry for several days before replanting.

Companion Planting and Design

Plant iris alone for impact or as part of a mixed border. Bearded iris bloom when spring bulbs have finished and summer annuals have not yet gotten up to speed. Try a large bed of iris with cleome planted all around. Cleome reseeds and blooms all summer but offers no competition while iris is in bloom. A single iris flower in a vase can dominate a room.

Did You Know?

"Iris" was a Greek messenger of the gods. She traveled on a rainbow that spanned the gap between heavens and earth. This is why iris is sometimes called "rainbow flower."

There is probably no other grouping of plants more complicated than the iris. The Siberian iris blooms in June with narrow leaves. The flowers have no "beards" (fuzzy filaments on the falls that look like a caterpillar), but they are very dependable. Japanese iris are stunning. They require acidic soil that is constantly moist. Yellow Flag can grow in shallow standing water and is thought to be the "Fleur de lis" associated with the kings of France. The most popular garden iris is probably the bearded iris. It is a mishmash of crosses and re-crosses resulting in breathtaking, enormous flowers. The standards are regally upright, and the falls re-curve gracefully with long, fuzzy beards, often in contrasting colors. Newer varieties may not produce as many blooms, but they can have flowers as large as softballs.

Other Common Names
Flag, Rainbow Flower

Bloom Period and Seasonal Color
Blooms from early spring to early summer in many colors, including yellow, pink, white, burgundy, orange, and purples.

Mature Height × Spread
4 ft. × variable spread

Maximilian Sunflower

Helianthus maximilianii

Maximilian sunflower deserves serious recognition. This tough-as-nails, drought tolerant, mid-west native blooms in October with a blast of yellow that rivals the impact of forsythia in spring. A mass planting is a show stopper. The shoots emerge in early spring from a solid knot of tangled roots. The stems are tightly packed together and look more like bamboo than the common sunflowers. They reach about three to four feet, depending on how much moisture they receive, and stay like that until early September. For the next month the branches elongate to about twice the height, producing a copious number of three-inch yellow blooms along the length. The branches glow with color that first shows in October and can last into early November.

Other Common Name
Perennial Sunflower

Bloom Period and Seasonal Color
Yellow flowers appearing in October.

Mature Height × Spread
12 ft. in bloom × variable spread

When, Where, and How to Plant
Plant seed indoors in late winter for first season bloom or plant potted plants in early spring. Plants are not always readily available, but seed can be purchased from many catalog companies. Choose a sunny location. Maximilian sunflower tolerates very dry soil conditions and grows just about anywhere. It will spread from the roots as well as seed, so don't put it in a small, tidy garden. Plant or transplant at the same depth it was in the container or in the soil. Better soil will result in more robust plants but may also cause overly rapid spread of the roots, so amend only the worst of soils.

Growing Tips
Water newly planted sunflowers until established. Afterwards they are extremely drought tolerant. Fertilize cautiously as better growing conditions will increase their spread. A light application of 5-10-5 in poorer soils in the early spring is all that may be necessary.

Care
Cut down sunflower stalks after they die back in early winter, or you'll have a flattened mess that can smother surrounding plants. Cull out seedlings or overly aggressive spreading roots in early spring when plants are young. Transplant or pot up divisions. They thrive in the pot for a while but don't display many flowers. Pests are not a problem.

Companion Planting and Design
At the edge of a field or on the side of a red barn, sunflowers create drive-by impact that is unexpected that late in the year. They are great to mix with naturalized daffodils. By the time the sunflowers bloom, the daffodil foliage is long gone and you have a completely different garden look for the fall. A few stems make an excellent display in a vase.

Did You Know?
Another perennial sunflower is *H. tuberosus.* This is the Jerusalem artichoke grown for its edible tuberous roots, making it one of few perennial vegetables. It is sometimes sold as "sunchoke." The plants produce 3-inch yellow flowers in early autumn. If left unharvested, it spreads so rapidly that it is considered a weed.

Mum
Chrysanthemum spp.

When, Where, and How to Plant
Plant mums in early spring after danger of frost has passed. Early fall is fine for autumn color, but plants offered at that time of year should be used as annuals. It may be difficult to think of mums in the spring, but you must if you want to grow them as perennials. Once flowering begins, plants don't make many roots and they will not get established well enough to handle winter weather. Choose a location in full sun with good drainage. Prepare the soil with plenty of organic matter to help keep soil moist and to improve drainage. Mums can get fairly large, so give them room. Mulch to help retain soil moisture and to control weeds. Mums are shallow rooted, so don't do much hoeing or digging around them.

Growing Tips
Water at planting and when soil gets dry. An annual dose of fertilizer such as 5-10-5 gives mums a healthy push.

Care
Pinch out the growing tips of the stems regularly until early to mid-July. This causes branching, creating more compact plants with more flowers, and the plant will be less likely to flop over when it rains. Cut back in late fall, after the plants brown, taking care not to damage the tiny green shoots (next year's plants) at the base. If you don't get around to pruning in the fall, then early spring is fine. It makes a nice project for a sunny day in February. Divide in early spring. Pests and diseases are seldom a problem.

Companion Planting and Design
Plant en masse, as a specimen, with other perennials, in containers, in rock gardens, in cutflower gardens, in front of foundation plantings, next to the mailbox, by the front walk, or in any nook or sun-filled cranny.

Did You Know?
Like many flowers, mums have meaning when sent as a gift. Red mum flowers say 'I love,' yellow flowers mean 'slighted love,' and white flowers symbolize 'truth.' Choose your flowers, and your message, carefully.

The world of chrysanthemums is another complex and convoluted maze. The American Chrysanthemum Society lists 15 official flower types and over 3,000 different varieties. However, gardeners will find that most of these plants give spectacular results with minimal effort. They come in an extraordinary range of colors that are rich rather than bright. Giant pompon "football" mums can be almost the size of softballs; little "button" mums, the size of a dime. "Doubles" have so many petals that you cannot see the center disc. Then there are "fried egg" types, whose large, domed, bright yellow discs are surrounded by white petals, truly resembling an egg. "Spoon" mums have tubular petals that open at the tip like long handled spoons. "Spider" mums have long, twisted petals.

Other Common Names
Chrysanthemum, Daisy

Bloom Period and Seasonal Color
Blooms in somewhat muted colors of gold, pink, white or red, from late summer through fall.

Mature Height × Spread
4 ft. × variable spread

Oriental Poppy
Papaver orientale

Poppies, irises, and peonies are important links between spring-flowering bulbs and summer annuals. Peonies and iris have soft colors that lean towards pastels. Poppies, on the other hand, are hot. Their colors, especially the reds, seem charged with electricity. The black centers and occasional black blotches at the base of the petals give intensity to even the lighter shades of pink. Flowers are large, 4 to 6 in., with delicate, crepe-paper petals. The coarse, bristly leaves are up to 12 in. long and pinnately dissected (very deeply lobed) much like a feather. Each lobe is also toothed. To use the vernacular, the leaves are big, pointy, hairy, almost raggedy things—and quite interesting. By midsummer, poppy plants will have completely died down. In late summer or early fall, the plants reappear in a tight clump and stay that way until the following spring.

Bloom Period and Seasonal Color
Blooms in white, pink, orange or red appearing in late May or early June.

Mature Height × Spread
2 to 4 ft. × 2 to 3 ft.

When, Where, and How to Plant
Plant potted poppies in early spring. Root divisions are made during summer dormancy, or divide clumps in early fall. Plant in plenty of sun and well-drained soil. They will not survive in soil that stays wet in winter. Plant root divisions 3 in. deep. If at all possible, start with potted plants. Plant at the same depth they were in their containers. Be sure to lighten heavy soils, as drainage is very important. Add organic matter (such as leaf compost) and sand in a 2:1 ratio prior to planting. Space the plants 2 to 3 ft. apart. They will eventually fill in.

Growing Tips
Water at planting and when soil gets excessively dry, but avoid soggy conditions. Fertilize in early spring with 5-10-5 or a water-soluble fertilizer.

Care
Plants need to be divided every 4 or 5 years. Do this in the early fall after the new rosette of leaves has emerged, and replant right away. Cut flowers for indoor use at night, just before the buds open. Sear the cut end before placing the stem in water. The flowers should open by morning. Poppies are generally pest free.

Companion Planting and Design
Poppy colors are spectacular en masse, but the plants die down over the summer. Hide the gaps with lots of annuals. Dahlias planted around poppies in the spring will grow large and leafy enough to cover the summer gaps. If you don't mind mixing colors, plant poppies with other perennials, but for harmonious colors, choose your poppies carefully. Poppies make excellent cut flowers. Combine with coral bells, *Heuchera sanguinea*, or branches of Vanhoutte spirea, which bloom at about the same time.

Did You Know?
Poppies have held magical qualities for me ever since I saw Dorothy and Toto fall asleep in the poppy field in *The Wizard of Oz*. Some gardeners, however, find that poppies spread with a bit too much enthusiasm. Their spread and their wonderful, intense colors make a few plants sufficient in a confined area. In a large area, let them go.

Peony

Paeonia lactiflora

When, Where, and How to Plant

Plant any time in the fall when the ground is not frozen. September and October are the best times to plant, but spring planting of potted plants is fine. Peonies need full sun and well-drained soil. Prepare the soil at least 1 ft. deep. Make sure the "eyes," or growing points, are facing up and no more than 2 in. below the surface. They can be planted closer to the surface in the south. Mulch is recommended, especially during the first season. (See chapter introduction for more planting information.)

Growing Tips

Water at planting and when soil gets excessively dry. A light application of 5-10-5 fertilier in early spring is beneficial.

Care

Peonies are not fussy. Some varieties benefit from the use of a support. The weight of the flowers, especially when they are wet, can bend the stems to the ground. Remove spent flowers to prevent seed formation. Cut back when foliage turns brown in the fall. The only problem peonies may experience is Botrytis, or gray mold. Flowers suffering from this disease turn gray and never open. Plants are more likely to be affected in wet seasons. Control with a fungicide, beginning when the flowers are pea-sized. Spray weekly until they finish blooming.

Companion Planting and Design

A mass planting can be appreciated at a slight distance, but specimen plants or a selection of varieties should be located where you can get very friendly. Avoid locating peonies close to large trees, as they will compete for nutrients and moisture. Peonies make excellent cut flowers.

Did You Know?

Ants are often found crawling all over the buds and open flowers. They do not damage the plant or the flowers. They are eating the sweet waxy substance that covers the buds. You may want to shake ants off before bringing in cut flowers, but there is no need to use commercial insecticides.

If peonies had a longer season, they would be a contender for the most wonderful flower of all time. The blooming period is fairly short, however, and a really good storm can blow apart the blooms like feathers in a pillow fight. Peonies make up for these weaknesses with longevity. A single plant can stay in the same spot for 50 years with minimum attention. New shoots, often red, emerge in early spring and unfurl into lovely compound dark green leaves. Four flower types are recognized: "Single," which has one or two rows of petals and many bright yellow stamens in the center; "Double," which produces numerous petals and is often fragrant; "Japanese," five or more rows of outer petals with a center full of "staminodium" or abortive anthers; and "Bomb," which has outer petals and a center tuft of very dense petals.

Other Common Names
Chinese Peony, Garden Peony

Bloom Period and Seasonal Color
Blooms in white, pink or red with yellow centers, appearing in May or June.

Mature Height × Spread
$1^{1}/2$ to 4 ft. × 3 ft.

Purple Coneflower

Echinacea purpurea

Purple coneflower can be found throughout the central, east, and southeastern United States. It is a wonderful native perennial that spreads but is not invasive, and it flowers its little heart out for much of the summer and early fall. With large coarse leaves and an open habit, it is not exactly delicate looking, but the enormous 6 in. flowers are cheerful and long lasting. Petals are often flat, like a classic daisy, but they sometimes droop in an appealing way. Purple coneflower tolerates heat, drought, and wind better than most. It is among the perennials suggested for shore planting where it is lovely with the fuzzy, silver lamb's ears. Plants are best placed at the back of a border where their less-than-meticulous growth habit won't be a problem. Bees and butterflies flock to purple coneflowers wherever they are planted.

Other Common Name
Hedgehog Coneflower

Bloom Period and Seasonal Color
Rose-purple or white blooms from July to frost.

Mature Height × Spread
3 to 6 ft. × 2 ft.

When, Where, and How to Plant
Plant in spring or early fall. Give purple coneflowers plenty of sun and a little room to stretch. They are not enormous plants but are likely to be among the tallest in the perennial border. They can tolerate moderately dry soils. This plant is not particular about its soil, but good soil preparation is always beneficial. Purple coneflowers are easy to establish and will usually bloom the first year. Potted plants will be the easiest but seed germinates readily. (See chapter introduction for more planting information.)

Growing Tips
Water at planting. You can maintain better flower production during drought by watering, but purple coneflower will tolerate dry soils. Plants thrive in the wild, so do not require fertilizer but an application of 5-10-5 fertilizer in early spring will result in more lush plants.

Care
Take lots of cut flowers and remove the rest as they fade. This will encourage flower production right up until frost. However, the seed pods can be used as long lasting dried flowers. Powdery mildew can be a problem but is not serious. Watch out for Japanese beetles. Spray or hand pick as soon as you see them munching.

Companion Planting and Design
The seeds of Echinacea are often included in wildflower mixes for meadow planting or along roadsides. They look lovely naturalizing with tall ornamental grasses like *Panicum* 'Heavy Metal', which is a tall, straight grass with metallic-blue foliage. Purple coneflowers make outstanding cut flowers that look fabulous with Queen Anne's lace for a wildflower bouquet or mixed with garden annuals like zinnias and cosmos.

Did You Know?
Purple coneflower is the *Echinacea* of herbal fame. The entire plant is used in the industry: leaves, stems, flowers, and seeds are usually processed together. The roots are processed separately. Until recently, plants were collected from the wild, but increases in demand have introduced the plant to commercial cultivation right here in the Garden State. Echinacea is often used to make a tea that is supposed to boost the immune system.

Rose Mallow
Hibiscus moscheutos

When, Where, and How to Plant
Plant potted plants in spring in moist-to-wet soil—rose mallow's native habitat is North American wetlands. Choose a spot in full sun, where they can stay put for a few years. In average to slightly dry soils you must water during hot weather. Rose mallow tolerates light shade. Add copious amounts of organic matter prior to planting. Space plants 3 ft. apart. Seed is readily available and can be sown indoors in March to bloom the following summer. Starting seed outdoors when the ground warms up will produce plants, but they may not flower the first year. Always use an organic mulch to retain soil moisture. (See introduction for more planting information.)

Growing Tips
Maintain moist soil conditions for the plant to do its best. Fertilize in early spring with 5-10-5.

Care
Don't bother to cut the flowers for indoor use. They wilt almost immediately. Keep mulch intact to prevent the soil from drying. Remove spent flowers to conserve plant energy. Cut back the plants when the stalks yellow in late fall. Don't divide. Rose mallow has no serious insect or disease problems.

Companion Planting and Design
Rose mallow has great 'drive-by' impact on the corner or by the mailbox. In a mass planting the flowers are spectacular. Mix with bulbs and the plants will fill in to hide deteriorating foliage. As part of a perennial border, they bloom later in the season when most other perennials have finished. They never spread out of their space or crowd out smaller plants.

Did You Know?
There is a road near me that goes through a very soggy patch of marshy woods. Early one late summer morning, I drove past this place as the sun streamed through the raggedy marsh trees. In an open area, in every nook and cranny right up to the tree line, pink rose mallows were opened with their faces tilted to catch the morning sun. The thousands of huge flowers were one of the most beautiful sights nature has ever offered me.

Rose mallow flowers are so enormous they don't seem real. The show stopping extravaganza of 12 in., five-petaled blooms is like nothing else in the garden. A mass planting will stop traffic. Happily, rose mallow provides these pleasures with very little effort. Once established, a plant will return for years. It actually does best when left undisturbed. Under the right conditions, rose mallow will spread from seed, but years of fabulous flowers may not produce a single volunteer. Then one year you may find a patch of seedlings to yank or transplant. One aspect of this plant's growth habit is worth noting: it shows no signs of life until very late in the spring. Rose mallow grows best in wet ground where many other garden favorites cannot survive. They make an excellent choice for planting at the shore.

Other Common Names
Mallow Rose, Swamp Rose Mallow

Bloom Period and Seasonal Color
Blooms in shades of white, pink or red in August and September.

Mature Height × Spread
3 to 8 ft. × 3 ft.

Shasta Daisy

Chrysanthemum × superbum

The Shasta daisy is the classic daisy flower. The large blooms (up to 6 in.) are single or double with white petals and sunny yellow centers. Shastas are cheerful, free flowering, unpretentious, AND they make people smile. This is one of the few mums that bloom early in the year. It was developed by Luther Burbank (1849–1926), who was an incredible plant breeder but a terrible recordkeeper. C. × superbum is probably a hybrid of C. maximum and C. lacustre, but there were so many crosses and selections that the pedigree is quite fuzzy. The shasta daisy is a wonderful addition to the perennial garden. It produces a big blast of flowers early in the season, and will continue to put out flowers for most of the summer. The leaves are quite shiny, toothed, and almost evergreen.

Other Common Name
Pyrenees Chrysanthemum

Bloom Period and Seasonal Color
White blooms with a yellow center, appearing in June and sometimes through August.

Mature Height × Spread
1 to 4 ft. × up to 2 ft.

When, Where, and How to Plant
Plant shasta daisies in spring. They prefer full sun but will adapt to a little shade. Short varieties stay about 1 ft. tall while others can reach 4 ft. Like other chrysanthemums, shastas need well-drained soil. Adding organic matter before planting is always a good idea, especially in heavy clay. Mulch to protect the shallow roots. Space most varieties 12 in. apart. Larger types may need a little more room. (See introduction for more planting information.)

Growing Tips
Water at planting and whenever soil becomes excessively dry. A light application of 5-10-5 fertilizer will get plants off to a good start in the spring.

Care
Regular removal of the dead flowers will encourage bloom throughout the season. Early pinching of tall varieties will make for more compact plants that produce a larger number of smaller flowers. If you prefer larger flowers, combine pinching with some disbudding (removal of flower buds) for compact plants that have big flowers. Control aphids when you see them. They can sometimes be hosed or wiped off. If they persist, check with your Cooperative Extension Service for current recommendations. Shasta daisies are not fussy, but they are not particularly long-lived. Divide every 2 or 3 years to keep them thriving.

Companion Planting and Design
Whether they should be planted in the back or front of the perennial border depends on the variety. Shasta daisies are a good choice for mixing in with bulbs and annuals. They bloom in June after bulbs have finished and before annuals really take off. The flowers are large enough and bright enough to be appreciated from a distance. They will even have "drive-by" impact if you plant a large patch or border. Shasta daisies make outstanding cut flowers.

Did You Know?
In the language of flowers, the daisy is said to represent "innocence." A very old-fashioned name is "bairn-wort," which means "children's flower." Choose this flower when you need to know if "he loves me" or "she loves me not."

Yarrow
Achillea millefolium

When, Where, and How to Plant
Potted yarrow can be planted any time from spring through fall. Seed started indoors in late winter will bloom the first year. It adapts to different soil types but will not do well in wet ground. Take advantage of its durability and plant yarrow in skimpy dry soils where most plants languish. The plants will do their absolute best in good loamy soil, but average garden soil will suffice as long as it is not soggy. Plant yarrow in a very sunny location. Space plants 1 to 2 feet apart. (See chapter introduction for more planting information.)

Growing Tips
Water at planting and whenever the soil gets excessively dry. A spring application of 5-10-5 will be beneficial. Yarrow is drought tolerant.

Care
Cut yarrow back after bloom to keep plants attractive and to encourage repeat bloom. To take advantage of its cooperative nature, mow it down after it blooms and it will start all over. Mow yarrow once a year when it is used as a ground cover. Divide plants every three or four years in either the fall or the spring. Powdery mildew can make an appearance but is not usually serious. This plant may spread with enthusiasm, but pulling out a few handfuls is usually sufficient to control it.

Companion Planting and Design
Yarrow is a primary ingredient in wildflower mixes. Yarrow looks natural rambling through a rock garden. Plant it on a slope or bank as a pretty ground cover, or mix with perennials and annuals in a cutflower garden. The delicate foliage and clusters of tiny blooms contrast well with large flowered daylilies which bloom at the same time. Choose colors carefully.

Did You Know?
Yarrow makes outstanding dried flowers. Cut at the peak of bloom and hang upside down in a dry, shady place. Even the dried brown clusters of wild yarrow or garden forms can be used. Cut them after they have dried in the field. They can be soaked upside down in a solution of household bleach and subsequently dyed with fabric dye.

Yarrow is native to Europe but has naturalized over much of North America. The wild type is almost always off white but may have hints of pink. Selection and hybridization have developed many wonderful pink-to-red varieties. Other species are brilliant yellow. Yarrow is outstanding for sunny, hot, dry places in less-than-ideal soil. Early summer flowers are followed by a significant number of re-blooms, sometimes lasting until late fall. Yarrow's feathery foliage is a dark, dusty green like an angry ocean. It can be used to make olive-green dye. The leaves are covered in soft hairs and have a distinctive aroma when crushed. The list of yarrow's medicinal uses in European and American Indian lore seems endless. With the rising interest in herbs today, it is in high demand.

Other Common Names
Milfoil, Sneezewort

Bloom Period and Seasonal Color
Blooms are commonly white but also pink, lilac, or red, appearing from July to September.

Mature Height × Spread
1 to 3 ft. × about 2 ft.

Plants with Winter Interest
for New Jersey

Once the leaves are shed in autumn, there is a definite lull in the excitement of most gardens. Winter tends towards a medium shade of gray with only an occasional snowstorm to break the monotony. There can be, however, a beauty to the winter landscape. It takes careful planning and an appreciative eye to find it.

Certainly evergreens are an important component of the winter scene. The massive green-needled trees move from background to center stage. When they become the focal point, their subtle differences become more obvious. You may suddenly notice that "ever green" comes in an infinite variety of shades, and that two blue spruces are not the same blue at all. The thick needles of the bluish white fir look nothing like the long, graceful needles of the Himalayan pine, which differ from the scalelike leaves of the arborvitae. Mixing species and adding an occasional young evergreen tree will provide differences in height and texture.

Redosier Dogwood in Snow

Perk Up Your Winter

Once you establish your landscape's character with a variety of elegant evergreens, you can get more daring. Add a weeping Norway spruce or a 'Zebrina' Himalayan pine, whose needles are variegated in green and yellow. A weeping blue atlas cedar is magnificent—you might almost look forward to leaf drop just to eliminate any distractions from its dignified grace. It is hardy only to Zone 6, but it might be worth a try in Zone 5 in a protected nook. A contorted white pine is another fascinating plant. It is a slow-growing pyramidal tree whose branches and needles are both slightly twisted.

Think beyond evergreens to perk things up in winter. Deciduous trees are sometimes more intriguing without their leaves. Harry Lauder's walking stick is a prime example. All summer it looks like

162

a green mound. Once it drops its leaves, it looks like it has a curly perm. The dangling catkins (flower stalks densely crowded with bracts) are an added bonus. The contorted mulberry sends twisted branches in all directions, and the corkscrew willow sends spiraling branches almost straight up. The Japanese fantail willow is more like a shrub. It has branches that grow flat and spreading, like a fan, but also twist and curl. You won't even notice the curling while it still has leaves. The redosier dogwood comes in several varieties. One variety has bright red stems on the current year's growth which are stunning against a backdrop of snow, and the red is an eye-catcher all winter long. There is even a bright yellow variety, 'Flaviramea'.

Vines that twist and turn add character. An old wisteria can ramble in impossible directions. The velvety seedpods dangle down and last well into winter, then they twist open to release the seeds. A thick tangle of silver fleece vine breaks up straight lines all year long.

Fruits and berries add another level of interest. The brilliant red berries of the winterberry holly are spectacular against the snow or a field of green. The paper lantern pods of the goldenraintree are so beautiful that they are used as dried flowers. They persist into early winter. Pyracantha can be covered in berries. These berries last most of the winter since the birds do not seem to favor them.

Beyond trees and shrubs is a world of interesting perennials that can add a surprising twist. The Christmas rose, *Helleborus niger*, produces three-inch flowers in December and can hold on to them until spring. The sensitive fern has tightly curled sporulating fronds that last all winter. These fronds are so engaging they are sometimes dipped in gold to be made into jewelry. Ornamental grasses offer many varieties that maintain decorative plumes for most of the winter. They are excellent for decorative indoor use.

Wonderful Surprises

If you just let your winter landscape happen, you might be surprised by something wonderful, but some things are best not left to chance. Gardeners sometimes struggle with cabin fever during a long cold winter. Plan your winter garden with as much care as your summer flowers. It will give you something to look forward to besides the winter blahs.

Planting for winter interest is no different than planning a spring garden or autumn color. Plant in spring or fall, but check the needs of the specific plant for details. Be sure to match the location with the growing requirements of the plant. Plants that provide winter interest can be any type of plant: a tree, shrub, vine, or even something herbaceous like a fern or ornamental grass. For each plant in this chapter, I will refer you to that plant type's chapter introduction for planting instructions. Follow the proper procedures to give your winter garden the best possible start.

Corkscrew Willow

Salix matsudana 'Tortuosa'

Gardening literature will not present a glowing recommendation for corkscrew willow, yet it is an outrageous novelty to spice up the winter landscape. It is neither sophisticated nor elegant. In spite of plant snobs mocking its appearance, it is fun, ridiculous, completely odd, and definitely needs to stand alone. The branches are held upright but are twisted and wavy like a pussy willow with a serious perm. The newest growth is yellowish green and generally abundant. It is a great choice for wet areas. Like all willows, it will tolerate wet ground as few other ornamentals can. Grown with a single trunk, it should be placed farther away for you to enjoy the entire quirky silhouette. The shrub habit can be appreciated up close and its branches are easier to prune for indoor use.

Other Common Names
Corkscrew Hankow Willow, Contorted Willow, Dragon-claw Willow

Bloom Period and Seasonal Color
Twisted yellowish green branches visible all winter.

Mature Height × Spread
30 ft. × 20 ft.

When, Where, and How to Plant
Plant in early spring or early fall in a sunny location (see Shade Trees chapter introduction for planting instructions). Cuttings rooted in water, potting medium, or even stuck in the ground will often root. Wet ground, stream banks, and low spots will all be acceptable choices. Because the root system is invasive, avoid growing near underground pipes as well as your foundation. Don't plant beneath any willow as the root system is thick and near the surface. Add organic matter to drier soils and mulch heavily. Early spring may be the best time to try this, but they are amazingly cooperative in propagation.

Growing Tips
Water thoroughly at planting and keep moist. Fertilize with 5-10-5 in early spring, especially if the branches are frequently harvested for indoor use.

Care
Tree forms require less pruning than bush forms. To maintain the bush habit, corkscrew willow needs to be pruned severely before the new growth emerges. This keeps the plant small, keeps the growing branches on eye level to be better appreciated, and provides copious material for decorative purposes. Like all willows, this one is prone to various leaf diseases, cankers, borers, and blights. For prevention, prune out dead or weak branches and let it grow. While subject to these annoying problems, it generally just keeps on ticking.

Companion Planting and Design
Keep corkscrew willow away from foundation walls, structures, and underground piping. It can be in the background of other deciduous plantings since it is of little interest except in the winter. This is not a plant for formal gardens or even small spaces. It doesn't add much in spring summer or fall, but if you have room, tuck one in somewhere. It will bring smiles in winter when they are most needed.

Did You Know?
In *Hortus III*, corkscrew willow is called "bizarre." The highly respected gardening authority Michael Dirr says it is "...a rather sickening site in any landscape." My corkscrew willow is a much appreciated addition to the winter landscape, and requests for the branches come in continually. Beauty is definitely in the eye of the beholder!

Dragon's Eye Pine
Pinus densiflora 'Oculus-draconis'

When, Where, and How to Plant
Plant in early spring or early fall (see Evergreens chapter introduction for planting instructions). Choose a sunny, well-drained location. As a general rule, variegated plants are a little more finicky than their all-green relatives, so pick the best location possible. There is nothing particularly difficult about establishing this plant. It would be wise to stake the tree, at least until it gets established. An evergreen's bulk causes it to capture wind and snow. A little support will keep it upright until the roots can take over the job.

Growing Tips
Water thoroughly at planting and whenever the soil gets dry. Fertilize in spring with 5-10-5, especially in poorer soils.

Care
Little pruning should be necessary. To make this naturally open plant a little fuller, you can pinch the candles back halfway when they elongate in the spring. Dragon's eye pine has no serious insect or disease problems.

Companion Planting and Design
Because its foliage is so unusual, dragon's eye pine makes a good specimen plant. While many plant professionals consider it an oddball, there is no reason it can't be mainstreamed if you like it. Mix it in with other evergreens as part of a border or mass planting to break up the monotony of green. This is especially appreciated in the winter where ever "green"or winter gray are pretty much the only other options.

Did You Know?
There are two other species of pine that have varieties called 'Oculus-draconis'. One is the Himalayan pine, *P. wallichiana*. It is believed to be the same as the variety 'Zebrina' and is more commonly available under that name. The other species, *P. thunbergiana*, is the Japanese black pine. The Japanese black pine version was not available in any of the catalogs or at any local nurseries. The Himalayan pine's needles are bunched together in fives, making it easily distinguishable from the Japanese black and red pines, both of which have needles in groups of two.

Dragon's eye pine is a novelty evergreen that is a compact, variegated version of the Japanese red pine. The species can sometimes reach one hundred feet, but this variety stays much smaller. The needles are quite distinctive; each one is marked with two irregular yellow bands. When you view the branch from its end, you can see alternating circular bands of yellow and green. This is (supposedly) absolutely identical to the pattern in a dragon's eye. The cones start out with a bluish tinge, turn brown as they age, and stay on the tree for several years. Dragon's eye pine produces cones at quite a young age. The habit of young trees is open and somewhat irregular in shape. The literature is completely inconsistent regarding the rate of growth, but it is not fast.

Bloom Period and Seasonal Color
Variegated needles in green and yellow all year.

Mature Height × Spread
35 ft. × 35 ft.

Harry Lauder's Walking Stick

Corylus avellana 'Contorta'

Harry Lauder was an entertainer who carried a twisted and gnarled walking stick as part of his act. The branches on this wildly contorted small tree are reminiscent of the famous staff, hence the name. It is a variety of the European filbert. Harry Lauder's walking stick is a fabulous choice for winter interest. When covered in leaves, it is impossible to see the twisting and spiraling of the. Once the season winds down and the wind blows away the wavy leaves, you are faced with the most outrageous of plants. The small catkins look like built-in Christmas ornaments and can reach up to six inches in length when they are in bloom. They blow in the wind like delicate threads of gold.

Other Common Name
Contorted Filbert

Bloom Period and Seasonal Color
Male catkins dangle all winter and elongate into golden wisps in April.

Mature Height × Spread
8 to 10 ft. × 10 ft. or more

When, Where, and How to Plant
Plant in early spring or early fall (see Small Flowering Trees introduction or Shrubs chapter introduction for planting instructions). Harry Lauder does well in full sun but is also tolerant of shade. Its rate of growth is slow. Choose well-drained loamy soil, however, it is fairly adaptable to different pH and soil types. There is nothing tricky about getting Harry established.

Growing Tips
Water thoroughly at planting and whenever the soil gets dry. Fertilize in spring with 5-10-5, especially if you harvest the branches heavily for decorative use.

Care
Most Harry Lauders are grafted, so it is critical that you remove any suckers emerging at the base. These will not be contorted and will have a much faster growth rate. If they are not removed, straight shoots will dominate the plant in short order. Pruning the contorted branches is rarely necessary. It is possible to layer one- to two-year-old shoots to get plants to grow on their own roots. Watch out for Japanese beetles. They can make quite a meal of the leaves. Spray at the first sign of damage. Leaf and twig blight may appear but is not common. Check with your Cooperative Extension Service for current pest control recommendations.

Companion Planting and Design
Harry Lauder makes a good choice for planting in a rock garden or mixing with small evergreens. When choosing a location for this tree, remember that it is at its peak in winter, so planting near the front door might be better than back by the pool. When covered in green leaves, it does not compete with summer annuals or even late spring perennials such as peonies or iris. Daffodils look beautiful with the dangling catkins in early spring. It is outstanding in arrangements, fresh or dry.

Did You Know?
Harry Lauder's walking stick was discovered growing in a hedgerow in England in the mid-1800s. It has been a featured plant in gardens designed for those who have visual difficulties. These gardens consist of plants that you can touch and smell. Harry Lauder's curling branches and dangling catkins are unmistakable.

Japanese Fantail Willow

Salix sachalinensis 'Sekka'

When, Where, and How to Plant

Plant in early spring or early fall in a sunny location with moist soil (see intro to Shrubs chapter for planting instructions). Japanese fantail willow is an excellent choice for wet sites or low spots in the yard. In sandy soil, you will need to add organic matter to help retain soil moisture.

Growing Tips

Water thoroughly at planting and keep it moist. This is especially true if you are trying to grow from rooted cuttings. Even when established, it will occasionally need a thorough watering in dry hot summers, especially in sandy soils. They are rapid growers so fertilizer may speed things up too much unless the soil is particularly poor.

Care

Prune Japanese fantail willow hard in the early spring to keep it from getting wild but also to use the amazing branches. Willows are among the easiest plants to propagate in moist sand or even a glass of water. When grown from cuttings, plants exhibit the variety's typical contortion within one or two years. If bunnies are a problem, be sure to cage this plant while it is young to protect the bark. Once established, it grows so quickly that what the bunnies eat can be sacrificed.

Companion Planting and Design

Japanese fantail willow can get a little wild looking and doesn't blend easily, so you may want to plant it in a featured spot by itself. Be sure to plant it where you can enjoy the contorted growth in winter when it is at its best. You will need easy access to prune regularly. For long term use, do not put them in water. Instead let them dry—they will last for years. If you use them as part of fresh flower arrangements, they may produce roots.

Did You Know?

The bizarre growth that distinguishes this variety from others is probably caused by a bacteria, *Corynebacterium fascians*. The phenomenon is called "fasciation," or cresting. The plant loses its ability to grow upright and grows as though many stems had fused together. The cause of fasciation is not entirely understood. In some cases it is thought to possibly be genetic.

Plants do not get much stranger than this one. Japanese fantail willow is definitely a novelty plant. You would probably not want more than one in your landscape, though it is absolutely remarkable in the garden as well as in cut arrangements. It produces catkins in early spring that are similar to those of the pussy willow, but smaller. They look particularly strange on the twisted, curled, fan shaped branches that are characteristic of this variety. Like other willows, Japanese fantail willow is an excellent choice for wet sites where many other plants "melt" in short order. It will do well in any moist soil. Willows are generally weak wooded and fast growing, and this plant is no exception.

Bloom Period and Seasonal Color

Fuzzy catkins in early spring.

Mature Height × Spread

10 to 30 ft. × very wide spread

Lacebark Pine
Pinus bungeana

There are many pines hardy in New Jersey. Lacebark pine is special because its bark sheds and peels like the bark of a sycamore. Young branches are green with bits of white and brown. As the bark matures, it turns chalky white, as if covered in a lace veil. It is always beautiful, but its subtle charm is better appreciated in the gray of winter. In many cases this tree is grown with a multistemmed trunk. This creates more trunk to see at eye level where it can be enjoyed. On occasion, the lower branches are removed to make the bark more visible. Lacebark pine is very slow growing. It can be pyramidal, though the branches spread with age and with the tree's number of trunks. The four-inch-long needles are dark green and in bunches of three.

Bloom Period and Seasonal Color
Lacy, multi-colored bark and dark green needles persisting up to five years.

Mature Height × Spread
50 to 75 ft. × 25 ft. or more

When, Where, and How to Plant
Plant in early spring or early fall (see Evergreens chapter introduction for planting instructions). Lacebark pine prefers a sunny location and well-drained soils. While lacebark pine would be lovely planted at the corners of buildings, watch out for any snow that may slide off the roof. The wood is weak and brittle, and winter ice and snow can cause damage. Balled and burlapped trees should be root pruned prior to digging. Many commercially produced specimens are now container grown, which eliminates the need for root pruning. Add organic matter and sand (2:1 ratio) to improve drainage on heavy clay soils.

Growing Tips
Water thoroughly at planting and whenever the soil gets dry. Fertilize with 5-10-5 in the spring in poor soils.

Care
Pines are subject to a variety of insects and diseases, but there is no specific pest or disease that affects the lacebark pine. You can prune by trimming the candles in the spring, but this tree is such a slow grower it may not be necessary. Proper removal of any winter damage is wise. Because lacebark pine is susceptible to damage from winter ice and snow, it may pay to shake off accumulations of snow, if possible, before the damage is done.

Companion Planting and Design
To use this tree to its best advantage, plant it in a location where you can see the bark. Because it grows so slowly, lacebark pine would be a poor choice for border plantings. Plant annuals at the base to provide summer color, or use ferns for a woodland look.

Did You Know?
Lacebark pine is grown by many wholesale nurseries and should not be difficult to locate. To see one "live"and get a better idea of this tree's appeal, visit the fifteen-foot specimen in the evergreen collection at Rutgers Gardens in New Brunswick, New Jersey. Several mature lacebark pines can also be found at the Willowwood Arboretum in Chester Township.

Mulberry
Morus spp.

When, Where, and How to Plant
Plant mulberries in early spring or early fall in full sun or partial shade (see introduction to Shade Trees or Small Flowering Trees for planting instructions). Weeping mulberries are an excellent choice for small urban yards. They take up little space and are tolerant of city growing conditions. The contorted mulberry needs a little more room—its branches grow in all directions. Mulberries have some tolerance for seaside conditions. They are flexible regarding both soil type and pH. Both varieties transplant readily and will survive with minimal soil preparation.

Growing Tips
Water at planting and during the first season when needed. Once established, the trees will withstand drought. No fertilizer is needed. Fruit is formed only on female trees.

Care
Mulberries are susceptible to leaf spot diseases and an occasional infestation of mites or scale. These problems are usually not serious and generally not worth treating. Prune in early spring. The contorted form can tolerate significant pruning if you want to cut branches for indoor use.

Companion Planting and Design
The long branches of the weeping mulberry form a curtain of strong vertical lines, creating a dramatic winter look. The spreading, twisted branches of the contorted mulberry have a completely different look, radiating from the trunk in all directions. These branches are prized for flower arrangements. Neither blends well with other plants, but either becomes the focal point of a stark winter landscape.

Did You Know?
The fruit of the mulberry is quite sweet. It has to be very ripe to develop its flavor and then it has almost no shelf life. Fruits appear as strawberries finish and as raspberries and blueberries are getting started. It is surprising mulberries have not become commercialized, but it may be due to the short shelf life and the tenacious green stems. Even so, they are delicious covered in heavy cream especially when mixed with other spring berries.

The weeping mulberry Morus alba 'Pendula' is a small tree with multitudinous slender branches cascading to the ground. These trees were popular with Italian immigrants early last century and were commonly found in Newark's Italian communities. People either love the fruit or hate it. It looks much like a blackberry but is infinitely sweeter. The contorted mulberry Morus alba 'Contorta' is sold under many botanical names, which makes finding one difficult. There is really only one variety of this fast-growing tree. It has an open spreading habit with branches that twist and turn fantastically. It makes a wonderful winter feature.

Other Common Names
Contorted Mulberry, Weeping Mulberry

Bloom Period and Seasonal Color
Insignificant flowers followed by $1/2$ to 1 in. almost black fruits on female trees in late June.

Mature Height × Spread
Weeping 12 ft. × 10 ft.
Contorted 25 ft. × 25 ft.

Paperbark Maple
Acer griseum

Paperbark maple is interesting all year, but its bark is a special bonus to the winter scene. This tree is smaller than many of the popular maples, which makes it useful in tight places. Its overall shape is oval to round but rather open. The winter silhouette is striking. The leaves are compound with three leaflets each, but the overview of the leaf is similar to more familiar maple leaves. The bark is a rich cinnamon brown. It peels in long strips, much like the bark of paperbark birch. This exfoliation begins at a very early age, usually when the tree is only two years old. Eventually the trunk stops exfoliating, but mature trees retain their lovely shades of red and brown.

Bloom Period and Seasonal Color
Leaves appear in late spring, turning orange and red in fall; inconspicuous red flowers mature into showy winged seeds.

Mature Height × Spread
25 ft. × 25 ft.

When, Where, and How to Plant
Maples generally do best when planted in late March or early April. Paperbark maple needs sun and moist, well-drained soils, though it tolerates clay soil better than some. It is wise to add organic matter to clay soil in order to improve drainage. Heavy clay soils sometimes have a hardpan several feet down. If you can, break up the soil with a pick. If you have heavy clay soil and improve the soil going back into the hole, watch out for the bucket effect: water follows the path of least resistance and flows into the soil around the roots, where it stays, waterlogging the plant. Make sure the water around your tree has a place to go.

Growing Tips
Water thoroughly at planting and whenever the soil gets dry. Fertilize sparingly with 5-10-5 in early spring.

Care
Paperbark maple has no serious insect or disease problems. Its slow rate of growth means it requires little pruning. Once established, this is a low maintenance tree.

Companion Planting and Design
Choose a place where you can enjoy this lovely small tree during the winter, such as outside a favorite window. Since the beautiful bark is one of its main attractions, paperbark maple works well as a specimen tree. It could be the perfect choice for condos or small suburban homes. Daffodils at the base will bloom before the tree's leaves come out.

Did You Know?
There are other delightful maples with interesting bark. *A. davidii*, the David maple, reaches 45 feet and has bark with white stripes. So does *A. grosseri*, which grows to 30 feet. Together they make up the "snake bark" maples. They provide wonderful winter interest but are difficult to locate. The literature varies greatly regarding hardiness, but they are probably hardy to Zone 5, possibly to Zone 4.

Redosier Dogwood
Cornus sericea

When, Where, and How to Plant

All dogwoods generally do best with spring planting. If you try fall planting, do it in early September (see Shrubs chapter introduction for planting instructions). Its native habitat is swampy ground, so it makes sense to plant redosier dogwood in a similar environment. While it may not thrive in extremely dry locations, almost anywhere else is acceptable. Sun, light shade, and deep shade will all be tolerated. Space plants 5 to 6 feet apart for a mass planting. Balled-and-burlapped or even bare-root specimens transplant easily. Add organic matter to dry, sandy soils.

Growing Tips

Water thoroughly at planting and before the ground becomes excessively dry. Fertilize with 5-10-5 in early spring to encourage new growth, especially after a serious pruning.

Care

Keeping it red requires frequent pruning to force lots of shoots from the roots. Individuals can be cut to the ground every spring for maximum color but not if you are using them for a privacy screen. Selective pruning of two- and three-year-old growth in the spring will keep a plant from becoming woody and brown. To control the plant's spread, prune the roots with a spade and prune branches that run along the ground. Redosier dogwood is subject to twig canker, scale, and the voracious bagworm. Check with the Cooperative Extension Service for the most current pesticide recommendations.

Companion Planting and Design

Plant en masse in open spaces for the best winter effect. Border plantings may be terrific, but remember that the roots will spread in all directions. They can be pruned to keep them under control but consider your neighbor's reaction if the plants should start to spread over the border. 'Flaviramea', the yellowtwig dogwood, has the same characteristics as redosier dogwood, but its twigs are bright yellow.

Did You Know?

You can see large plantings of this shrub along the ramps of Route 18 in the New Brunswick area, proving that redosier dogwood along highways is attractive as well as functional as a bank stabilizer.

Winter is far more colorful if it includes a bank of redosier dogwood. The new growth is very red. It spreads from the roots and rapidly becomes a thicket. This, and its tolerance for wet locations makes it the plant of choice for stabilizing banks along streams and the water's edge. Spring flowers are attractive, if not spectacular. Redosier dogwood also occasionally blooms in summer. White fruits appear in late summer and are very pretty up close. Fall color varies but can sometimes be a very attractive red-purple. Choose your location carefully. Since this shrub does spread, it can be overpowering in a confined space. Redosier dogwood is native to eastern North America from Newfoundland to Virginia and Kentucky.

Other Common Name

Redtwig Dogwood

Bloom Period and Seasonal Color

$1^{1}/_{2}$ to $2^{1}/_{2}$ in. clusters of small white flowers in late May; purple fall foliage and red twigs all winter.

Mature Height × Spread

10 ft. × 10 ft.

Weeping Norway Spruce

Picea abies 'Pendula'

This weeping form of Norway spruce is an attractive alternative to the species. Weeping trees generally grow at a slower rate than that of uprights. It is difficult to measure the growth rate since weepers grow up a little, then arch over and down or out and along the ground. Training young trees to establish a trunk and primary branches can affect their growth pattern and ultimate shape. The cones of Norway spruce are up to six inches long and persist through most of winter. The bright green new growth of spring seems to glow against the dark green of older needles. The needles stay on the plant for several years. Traits can vary by specimen, so make your choice carefully.

Bloom Period and Seasonal Color
Young cones are pink and purple in spring; bright green new growth turns dark green later in the year.

Mature Height × Spread
20 ft. × 20 ft., but variable

When, Where, and How to Plant
Plant in early spring or early fall in full sun (see intro to Evergreens chapter for planting instructions). Weeping Norway spruce is fairly flexible regarding soil type, though it does prefer well-drained sandy soil that is moist. Weeping Norway spruce transplants readily. Even larger trees do well since they have shallow, spreading root systems rather than a tap root. Weeping trees grow slowly, so starting with a larger plant will show you the habit of the particular tree you choose. Consider staking newly planted trees. Their less than symmetrical shape may make it harder to stay upright in a strong wind, at least until they get established.

Growing Tips
Water at planting and when soil gets dry. It is important to keep Norway spruce well watered, especially in hot, dry weather, for the first few years. After established, use 5-10-5 fertilizer in early spring as needed.

Care
Prune weeping Norway spruce in early spring if necessary. Weepers occasionally throw off an upright or vigorous shoot that must be removed to maintain the form. Watch out for mites. Control them if necessary in May and September. Your Cooperative Extension Service can offer advice for controls.

Companion Planting and Design
Weeping forms are usually used as specimen trees. Be sure to give your tree a prominent place in the landscape. A clear window view as you sit by the fireplace might be nice, or you could plant it by the mailbox, where you will be able to see it at least once a day. Weeping Norway spruce is always interesting but moves out of the spotlight while summer color dominates.

Did You Know?
The contrast of weeping Norway spruce's soft bright green new growth against the stiff dark green growth seems artificial, prompting people to touch it. This is another good reason to place it where you can get up close. At Blooming Acres, we have two. One is S-shaped growing up, down, and up again. The second almost hugs the ground. Visitors are intrigued by the appearance of these odd trees, but even more so when the new growth is out.

Winter Jasmine
Jasminum nudiflorum

When, Where, and How to Plant

Plant in early spring or early fall (see intro to Shrubs chapter for planting instructions). Winter jasmine will tolerate full sun to significant shade but will produce fewer flowers in a shady location. In an ideal world this plant prefers well-drained, better soils but will tolerate a very wide range of soil conditions. It is even somewhat drought tolerant. Potted plants transplant with extreme ease. Transplanting rooted shoots is best done in early spring, but with extra care it can be done any time the ground isn't frozen.

Growing Tips

Water at planting and whenever the ground gets dry until established. After that, winter jasmine is drought tolerant. Fertilize with 5-10-5 in early spring if it has been significantly pruned, to help rejuvenate it.

Care

Winter jasmine will grow to become a "patch." This is fine to stabilize banks or to create a ground cover but can overpower other smaller plants in the vicinity. Prune back in early spring to prevent crowding and to let the plants regenerate healthy new growth. Other than a touch of over enthusiasm, this plant has few problems.

Companion Planting and Design

Since winter jasmine can get thick and somewhat aggressive, plant it by itself or around things too large to overpower. It is very effective trailing over a wall or trained up a trellis. A spot by the mailbox works well with winter jasmine, giving you a location where it can be seen regularly, without its taking up a focal point in the landscape.

Did You Know?

Winter jasmine is a great plant to force into bloom indoors over the winter. To do this, prune away some of the excess branches and place the long shoots in a vase with water. They bloom readily, and you can do this repeatedly during the winter. Not only will you get to enjoy the flowers, but also you will get your pruning done at the same time.

This plant is to gardeners what a sun lamp is to people who suffer from light deprivation. The habit is somewhat gangly. It spreads thickly as the shoots root along the soil surface. The branches are stiff although the leaves are small and delicate. The variegated leaves are a bit more interesting. Winter jasmine is not exactly a show stopper in spring or summer. It is amazing, however, what six or eight bright yellow flowers can do for the spirit on a warm day in January. In a mild winter a handful of blooms appear almost continually throughout the season. In a severe winter, winter jasmine is probably the first shrub to show color, which comes in a blast of yellow.

Other Common Name
Winter Blooming Jasmine

Bloom Period and Seasonal Color
One-inch yellow flowers throughout a mild winter, or many flowers in very early spring.

Mature Height × Spread
3 to 4 ft. × variable

Roses *for New Jersey*

In order to create a list of the best roses for New Jersey, it seemed wise to consult with the ultimate in rose specialists. There are thousands of species and cultivars, and unless one dedicates one's life to the thorny genus *Rosa*, it is difficult to evaluate all the possibilities.

The Dawn of a Winner

One of the best people to answer questions about New Jersey roses is Frank Benardella, a past president of the American Rose Society and long-time New Jersey resident. Mr. Benardella now lives in my own neighborhood. He has grown thousands of roses and has firsthand experience in our climate. My meeting with him and his wife was delightful; he is knowledgeable and full of enthusiasm. One of his suggestions for an outstanding climbing rose was 'New Dawn'. This was introduced in 1932 and was developed in New Jersey. It received the very first plant patent, #0001, and in the late 1990s was voted the favorite rose by the World Federation of Rose Societies. This international organization represents thirty-three countries. They normally have a painting done of the honored "favorite" to present to the party responsible for the winning rose's introduction. In this case, because the rose was introduced so long ago, there was no trace of the originator.

Life works in mysterious ways. It turns out I know the family of the man who first discovered 'New Dawn'. Years prior, in the course of everyday business, I had been told the family of Carl Bosenberg (a friend of mine) held the first plant patent ever issued; however, I did not know what kind of plant it was. After meeting the Benardellas, I contacted my friend Carl who is a retired landscape contractor in North Brunswick. It turned out that his father and founder of the family business, Henry F. Bosenberg, was the person who actually discovered the rose. It was a "sport" of 'Dr. W. Van Fleet', a popular rose of the time. (A sport is a naturally occurring branch that differs from the rest of the plant.) The sport appeared on a plant growing in the yard of the Bosenberg's company headquarters. It was cultivated and released by the Somerset Rose Nursery, another family business.

Hybrid Tea Rose
'Double Delight'

Shrub Rose 'Carefree Delight'

Weighing the Pros and Cons

It has been over 2000 years since the Greek poet Sappho first called the rose the "Queen of Flowers." There are other flowers that may try to seize the title, but roses have reigned for too long to easily give up the throne.

To plant roses in your garden requires serious deliberation. You'll have to find the right location. A sunny, well-drained bed is essential. Trying to grow roses in less than full sun or in wet ground is futile. You will need to do some research to discover the type of rose you want to grow. A climbing rose is not a shrub rose, and neither is likely to produce the flowers of a hybrid tea. The type of rose you choose will also affect the location you choose, so you are back to square one. A climbing rose needs to climb on something. A hybrid tea is not the best choice for blending into a landscape planting, but shrub roses may be better for that application.

Roses are not stick-them-in-the-ground-and-forget-about-them plants. All roses need some attention. If you want your roses to bring you pleasure, you have to tend them. Hybrid teas may require the most care, but then they are the classic image of a perfect rose. As is true of most things in life, if you want the best, you will have to work for it. Some shrub roses, including the rugosa roses, may be less demanding and are truly lovely, but you will never get a perfect long-stemmed beauty from a rugosa rose.

Getting Started

Once you have chosen your planting location and have decided you have the time and willingness to do what it takes to grow roses, you can get started. Some gardeners prefer to keep all their roses together in one spot. In Victorian times this was called a "rosary" and is the origin of the term "rosarian," which means rose gardener. Such a grouping certainly makes caring for roses easier and draws attention to their magnificent flowers while in bloom. The plants themselves, however, are often not very exciting when not in bloom. And not everyone has room for a special "rosary."

Whether your roses will stand alone or be part of your landscape design, you will have to do some serious soil preparation. Drainage is critical. The addition of organic matter to heavy clay soil will help prevent the soil from staying waterlogged. It may be necessary to raise the bed or install a drainage pipe to remove excess water. The addition of organic matter will help sandy soil hold moisture. It is especially important in hard-packed clay soil to double-dig the soil in order to prepare it deeply, enabling a root system to expand.

Planting Your Selections

When you are ready to purchase your roses, you may be able to find the types you want locally. These will, in most cases, be available in containers. The best time to plant is early spring. Plant them very carefully. Try not to let the soil fall away from the roots as you pull the plant out of the pot or you may tear the delicate feeder roots that are just developing.

Roses shipped to you will arrive bare root, usually at the time of year best suited for the planting of roses in your area. When they arrive, check them right away to see that their roots are moist. If your new roses cannot be planted immediately, moisten the roots and wrap them in damp newspaper in plastic. Store at 35 to 40 degrees Fahrenheit. Check them every two or three days to make sure they don't dry out. Two weeks is about as long as you can keep them like this. If you must wait longer to plant, bury the plants about a foot down with their branches pointing up at a 45 degree angle. If the temperature is expected to drop below freezing, cover them with leaves and plastic. If temperatures go above freezing, be sure to get out there and pull off the protection or the plants will cook.

Soak the roots overnight or up to twenty-four hours before planting. Cover the whole plant with water for the last two or three hours before planting. When you are ready to plant, prune off any broken roots and damaged canes. Prune all the canes to ten to twelve inches.

When digging the hole, keep in mind you will want the entire root system to fit inside. Make it big enough; then make it a little bigger. Put most (not all) of the soil back in the hole, forming a mound in the center. Put the plant in the hole, spreading the roots evenly over the mound. If you are growing roses where the temperature goes below zero degrees Fahrenheit in winter, the bud union, a fat knot, should be planted two inches below ground. Since temperatures in some New Jersey winters can hit zero throughout the state, this is a good rule to follow. Orient the bush so the bud side of the knot faces north. The bud side is the side where most of the canes will develop. The canes will reach for the sunnier side, helping to establish a well shaped bush. Fill the hole and tamp it down firmly with your hands. If you use your foot for tamping, it may get packed too hard. Water thoroughly. Let the water soak in and water again.

When and How to Prune

If you want long, straight stems and large blooms, it will be necessary to remove the side buds that grow along the canes below the terminal bud you want to keep. If all the buds grow, you will have many shorter branches with many smaller flowers. You can prevent unwanted branching by snapping off the buds with your thumb.

Pruning will encourage branching and future flower production. You will know how far to prune a branch back by looking at the leaves. Complete rose leaves contain five leaflets. Beneath the flower they may have only three or even just one leaflet. Pruning to remove dead flowers is done by cutting the stem back to the first complete leaf. Cutting back to the second complete leaf will result in longer stems and larger blooms but fewer flowers.

In the autumn, allow the last flowers to die on the plant. Pruning them late in the season may trigger new growth that will be tender going into winter. When the plant is dormant, prune the branches lightly to prevent injury due to wind, ice, and snow.

Major pruning is done in late March or early April. First remove any dead, diseased, or broken canes. Then remove canes growing towards the center, or these will crisscross and make a mess. If two canes are rubbing, even if they are both arching out nicely, one must be removed. You want to leave three to five healthy canes that are as large as a pencil or larger. The secondary canes that emerge from the canes you keep will usually stay smaller than the original, and they will never be larger.

Roses in a Cottage Garden

Prune to a height of 18 inches, pruning to a bud that points to the outside. Buds develop into branches that grow in the direction the bud was pointing. Inside buds eventually become crisscrossing branches. Make your cut at a 45 degree angle pointing down towards the center of the bush. After making the cut, examine the "pith" or center of the cane. If it is white, the cane is in good shape. If it has a brown center, continue to remove small increments until you reach healthy tissue. After a severe winter, there may not be much left. You may be forced to settle for a little brown in the center to save the cane. Sealing the cut ends with nail polish, white glue, petroleum jelly, or tree wound compound helps prevent borers from getting into the canes.

Climbing roses may bloom once in the spring, or they may repeat-bloom in the summer. Even on those varieties that bloom again, the bulk of the flower display will be in the spring. The spring flowers are all on "old wood," which means wood that grew the previous growing season. In early spring, prune away only those canes that suffered winter damage or die-back; anything else will remove the blooms. Any major pruning should wait until after they bloom. The dead flowers of repeat bloomers should be removed to the first complete leaf. If they are not eliminated, the dead flowers will make "hips," or seeds, and plant energy will go into seed production instead of into making new flowers.

Feeding Your Roses

Apply fertilizer to new roses after the first round of blooms. Established roses can be fed once a month beginning six weeks before the first bloom (the first feeding will be mid to late April). Finish fertilizing six weeks before the last bloom (early September). If you are not religious about your fertilizer schedule, at least remember to feed on three holidays: Memorial Day, Fourth of July, and Labor Day.

There are many commercial formulations available for roses. The three numbers on the bag represent the percentage of nitrogen (N), phosphorus (P), and potassium (K), always in that order. How much you should apply depends on the exact formulation of the product you buy. Follow the directions. A soil test will supply the exact requirement for your garden (see main introduction). Contact your Cooperative Extension Service to have your soil tested through Rutgers University.

Controlling Insects and Disease

Unfortunately, roses have many pest problems. Breeders are paying particular attention to these issues as they develop new selections. Disease-resistant varieties are extremely helpful. Some old types, including shrub roses, may have more natural resistance than the more popular hybrid teas.

Starting in late May, a weekly spray schedule of an all-purpose rose spray will keep the problems from getting out of hand. Of the many insects you may encounter, spring caterpillars, Japanese beetles, aphids, and mites are probably the biggest offenders. Blackspot and powdery mildew may be the worst of the diseases.

Floribunda Rose 'Iceberg'

Certainly some handpicking of Japanese beetles and spring caterpillars can be helpful. Squishing them is unpleasant but effective. Wearing gloves is always a good idea since roses have thorns, and it makes the task of picking more tolerable. You can also drop these pests into a can of kerosene or gasoline. Aphids often appear in high concentration on the buds and branch tips. These, too, can be squished. Mites can be hosed off with a strong spray of water, but once established they are difficult to eliminate without an insecticide.

It is very important to rake up old leaves and dispose of them in a way that eliminates the decaying leaves as a source for future infections. Watering directly into the soil rather than with overhead sprinklers will minimize the spread of diseases from leaf to leaf. Spraying as soon as leaf diseases show up will be more effective than trying to control a serious problem. Make sure you are informed as to the insect and disease susceptibility of the varieties you choose to grow.

Winter Care

The final pruning is done after the plants are fully dormant, and it is done only to prevent winter damage from snow and wind. It is a good idea at that time to mound soil, or a mixture of soil and mulch, or even mulch alone, to a height of ten to twelve inches around the base of the plant. This is particularly important for white and yellow roses, which have the most difficult time surviving winter.

Suggested Roses for New Jersey

Mr. Benardella offered many suggestions for roses to be grown in New Jersey. He also went to a meeting of the Garden State Rose Club and had the members vote on their favorites. The varieties suggested here are the results of these many rose specialists working together to compile the list. All of these selections are generally available in the trade.

Climbing Rose

Climbers are roses that can be trained to grow up a trellis, arbor, pergola, or other support. They bloom profusely in spring on previous year's growth. Some climbers have large blooms, and a few will even rebloom in the summer.

The difference between a climber and a true rambler sometimes gets a little fuzzy. In fact, ramblers are a type of climbing rose. They have very pliable canes for training over archways and around gazebos. Ramblers bloom only in spring on old growth, and they generally have an abundance of small flowers. When left on their own, they can grow in all directions. Some rosarians prune ramblers to the ground after they bloom to start over for the following year.

Climbing rose varieties include: 'Autumn Sunset' (apricot gold), 'Westerland' (apricot blend), 'New Dawn' (light pink), 'Handel' (pink blend), 'Red Fountain' (bright red), 'Dortmund' (red and white single), 'Sally Holmes' (white single, sometimes considered a shrub), 'Climbing Iceberg' (white), and 'Jeanne LaJoie' (pink miniature).

Floribunda Rose

Floribundas are modern roses, the result of crossing polyantha roses with hybrid teas. This cross was first successfully accomplished as part of a breeding program in Denmark in the 1920s. Floribundas have an extended season of bloom and are available in a wide range of colors. The flowers are not as large as those of hybrid teas, but they grow in clusters with many flowers per cluster. The flowers are becoming larger as new varieties are developed. They may soon approach the size of those of the large-flowered parent.

Floribundas may not be quite as finicky as hybrid teas, but they are far more demanding than many shrub roses. To keep them blooming, remove the spent blooms and follow a regular maintenance program.

Floribunda selections include: 'Iceberg' (white), 'Sunsprite' (yellow, fragrant), 'Showbiz' (medium red), 'Scentimental' (red and white stripe, fragrant), 'Playboy' (orange and scarlet with a yellow center, single), 'Sexy Rexy' (pink), 'Dicky' (pink), 'First Edition' (coral orange), and 'Trumpeter' (orange red).

Grandiflora Rose

Grandifloras are even newer than floribundas. They are the result of crossing floribundas with hybrid teas. The first grandiflora was introduced in 1954. It took an act of Parliament to establish formal approval to name the lovely new pink rose 'Queen Elizabeth'. It is still considered the standard by which other grandifloras are judged.

The idea behind the hybridization was to combine the hardiness of the floribundas with the long stems and flowers of the hybrid teas. In England, this classification is not even recognized; what are called grandifloras in the United States are lumped in with floribundas by English gardeners. Even so, many hybridizers continue to work with this group, and new varieties are being introduced all the time.

In general, grandifloras are taller than both parents, more vigorous and slightly hardier than the hybrid tea. Their numerous blooms have the form of the hybrid tea.

Grandifloras include: 'Queen Elizabeth' (pink), 'Love' (red and white), 'Gold Medal' (medium yellow, needs winter protection), 'Tournament of Roses' (pink), 'Pink Parfait' (pink), 'Aquarius' (light pink), and 'Camelot' (coral pink).

Hybrid Tea Rose

When the romantic image of a large, beautiful red rose on a long stem comes to mind, that is a hybrid tea rose. They are the result of crossing the hybrid perpetual rose with tea roses introduced from China.

The hybridization was started late in the 1800s. The targeted traits were the repeat blooming capabilities of the tea roses and the flower form of the hybrid perpetuals. The early experiments resulted in repeat bloomers but fewer flowers in the first flush. The flowers and hardiness were an improvement over the teas, but they were less hardy and sturdy than the perpetuals.

Over the years, breeders have expanded the palette of colors to an incredible range. These are, hands down, the most popular roses under cultivation in greenhouses and backyards and have been for over fifty years. Unfortunately, hybrid teas continue to be the most difficult to grow successfully. In recent years, breeders have put more efforts into developing insect and disease resistance as well as hardiness. Some new introductions show marked improvement in these important characteristics. There are also older varieties that are extremely worthwhile. Keep in mind that there are no pure yellow hybrid teas that are truly hardy in New Jersey.

Hybrid tea varieties include: 'Mr. Lincoln' (dark red), 'Olympiad' (medium red), 'Touch of Class' (coral pink), 'Elina' (creamy white), 'Pristine' (white), 'Peace' (yellow blend), 'Double Delight' (red-and-white blend), 'Signature' (deep pink), 'Fragrant Cloud' (orange red), and 'Sheer Bliss' (white).

Miniature Rose

There is a miniature rose planted outside my office window in plain view. Every year it blooms in profusion until December. When all the other roses and everything else are long gone, it still blooms. It brings great joy.

Miniature roses are generally about twelve inches tall but they can be up to eighteen inches. A few climbing miniatures can reach five feet. They are hardy little things and extremely floriferous. They have been crossed and recrossed with so many traditional roses that the color options are phenomenal.

Miniature roses grow on their own roots, so you can root some cuttings and have many miniatures. Minis can be cultivated indoors, but only if you have an abundance of light. At the very least, you need an unblocked southern exposure window, and you may want to supplement that with florescent light in the winter.

Miniature rose varieties include: 'Kristin' (red blend), 'Jean Kenneally' (apricot blend), 'Figurine' (white), 'Starina' (orange red), 'Black Jade' (dark red), 'Snow Bride' (white), 'Rainbow's End' (yellow blend), 'Old Glory' (medium red), 'Rise 'N' Shine' (yellow), and 'Loving Touch' (apricot blend).

Rugosa Rose

Rugosa roses are shrublike, with heavily textured foliage. They make an excellent choice for mass planting and are probably among the most care free plants in the world of roses.

Their flowers are usually single, but they are large, fragrant, and produced most of the season. Their hips, commonly used for tea, are among the best—they are bright orange-red and grow the size of cherry tomatoes. All rose hips are very high in vitamin C. The rugosa rose is also one of the best plants for use at the shore. It is especially tolerant of cold, wind, sand, and salt spray.

Rugosa rose varieties include: 'Alba' (white), 'Rosa rugosa' (deep pink), 'Linda Campbell' (velvety bright red), 'Blanc Double DeCoubert' (white double), 'Grootendorst Pink' (pink), and 'F.J. Grootendorst' (red).

Shrub Rose

Shrub roses are a broad group that often includes roses that don't quite fit anywhere else. These roses are generally among those best suited for landscaping purposes. They are bushlike in habit, but they may be tall and arching or compact and tidy. They have very diverse origins. Shrub roses are usually vigorous, low maintenance, hardy, and pest resistant.

Shrub rose varieties include: 'Carefree Beauty' (pink), 'Bonica' (pale pink), 'Sea Foam' (white), 'Flower Carpet' (pink, very disease resistant), 'Scarlet Meidiland' (bright red), 'White Meidiland' (white), and 'The Fairy' (very pale pink).

For more information on the pests of these finicky beauties and the latest preventions, consult one of the many good rose references available, or contact your local Cooperative Extension Office.

Shade Trees *for New Jersey*

When Joyce Kilmer wrote, "I think that I shall never see a poem lovely as a tree," he was referring to a white oak growing on Cook College campus in New Brunswick. A mature shade tree is a thing of beauty that has tremendous impact on a property in both its appearance and function.

Majestic White Oaks

When there is new home construction on wooded lots, there is often an effort to save existing trees. When the effort is successful, these older trees give a feeling of maturity and dignity that can take years to achieve with newly planted trees. Unfortunately, even when trees are protected during construction, the constant moving of heavy machinery across their roots causes a compaction that can take its toll. A change in grade six inches up or down can eventually kill a tree as can changes in the flow of water. Within five years of new construction, many established trees often begin to die. It is very expensive to remove large dying trees from around buildings, so carefully choose the trees you intend to save.

Location Is Key

Whether you start out with a wooded lot or have a yard that is a blank canvas, plant shade trees in key locations as your first step in making your grounds all you want them to be. The newly planted shade trees in a wooded lot will have gotten fairly large if and when you lose what was already growing there.

Adding a shade tree to an established landscape requires even more consideration than when starting with a blank canvas. Established plants that thrive in the sun may suffer as your shade tree grows. If the lawn is your pride and joy, remember that many shade trees compete with lawngrasses and make growing grass difficult, if not impossible.

It is important to think about why you want a shade tree. A nice shady tree or two in the backyard is greatly appreciated in summer. They are terrific on the south side of a property, where they block intense sunlight in the summer but allow warm rays through in the winter. If you are planting trees in the front yard, decide whether you want to frame the house or hide it for privacy. Keep in mind the location of sewer and water lines, since roots may grow to seek water and cause problems down the road.

A vegetable or flower garden needs full sun to thrive. Be sure to leave an open area on the grounds if you intend to grow an annual garden.

There are many trees from which to choose. It is hard to go wrong with the sturdy tap-rooted oak. Sweet gum is hardy with very attractive leaves, but many object to the gumballs that drop every fall. Sycamores and London planetrees are similar in appearance, with lovely peeling bark, but you should avoid these two as well if you don't like trees that "drop things" like bark, gumballs, and leaves. Gray birch is a graceful tree, but the birch leafminer and the bronze birch borer are serious pests.

Maples are classic shade trees. Their shape and dense masses of leaves produce terrific shade. Most maples have excellent fall color, but the roots stay close to the surface, making wicked competition for lawngrasses. Many maples have trouble with wilt disease, for which there is no control.

Planting With Care

There are certain procedures to follow when planting shade trees. Always pay close attention to the light, space, soil, and moisture requirements of each tree. Choosing the right tree for your location and needs is key to having a thriving tree you will enjoy for many years to come. When planting, dig a "$5 hole for a 50¢ plant." Make the hole at least twice as wide and as deep as the root ball. Back fill with soil amended according to the needs of the plant. Always remove wires, tags, strings, and labels. Plant at the same depth as it was in the ground or the top of the soil in the pot. In very wet ground you may need to plant high, but that is more site specific than tree specific. Be sure to untie burlap. Natural burlap can be left intact, as it will rot. Plastic needs to be removed, which is unfortunate since in the removal process, soil will fall away possibly damaging tiny hair roots critical in water absorption. Always water newly planted trees deeply. Staking is a good idea in windy environments or very loose soil. Never fertilize at planting. Wait until the tree is established for at least one full growing season. To fertilize the shade trees in this chapter, an application of 5-10-5 fertilizer can go down in the early spring, or use 5-10-5 as a deep root application on mature trees in October. In average soils, especially when planted in lawns that are fertilized, shade trees often do well without supplementary fertilization.

Choose and plant your trees with care. If you have your heart set on a particular look for your grounds, be sure to plant a named variety with the fall coloration you desire. Planting a shade tree is an investment in the future. It will mark the passage of time and store memories as it grows with you.

Ginkgo
Ginkgo biloba

The ginkgo is a wonderful tree with a fascinating history. It is one of the oldest trees known to humankind, dating back 150 million years. At one time, ginkgoes grew worldwide but are now only native to China and possibly currently exist in China only in cultivation. Gingko leaves are works of art, with interesting fan shapes and lovely golden-yellow fall color. The leaf pattern is often used in fabric design and in jewelry. The open-growth habit and spurred branches are also unique. Its winter silhouette is unusual and very attractive. Many experts recommend planting only male specimens. Since sex determination is impossible until the trees bloom and they often do not mature until they are twenty years old, take care to purchase a named male variety that has been asexually propagated.

Other Common Name
Maidenhair Tree

Bloom Period and Seasonal Color
Spectacular golden foliage in fall.

Mature Height × Spread
80 ft. × 30 to 100 ft.

When, Where, and How to Plant
Plant ginkgoes in late March or early April. Spring planting is generally preferred, but since they establish without much difficulty, these trees may also do well planted in September. Choose a sunny location. Ginkgoes are not particular about soil type but prefer moderately moist soil conditions. If planting the tree in the fall, be sure to stake it securely so that it will be better able to withstand winter winds.

Growing Tips
Water thoroughly but do not fertilize at planting time. Ginkgoes are not fast-growing trees, but if watered and fertilized appropriately (not to excess!), they will grow at a much faster rate. An application of 5-10-5 in early spring can be used to encourage growth.

Care
The ginkgo is a low-maintenance tree. Any necessary pruning can be done in the spring before bud-break. Ginkgoes are extremely hardy and suffer few, if any, insect or disease problems. They tolerate air pollution and also withstand some salty soil conditions.

Companion Planting and Design
Ginkgoes are often used as specimen trees. Since they spread so far, one tree is usually enough for most yards, although a pair flanking the house or drive can be stunning. The open habit produces a light shade. Be sure to allow plenty of room for growth. The tree will tolerate streetside planting, though the spread usually makes this inappropriate. 'Sentry' is a male with an upright growth habit that makes it an excellent selection for a street tree.

Did You Know?
The gingko is a primitive tree. Although deciduous, it is more closely related to our needled evergreens than oaks or maples. It is a gymnosperm, meaning "naked seed," and does not produce flowers. Ginkgo leaves are currently in demand as an herbal treatment for a variety of ills, including its use to dilate blood vessels with the hope of enhancing memory. The seed is considered a delicacy in Japanese cuisine, but the plum-like fruit has a slimy, smelly flesh. Male trees will not produce fruits, so look for either 'Santa Cruz' or 'Autumn Gold'.

Heritage River Birch

Betula nigra 'Heritage'

When, Where, and How to Plant

Plant in March or early April. River birch requires high soil moisture to do its best. Since it is tolerant of wet ground, plant along streams or in places where the ground is wet for part of the year. It requires a pH of 6.5 or below, but in New Jersey that should be no problem. River birch is not difficult to get established, but selective pruning at the time of planting may be helpful, especially for balled trees.

Growing Tips

Keep the tree well watered during its first summer. Deep watering during severe drought conditions is recommended. Fertilizing is not usually necessary.

Care

River birch is resistant to most major pests of birches, so you should not have to spray it. Expect some minor damage from birch leafminers, but there are usually not enough to be problematic. Clump forms of river birch may need occasional removal of crossing, or sucker branches.

Companion Planting and Design

River birch is very effective as a specimen tree or in groups. In its clump form, its branches reach down almost to the ground, providing privacy in summer. Allow daffodils to naturalize around the base of river birch and tuck in a garden bench or hammock for a delightful "secret garden" nook.

Did You Know?

Each species of birch has a particular appeal. The gray is favored for its clump habit and graceful branches. The white is majestic in both color and stature. The black and yellow birches are the least popular but are perhaps under appreciated. They have a wonderful, oil-of-wintergreen smell under the bark and in the twigs, and black birch is resistant to the bronze birch borer, a pest that can devastate white and gray. The white does best further north while the gray, though amazingly pliable, often snaps under the weight of snow and ice.

Of all the birch species, the river birch may be the best choice for New Jersey gardens. River birches are ideal for wet spots where many other trees do not survive. They can even tolerate short periods of standing water. One of the river birch's greatest attractions is its peeling bark. The bark of the colorful 'Heritage' peels back to reveal many shades of pink, peach, and cream. Bark begins peeling at an early age; larger scrolls fall away as the tree matures. 'Heritage' is available as a single trunk or clumping specimen. It is very dense when in full leaf; its spreading habit will require room to grow. In winter, its multi-colored bark and delicate, thin branches give 'Heritage' river birch a special place in the landscape.

Other Common Names
River Birch, Red Birch

Bloom Period and Seasonal Color
Beautiful peeling and soft-colored bark provides winter color.

Mature Height × Spread
40 to 70 ft. × 40 to 60 ft.

October Glory Red Maple

Acer rubrum 'October Glory'

The dense foliage and beautiful fall color of maples make them classic shade trees. They can be found from Maine to Florida, but many species are native, so we can expect them to do well in New Jersey. Seedlings selected from locally grown trees do best. This is one reason 'October Glory' is such a good choice—it was developed in the center of New Jersey at Princeton Nursery. Red maples get their common name from the color of their flowers. Many maple trees do turn red in the fall, but colors vary from yellow to dark red. Because the leaves are relatively free of disease and the wood is strong, red maple is one of the best maple species. This tree will not thrive in areas of heavy pollution.

Other Common Name
October Glory Maple

Bloom Period and Seasonal Color
Clusters of small, intense red flowers appearing in late March or early April. Rich red fall foliage.

Mature Height × Spread
50 to 60 ft. × width less than or equal to height

When, Where, and How to Plant
Red maples do best when planted in late March to early April. Choose a sunny location and plant where you will be able to appreciate its fall color. It will tolerate wet ground. Soil with a high pH can cause chlorosis of the leaves, though this should not be a problem in our acidic Jersey soils. Red maple is not difficult establish. Very young trees can be moved bare-rooted, but you will most likely find 'October Glory' balled at your nursery in the spring. In general, maples have shallow, fibrous roots that can present problems such as lifting sidewalks or extending into water lines.

Growing Tips
Water deeply under dry soil conditions. A mature tree may benefit from deep root fertilization in October every few years with 5-10-5, or have a soil test for specific recommendations (see book introduction regarding soil testing).

Care
Maples may be attacked by cankerworms (commonly called "inchworms") in the spring. Spray if necessary with carbaryl or *Bacillus thuringiensis* (Bt). Maples also drop their fruits, or "samaras" ("whirlybirds," if you're under ten years old), sometimes in large numbers. Mature trees may require occasional limb removal, but if you can't do it from the ground, hire a professional.

Companion Planting and Design
'October Glory' is a patented variety. The intense red fall color is outstanding, and the tree holds its leaves longer than most other red maples. 'Armstrong' red maple is a columnar form that works well in confined streetside plantings. 'Red Sunset' is an excellent cultivar whose brilliant orange-red fall color appears about three weeks earlier than 'October Glory'.

Did You Know?
Acer saccharum, the sugar maple, is the most common source for maple syrup. It is a beautiful, hardy, long-lived tree with dense foliage and a pleasing shape. It is famed for its fall color but does best in the northern part of its range. Sugar maple does not tolerate air pollution or crowded situations. While it will do well in much of the state, specimens planted in the mountainous northwest will produce the best fall color.

Purple Beech
Fagus sylvatica 'Riversii'

When, Where, and How to Plant
Plant beech trees in late March to early April, but there are no serious objections to planting container stock in September. Nursery plants may be grown in the ground as well as container grown. Digging up a beech in the fall is not recommended as it damages the roots. If you want to transplant and have to dig it first, wait until spring to do this. Avoid wet sites and compacted soil. Do not plant a beech where roots will receive heavy foot or vehicle traffic as the tree matures. Beeches require oxygen in the soil; prepare the soil thoroughly. Heavy clay soils need both organic matter and sand to open up air spaces. Always mix 2 parts organic matter to 1 part sand before adding it to the soil. Dig a hole at least three times the diameter of the rootball.

Growing Tips
Water deeply at planting and when soil is dry. A mature tree will benefit from deep root fertilization every few years. Have a soil test for specific recommendations or use 5-10-5 fertilizer.

Care
Beech trees can tolerate severe pruning. It is best to prune in late summer or early fall. Remove crossing branches on young trees to prevent damage. Bagworms are an occasional problem. Remove bags when you see them and spray in mid-June and late June with *Bacillus thuringiensis* (Bt). People carving their initials in the bark make it more susceptible to disease.

Companion Planting and Design
Beech's dense foliage and low branches make it difficult to grow grass beneath it. The purple beech makes an excellent specimen tree, but other forms have unique qualities as well. 'Asplenifolia' is the best of the cutleaf varieties. 'Cuprea' is the copper beech, a pale-purple-leafed variety, though there is little consistency among specimens. 'Fastigata' and 'Dawyckii' have upright growth habits, and 'Pendula' weeps gracefully.

Did You Know?
The American beech, *Fagus grandiflora*, is a fine shade tree, and the edible nuts are an important food source for wildlife, especially squirrels, chipmunks, and bears. *F. grandiflora* is easily identified in the forest by its smooth, gray bark that often, unfortunately, has initials carved in it.

Beeches are magnificent trees. The European beech, F. sylvatica, has long been cultivated in Europe, with many named selections dating back to the 1800s. 'Riversii' has all the majesty of the species. Its rich maroon-colored leaves add focus as well as beauty to the summer landscape. Be patient; this tree is not a fast grower. Do not overlook the many other varieties. Mature weeping beeches create magical havens under which one can hide. There are variegated as well as cutleaf varieties, upright growth forms as well as weeping. Each one is more beautiful than the next. It is interesting to note that few if any varieties or cultivars have been developed of the American Beech.

Other Common Name
Rivers Purple Beech

Bloom Period and Seasonal Color
Deep purple foliage that retains its color well.

Mature Height × Spread
50 to 60 ft., up to 100 ft. × 35 to 40 ft.

Red Oak
Quercus rubra

It is hard to go wrong with the mighty oak. They are fine trees. The red oak is the state tree of New Jersey. It is native to our forests, where deer, bears, raccoons, squirrels, turkeys, and bluejays feast on its acorns. Deer also feed on the twigs of low-growing branches. Red oak transplants well to the city; it is tolerant of air pollution and grows more rapidly than other oaks: about two feet per year when young. Its deeply lobed leaves sport bristles at the leaf tips. As the tree matures, flat white surfaces resembling "ski trails" develop on the bark. These are one of the red oak's identifying characteristics. The rich red wood is important to the lumber industry. Because oaks in the wild often hybridize, specific identification can be difficult.

Bloom Period and Seasonal Color
Summer foliage is dark green, turning a rich, deep red in the fall.

Mature Height × Spread
75 ft., up to 100 ft. in the wild × 40 to 50 ft.

When, Where, and How to Plant
Red oak does best planted in late March or early April. It prefers well-drained, sandy loam soils, so avoid wet sites. It thrives with an acidic pH, so do not add lime. Because it doesn't have a significant tap root, red oak is easier to establish than many other oaks. Tap-rooted trees are often difficult to transplant. When planted as a specimen, be sure to allow plenty of room for red oak's wider spread.

Growing Tips
Water newly planted trees whenever the soil gets dry. Established trees only require water under very dry conditions. When needed, water deeply. No fertilizer is needed.

Care
Oaks are susceptible to a variety of pests, but they are usually not serious. Watch out for gypsy moth caterpillars. In a bad year they can completely defoliate an oak tree. Use *Bacillus thuringiensis* (Bt) for control. One year of defoliation may not kill a well-established oak, but two years will put even an old established tree at risk. Major limbs can be removed at any time. Pruning and shaping is best done while dormant in winter.

Companion Planting and Design
The red oak has been successfully used as a street tree but is happier with more room to grow. It is an excellent choice for parks, golf courses, or lawns. Since squirrels love the red oak's acorns, you may not want to plant one so close to the house that it will eventually touch the building. This may encourage squirrels to take up residence in your attic. Dogwoods planted beneath oaks benefit from the shade and add both dimension and color to the landscape.

Did You Know?
It takes twenty to twenty-five years before oaks flower, and perhaps twenty-five more years before they produce much in the way of a crop of acorns. At that time, you can expect a large production of acorns every two to five years.

Tuliptree
Liriodendron tulipifera

When, Where, and How to Plant
Only plant the tuliptree in late March or early April. Plant it in wide open spaces in full sun. Avoid wet sites or very dry, sandy soil. Tuliptree prefers a deep loam soil, so be sure to add plenty of organic matter to existing soil. Prepare the soil deeply before planting. Tuliptree's fleshy roots do not usually branch very much, and they need a little extra attention while being established. A tuliptree grows quickly. Its annual rings can be as much as one centimeter wide.

Growing Tips
Take extra care to keep the tree well watered while it is getting established. Water mature trees deeply under very dry conditions. Fertilizing is not needed.

Care
The tuliptree is slightly weak wooded, but this weakness varies greatly among individual specimens. You may have to tend to occasional storm damage. Winter pruning is best. Tuliptree is subject to tuliptree scale, but this is seldom a problem. You can control tuliptree scale when it appears by applying a dormant oil in April and carbaryl or malathion in late August. Treating the tops of large trees for tuliptree scale may require professional services.

Companion Planting and Design
The tall, straight trunk of the tuliptree will eventually be bare for 70 to 80 percent of its height, so plan to utilize the space below it. Dogwoods are native understory trees and will do well shaded by the tall tuliptree. The deep loam soil preferred by the tuliptree will also keep rhododendrons and azaleas very happy. The tuliptree offers spring flowers, unusual foliage, and great fall color. Combined with small flowering trees and shrubs, it can contribute to an exceptional landscape.

Did You Know?
The wood of the tuliptree is important in the lumber industry. It is used for furniture, for the interior finishes of buildings, and in general construction. Tuliptree seeds feed many birds and small mammals. Young seedlings are nibbled by rabbits and deer.

The straight, majestic trunk of the tuliptree is dramatic but requires space to be appreciated. It is one of the few shade trees that also contributes significant bloom to the landscape, although the trees are quite tall by the time they are ready to flower. Bees love the flowers; the honey they produce from them has a reputation for excellent quality. Even the tuliptree's foliage is interesting. The unusually shaped leaves are large and bright green. Fall color is a rich yellow. Though fast-growing trees are generally less desirable due to weak wood and pest problems, tuliptrees may be the best of the fast-growing shade trees. They are one of our tallest native deciduous trees and have been known to reach two hundred feet.

Other Common Names
Tulip Magnolia, Tulip Poplar, Yellow Poplar, Whitewood

Bloom Period and Seasonal Color
Beautiful pale-greenish blooms with orange centers appearing in June; rich yellow fall foliage.

Mature Height × Spread
90 to 150 ft. × 35 to 40 ft.

Shrubs *for New Jersey*

Landscaping projects begin to be a lot of fun when you start to select garden shrubs. The options are almost limitless. If new gardeners are uncertain where to begin, it may be worthwhile to have some professional direction. At least take the time to learn which plants will do well in your area and what constraints your soils and sun exposure may offer. The shrubs offered in this chapter are a good start.

After you have gathered some basic information, let the games begin. Your yard and garden need to be places you enjoy. For a low-maintenance garden, select shrubs that thrive with a minimum of attention. Avoid formal plantings since they often require rigid pruning and constant attention to detail. Acquire a taste for the natural growth habit of the plants you choose. It's that electric hedge shears addiction that turns normal, reasonable gardeners into buzzing, glassy-eyed maniacs. Nothing is uglier than a butchered forsythia, massacred with electric hedge shears. The natural arched branches are breathtaking while in bloom, yet people work so hard to keep them ugly.

Azalea

Building a Good Foundation

Foundation plantings are important. Take care to choose plants that will be pleasing but stay in bounds. All too often, gardeners overplant to attain a mature look right at planting. There is not much room to grow in the confines of foundation beds, so overplanted shrubs all grow together. Some will get too large. Others will become such a mess they cannot be salvaged. It is better to plant smaller, slow-growing varieties. Fill in with perennials, ornamental grasses, and annual flowers until the bed matures. Starting small gives the plants a better chance to become established, and the bed stays attractive longer. In the long run it will be less work.

If you are a flower fancier, shrubs can supply a blast of seasonal color without replanting every year. Witchhazel will bloom as early as February. Cornelian cherry, related to the dogwood, is another early bloomer. Caryopteris produces blue flowers from August until frost. The large panicles of PeeGee hydrangea stay dry on the bush into late fall. *Lespedeza thunbergii* has panicles of rosy purple pea-like flowers in September and October. Don't forget old favorites: azaleas, rhododendrons, mountain laurel, and many others. Summer bloomers include rose-of-Sharon, St. Johnswort, potentilla, and itea. The white berries of *Symphoricarpos* are so abundant they can weigh the branches down. Winterberry holly is covered in red fruits which last well into winter.

Beautyberry

There are shrubs for shade, shrubs to add winter interest, others for flowers, and some to attract butterflies. Choose a few old friends, and mass-plant something colorful for a dramatic impact. Create privacy with a hedge but make it informal to minimize maintenance chores. Then get a bit daring. Plant something odd or new or twisted. Try some variegated foliage, or purple, or a cutleaf variety. Add a weeper or a creeper or a dwarf. Do something dramatic or silly or elegant. This is your garden and needs to be an extension of your personality. You will want your shrubs to be successful, but planting shrubs does not require the same commitment as planting a mighty oak. If you don't like a shrub, you can change it or move it or prune it; but first, you have to plant it.

Planting Your Selection

As with anything, be sure to match environmental conditions to the growing requirements of the plant. Trying to maintain a shade loving plant in the sun is a bit like trying to empty the ocean with a bucket. You just can't keep up. You can modify soil conditions to some degree by adding organic matter to sandy soil or lime to change the pH, but soggy ground will require tolerant plants or you are back to emptying the ocean. Also match the space limitations to the growth habit of the shrub. Your maintenance will be so much easier if it is a good match.

To plant shrubs, prepare the soil according to what you have and what you need. See individual plant listings in this chapter for details on preparing the soil. Dig a much larger hole than you think you need; twice as wide and deep is generally acceptable. Plastic-type burlap must be removed. Backfill with amended soil and place the shrub at the same height it was in the ground or pot. Tamp down firmly but gently, taking care not to tear roots. Staking is more necessary with fall planting, especially of evergreens, or in windy locations. Remove all wires, strings, ribbons, and ropes. Water deeply. An organic mulch is always beneficial. Never fertilizer at the time of planting. Wait until the plant is established for at least one full growing season and then fertilize the following spring. A standard fertilizer is 5-10-5, but water-soluble fertilizers are also suitable. Be sure to follow the directions on the type of fertilizer you purchase. You will be doing the best for the plant if you have a soil test (see book introduction) and then match the fertilizer to the existing soil conditions as well as the needs of the plant.

Andromeda

Pieris japonica

Bronze to bright red (sometimes even pink!) new growth, combined with long lasting flowers have earned andromeda a place in many gardens. The three- to five-inch flower clusters are similar to lily-of-the-valley, but the clusters are dense and slightly more pendulous. The evergreen leaves mature to a rich dark green. They are arranged in whorls with the abundant leaves packed in around the stem. The plants continue to put out new growth during much of the summer, so the splashes of color keep appearing. The plant tolerates shade but needs some sun to flower with enthusiasm. The flower buds are set by fall, and the beady-looking clusters add a touch of winter drama as they wait for their chance to perform.

Other Common Names
Japanese Pieris, Lily-of-the-Valley Bush

Bloom Period and Seasonal Color
Clusters of white (red has been recently introduced) flowers in early April; red new growth in early spring through the summer; golden flower buds and dark green leaves in winter.

Mature Height × Spread
9 to 12 ft. × 6 to 8 ft.

When, Where, and How to Plant
Plant in early spring or early fall. Provide a little protection from winter wind. Avoid western exposures where in the winter it may be warmed prematurely by afternoon sun. Andromeda prefers light shade during hot summer afternoons but requires some direct sun to bloom its best. Avoid wet spots—check carefully for the location of downspouts before planting near the house. Andromeda needs an acid soil, so planting right up against a foundation wall can sometimes present difficulties. Most New Jersey soils are fine, as long as you do not add lime. Adding lots of organic matter at planting time is the best thing you can do to help this plant get started.

Growing Tips
Water thoroughly at planting and whenever the soil gets dry. A light application of 5-10-5 fertilizer in early spring will encourage new growth.

Care
Any pruning should be done after blooming. Pruning any time between midsummer and the following spring will remove the flower buds. An organic mulch is beneficial. Do not use white marble chips as a mulch; they are a form of limestone which will make the pH skyrocket. Since Andromeda requires an acid pH (4.0 to 5.0), this could be deadly. (Besides, marble chips are really ugly!) Watch out for lace bug and use carbaryl as a control.

Companion Planting and Design
Andromeda mixes well with azaleas, rhododendrons, and mountain laurel. Sarcococca is a wonderful broadleaf evergreen ground cover that performs beautifully in the same locations as Andromeda and provides a lovely early spring scent. Andromeda stays compact and tolerates containers on the deck or patio but will have to be protected from the freezing and thawing of winter.

Did You Know?
Andromeda is a member of the family Ericaceae. This is the "acid-loving" family that includes rhododendrons and azaleas. The use of acid fertilizer is fine but not necessary. The use of any fertilizer renders the soil slightly more acidic, and most New Jersey soils are acidic without any help. Don't add lime unless a soil test tells you it is necessary.

When, Where, and How to Plant
Plant in late March or early April. Azaleas all need some shade and almost all need acidic soil. Avoid wet ground. Before planting, check for downspouts, which may create waterlogged soil in your beds. It is especially important to avoid locating your azaleas facing west where they will receive afternoon winter sun. This can force them out of dormancy and cause subsequent winter injury. Improve the soil with the addition of organic matter. In heavy clay soils it is important to prepare a large area prior to planting. This is because a small hole with improved soil can fill with water like a bucket. Do not lime.

Growing Tips
Water thoroughly at planting and during hot, dry weather. Use an organic mulch. Fertilize in early spring with a 5-10-5 or water-soluble fertilizer, and possibly again after blooming. Acid fertilizer is fine, but any fertilizer renders the soil more acidic over time.

Care
Prune after azaleas finish blooming in the spring. Be sure to use hand pruners and selectively remove the branches to maintain a natural shape. Prune to a 'V' or the main trunk. Never use electric hedge shears on an azalea. Keep an eye out for lace bugs and spray with carbaryl when you see them.

Companion Planting and Design
Azaleas are the perfect shrubs to mix with andromeda, rhododendrons, mountain laurel, and drooping leucothoe. Ferns scattered about give a nice woodsy look. Sarcococca makes a companionable ground cover, but don't forget sweet woodruff, a perennial ground cover with delicate white flowers. Mix in a few spring wildflowers such as trillium, spring beauties, or bloodroot. For summer color, fill in with impatiens.

Did You Know?
Azalea's cultural requirements, regardless of zone, demand a protected spot in the landscape. While it might be risky to grow a variety of questionable hardiness around the mailbox, the same type may thrive if tucked into a nook by the front door. New varieties are constantly being introduced. Contact the New Jersey Rhododendron Society for the most current information.

All azaleas are rhododendrons, but not all rhododendrons are azaleas. There are over nine hundred species which hybridize freely. This is one of the most confusing groups of plants to try to organize in a way that makes sense. Most people have a very clear image of a rhododendron, with its large leathery leaves and softball-sized clusters of flowers. Azaleas are smaller plants with smaller leaves and a more evenly dispersed array of flowers. Some are deciduous while the more popular are evergreen. There is a gray area between these two categories in which the differences in appearance are not so clear cut. It is best to use cultivars that have been developed and produced locally to be sure of having suitable specimens.

Bloom Period and Seasonal Color
Flowers appearing in spring in many shades of white, pink, coral, red, burgundy, or lilac.

Mature Height × Spread
4 to 5 ft. × 4 to 5 ft.

Bumald Spirea
Spirea × bumalda

Flowers in midsummer always get a gold star, but this plant also has pink leaves when new growth first emerges. Its low, rounded habit is easy to maintain. It can take severe pruning since it blooms on new growth. (Mine was accidentally mowed one year, and it still bloomed beautifully.) The bumald hybrids are a cross between S. albiflora and S. japonica. The first is quite small, reaching only one and one-half feet in height, and has white flowers. Japonica can reach five feet and has white to pink flowers. The hybrid is a combination of the best characteristics of both. 'Anthony Waterer' is the variety most plant people think of when you mention bumald spirea. It may be close to the truth to say it is the only one. It has been around for over seventy years.

Bloom Period and Seasonal Color
Pink to white flowers June through August; foliage in many changing colors.

Mature Height × Spread
2 to 4 ft. × 5 ft.

When, Where, and How to Plant
Plant in early spring or early fall in a full-sun, open area. These plants are tolerant of many soil types, but avoid soggy ground. Bumald spirea transplants easily. Container plants can be planted in the summer while in bloom if you take extra precautions. If you can't resist popping in a container-grown plant in the heat of summer, be sure to water the bed (not just the spot) thoroughly the day before planting. Water the pot well several hours before transplanting. Plant on a rainy or at least cloudy day; the end of the day is best. Water thoroughly and apply organic mulch. If it is very sunny the next few days, provide some light shade. Keep well watered.

Growing Tips
Water thoroughly at planting and during hot, dry weather. Fertilize in early spring with 5-10-5, especially after any serious winterkill or major pruning.

Care
Bumald spirea plants can have a few problems, but these are tough little plants. There may be some winterkill of branches, but if you prune the plants in early spring then they will flourish. Since they bloom on new growth, this will have little impact on summer flowers.

Companion Planting and Design
You may be able to find other Bumald spireas to blend with 'Anthony Waterer'. Any listed here make interesting choices for the small condo yard or for tight, almost urban places. They can be tucked into a rock garden or massed together in open spaces. 'Crispa' has twisted leaves. 'Gold Flame' has orange new growth that turns yellow-green and orange again in the fall. It has given rise to 'Fire Light', with deep red-orange new growth. 'Norman' hits full size at 10 inches. 'Shibori' is the peppermint spirea with red, white, and pink flower clusters. Scattered in the front of beds on the sunny side of the house, they will provide interest most of the season with flowers throughout the summer.

Did You Know?
The Bumald spireas are easily rooted from cuttings or can be propagated by division. If you have one, you can easily make more. Keep your eyes open for other varieties.

Doublefile Viburnum

Viburnum plicatum var. *tomentosum*

When, Where, and How to Plant

Plant in early spring or early fall in a sunny location. Some gardening references indicate partial shade is fine, but that is really more for the viburnums down south. Try to avoid wet, heavy clay soil; add organic matter if necessary. Since viburnum can grow wider than its height, make sure these plants have enough room to spread. After all, that is one of their most beautiful features. This plant is not fussy. (We once stuck twelve rooted cuttings in the ground in late fall in an open, windy location. Ten of the twelve survived the winter and are now thriving.)

Growing Tips

Water thoroughly at planting and in the heat of summer. An occasional early spring application of 5-10-5 fertilizer, especially after a tough winter, will keep it robust.

Care

This plant doesn't need much care. Wait to prune until after it blooms so you will be able to fully enjoy its blossoms. Some removal of winterkill branches may be necessary in early spring. Insects and diseases are generally not a problem.

Companion Planting and Design

Mass planted doublefile viburnums are spectacular. The flowers are magnificent on the shrub or cut and roughly shoved into a vase. Doublefile viburnums don't make the best foundation plantings since they like to spread out, but they can be fabulous in a border planting or natural hedge. Even a single specimen can be effective. The beauty of the doublefile viburnum has been compared to the beauty of the dogwood. Plant them both and compare them yourself every spring.

Did You Know?

Doublefile viburnum is one of the easiest plants to propagate from cuttings. The cuttings can be taken almost any time of year, but late June is probably the best time. Use a rooting hormone to help them get started. If you can find 'Summer Snowflake,' grab it. It blooms all summer.

When covered in its horizontal paired clusters of white flowers, this plant is breathtaking. The arrangement appears as if each cluster were being served up for your personal inspection. The center is so delicate it could have been made by an industrious spider. The tiny, fertile flowers in the center are surrounded by a circle of showy white sterile blossoms, giving the overall appearance of a pretty hat from the 1940s. The center flowers may be followed by red fruits in summer that will eventually turn black if the birds don't get to them first. The leaves are "opposite" (arranged in pairs along the stem) and droop slightly. The fall foliage color is a red purple. In winter, the naked spreading branches have an interesting effect, especially when covered in snow.

Bloom Period and Seasonal Color

Flat clusters of white flowers in summer; black berries in late summer; red purple fall foliage.

Mature Height × Spread

8 to 10 ft. × 10 to 12 ft. or more.

Dwarf Alberta Spruce

Picea glauca 'Conica'

The dwarf Alberta spruce is one of the most common dwarfs. It has a natural almost-perfect cone shape. It grows very slowly: a forty year old shrub may be only ten feet tall. The light green color and dense, short needles have a soft appearance. While the new growth is very soft, it stiffens up quickly. Dwarf Alberta spruce could be the result of a "witches'-broom," (a very dense, compact shoot) which causes all the dormant buds to grow at once. Rooted cuttings from the witches' broom almost always grow more dwarfs. Occasionally one of these dwarfs will grow a witches' broom, such as P. abies 'Little Gem', which is so compact it's tiny. Witches' brooms are thought to be the result of a mite and fungus, but no laboratory has produced one.

Other Common Name
Dwarf White Spruce

Bloom Period and Seasonal Color
Light-green new growth; dark green the rest of the year.

Mature Height × Spread
12 ft. × 5 to 10 ft.

When, Where, and How to Plant
Plant in early spring or early fall. It is best to plant in a sunny spot, but a bit of shade is okay. The dwarf Alberta spruce is not too difficult to get established. It likes moist, well-drained soil so be sure to add lots of organic matter such as leaf compost. As is true of most plants, it will appreciate an organic mulch.

Growing Tips
Water thoroughly at planting and keep it well watered. A light application of 5-10-5 in early spring will speed up its growth a bit.

Care
Pruning is generally superfluous. You may need hand pruners if the plant throws out a reversion-type (larger, non-dwarf) branch. Mites can be a problem. Some warning signs: the plant loses color, and in the morning you will see webbing resembling not-very-artistic spiderwebs. Shake a branch onto a white paper towel to more easily see the dust-sized insects. Infestations are more likely in hot, dry weather and are worse on drought-stressed plants. The first defense is to hose them off with a hard stream of water, which also gives the plant a thorough drink. This treatment may be sufficient. Mites reproduce rapidly, so hose them off every few days until you are sure they are under control. If the mites persist, contact your County Extension Service for current pesticide recommendations.

Companion Planting and Design
Since it is so small and grows so slowly, this dwarf makes a terrific foundation plant. It can also be used in containers but will need winter protection. It works well in rock gardens, in planters, and around condos. These trees are very popular for use as container Christmas trees. Keep them cool and don't keep them indoors any longer than absolutely necessary.

Did You Know?
Dwarf Alberta spruce was discovered in 1904 by J. G. Jack and Alfred Rehder at Lake Laggan, Alberta, Canada. These gentlemen were botanists from the Arnold Arboretum of Harvard University. While waiting for their train home, they happened to discover this unusual plant at the base of the Canadian Rocky Mountains.

Eastern Red Cedar

Juniperus virginiana

When, Where, and How to Plant

Plant in early spring or early fall. Red cedar prefers sun, but you may find seedlings popping up in shade. Very young plants tolerate light shade. The soil is best if deep, moist, and well-drained, but this plant will tolerate a wide range of conditions. Red cedar is not fussy, but transplanting will be more successful if you root-prune first. The young plants have a very soft, fluffy appearance which differs from the adult foliage. If you find one, transplant it carefully while it is still quite small. It is best to have the planting hole ready before you dig the tree. When digging, get as large a clump of soil around the roots as possible.

Growing Tips

Water thoroughly at planting and whenever the soil gets dry. Once established, red cedar is very drought tolerant. This is a native plant and usually grows fine without fertilizer.

Care

You can prune lightly to shape in April and again in June if necessary. Avoid the use of electric hedge shears; a light touch with hand pruners will maintain a natural shape. Bagworms are the most destructive problem. The bags are made from bits and snips of twigs and leaves. They dangle from the branch tips as if they belong there. Remove whenever you see them and spray in mid-June and late June with *Bacillus thuringiensis* (Bt).

Companion Planting and Design

The beautiful cedar waxwing is particularly fond of red cedar fruits. It is a thrill to see a migrating flock stopping for a snack. On the down side, it is not the most interesting plant for specimen planting, and many turn an unattractive brown in the winter. Red cedars are great for grouping, borders, or backgrounds. They are among the better choices for use as a windbreak.

Did You Know?

Eastern Red cedar is the cedar used to line closets and chests. It has a lovely scent which is effective in keeping away clothes moths. The wood is also important in the production of pencils. The berries are used in making gin, and they smell like gin if crushed. Red cedar is also considered a good choice for bonsai.

One of the fine personality traits of the red cedar is that it is one of the first trees to reforest an abandoned field. Since it is also tolerant of soil conditions that would make many plants choke, it is an essential plant for land reclamation projects. While it can grow much taller than your average "shrub," if controlled, J. virginiana can be used for affective borders and windbreaks. It is an attractive, easy care, practical landscape plant. Root-pruned plants will transplant easily. It is extremely drought resistant and will live a respectable 200 to 350 years. For uniformity, choose young plants carefully or use named varieties. If you are using them in a mixed evergreen grouping, you may enjoy the natural variation. Eastern red cedar is the most widespread native evergreen in North America. Young seedlings can pop up almost anywhere, with help from bird friends.

Other Common Name

Pencil Cedar

Bloom Period and Seasonal Color

Green but may be brownish in winter.

Mature Height × Spread

40 to 50 ft. × 8 to 20 ft.

Forsythia

Forsythia × intermedia

A gracefully arching forsythia covered in masses of yellow flowers is spectacular. These are easy-care, fast growing shrubs that need little attention when properly sited and are horrid beasts when shoved into the wrong spot. It is an enormous amount of work to fight forsythia's programmed growth habit. When used as a border planting in tight quarters or as a foundation plant, they need constant pruning to keep them in line. This results in lots of short, twiggy growth with little flower production and a total loss of natural elegance. The worst scenario is when they are pruned repeatedly with an electric hedge shears and then pruned again just before they bloom. All you will see is old bare trunks with a few specks of pitiful yellow drips inside. Let it be itself!

Other Common Name
Golden Bells

Bloom Period and Seasonal Color
Many bright yellow trumpet-shaped flowers in April.

Mature Height × Spread
8 to 10 ft. × 10 to 12 ft; sometimes up to 15 ft.

When, Where, and How to Plant
Plant in early spring or early fall. Forsythia needs full sun to flower brilliantly. It tolerates a wide range of soil conditions and will even do well in an urban setting. Just be sure to pick a place where it has enough room to spread. Balled-and-burlapped, container-grown, even bare-root plants all transplant easily. Sometimes branches forced into bloom indoors will root in the vase. Even they can get established with relative ease.

Growing Tips
Water thoroughly at planting and whenever soil dries until the plant is established. After that it will tolerate dry conditions unless they become extreme. Fertilization of young plants will encourage rapid growth, but that may not always be desirable. An application of 5-10-5 after a severe pruning will help forsythia to fill in.

Care
Prune properly. The first step is to retire your electric hedge shears for everything but hedges (maybe even for hedges). Forsythia can be pruned severely after bloom (or during bloom for big indoor bouquets), but start by taking the oldest wood out at the base. That step will remove much top growth. Selective pruning of the rest with hand pruners will be easy. The young growth you keep will continue to bloom while the rest of the shrub fills in. Forsythia can get a variety of insects and diseases, but they rarely amount to much.

Companion Planting and Design
Forsythia makes an excellent specimen plant and can be incredibly dramatic when planted en masse. For a border planting, consider mixing it with weigela and/or spirea, then your planting will have more than one season of bloom. If you plant a staggered row, you can have the front row bloom yellow and the back bloom another color.

Did You Know?
If you inherit a really overgrown or over-pruned forsythia, it can be salvaged. Right after it blooms, cut it down to the ground. Give it a dose of fertilizer, and it should re-grow more to your liking. With a small amount of annual pruning each spring, you should be able to maintain an attractive shrub for many years.

Fothergilla
Fothergilla gardenii

When, Where, and How to Plant

Plant in early spring or fall in sun to partial shade. The best flowers and fall color will appear in more sun. Fothergilla prefers acid soil with good drainage. That indicates no need for lime, but do add organic matter, especially to heavier soils. Provide an organic mulch, especially in full sun, to keep soil from drying out. In its native habitat, it is often found by the edge of ponds and streams, so avoid arid soils.

Growing Tips

Water thoroughly at planting and before soil dries out. A light application of 5-10-5 or water-soluble fertilizer in early spring will encourage it to stay full.

Care

Fothergilla is virtually pest free, slow growing, and stays small. Apart from pruning the occasional stray branch, this small shrub should be care free.

Companion Planting and Design

Fothergilla is fabulous around pink or white dogwoods. Planted in front of evergreens, it will draw attention both while in bloom and with its brilliant fall foliage. Fothergilla mixes well with or is an alternative to azaleas. In foundation plantings, place it near the door or walkway to enjoy the sweet scent of the flowers. The green foliage in summer is lovely as a backdrop to annuals. Choose impatiens, begonias, or trailing lobelia in the shade and marigolds, salvia, or petunias when planted in a sunnier spot. A larger relative, *F. major*, can reach 10 feet and boasts many of the same attributes.

Did You Know?

At one time, *F. monticola* was considered a third species. It sometimes still appears in the literature. It was intermediate in height between *F. gardenii* and *F. major*. In more recent years it has been lumped in with *F. major*, as the differences were anything but clear cut when grown together. Under either name, it will serve your garden well.

Fothergilla packs quite a bit of interest into a small compact plant. It is a delightful small shrub with showy white flower spikes in late April or early May. Its bloom-time overlaps with the native dogwoods, and together they make a grand show. Fothergilla is related to witchhazel and is native from Virginia to Georgia. The flowers are fragrant, appear before the foliage, and last up to two weeks. Each one looks exactly like a bottle-brush. The fall foliage is spectacular and comes in a variety of shades, often many appearing at the same time. While not common, it is available without too much searching. Expect to see more of these plants as they are a worthwhile addition to any garden.

Other Common Names

Dwarf Fothergilla, Dwarf Alder

Bloom Period and Seasonal Color

Late April, early May spikes of fragrant white flowers; multi-colored fall foliage.

Mature Height × Spread

2 to 3 ft. × 2 to 3 ft.

Juniper

Juniperus spp.

Two species of Juniper, Juniperus scopulorum *and J.* chinensis, *have given rise to some of the best-known and popular juniper varieties. Their care is similar, but their growth habits vary. There are tall junipers, fat ones, creepers, and weepers. Junipers in general, and these two species specifically, are among the most commonly planted landscape plants. Junipers transplant easily and are very adaptable. They can handle some pruning to keep things in line, but when they get severely overgrown, they should not be pruned back to bare wood. You might as well pull out the plants and start over with something more appropriate for that particular spot. Michael Dirr offers the following opinion in his book regarding the ease of junipers: "If you cannot grow junipers, then do not bother planting anything else."*

Bloom Period and Seasonal Color
Green, sometimes bluish year-round.

Mature Height × Spread
Variety dependent

When, Where, and How to Plant
Plant in early spring or early fall. Junipers prefer a sunny location and will get loose and ratty in too much shade. Their tolerance for a range of soil types and pH contributes to their popularity. They are also tolerant of urban conditions, can be used as windbreaks, and a few exhibit salt tolerance. They are easy to get established. Follow good planting practices (see introduction) and watch them grow.

Growing Tips
Water thoroughly at planting and whenever the soil dries. Once established, junipers will tolerate drier soil conditions. A light application of 5-10-5 or water-soluble fertilizer in early spring will help heavily pruned plants regenerate.

Care
Light pruning of new growth can be done in April with a second pruning of rebellious branches in June. Always prune to a side shoot, not bare wood. Bagworms infest all junipers. Their spindle-shaped bags are constructed so they look like part of the shrub, and the worms can completely strip a plant. Remove the bags whenever you see them. Spray in mid and late June with *Bacillus thuringiensis* (Bt.). When pruning to remove the occasional diseased branch, be sure to dip your pruners in a 10 percent solution of chlorine bleach to prevent contamination. In general, junipers are very resilient.

Companion Planting and Design
Junipers are sometimes used to the point of total monotony and boredom, but as screens, hedges, and windbreaks they have no equal. As specimen plants they are ho-hum and are an overgrown tangle most of the time; however, they can be a dependable foundation for your garden. While useful, I advise that less is better than more.

Did You Know?
The word "gin" is derived from the Dutch "jenever," which means juniper, and we can credit the Dutch for inventing it. All juniper berries can be used to make gin. Only females produce the small bluish fruits. After the grain is distilled, juniper and sometimes coriander can be added. After a second distillation, you will have gin.

Lilac

Syringa vulgaris

When, Where, and How to Plant

Plant in early spring in a sunny spot. Late March or early April is best. Lilacs are not too particular about soil type, but they are fussy about pH, which needs to be neutral. In New Jersey most soils will require a thorough lime application at planting time. A soil test will tell you the exact amount needed (see book introduction for details on testing).

Growing Tips

Water thoroughly at planting and whenever the soil gets dry, especially while in bloom. Fertilize in early spring or after bloom with 5-10-5 or a water-soluble fertilizer according to directions.

Care

Prune lilacs while in bloom. Much of the plant energy will go into new growth further back on the plant where you want it. Take some of the old wood out at the base; it doesn't make many flowers. Thin suckers as needed. Check regularly for borers, controlling them in early May and mid-June. Contact the Cooperative Extension Service for up-to-date control measures. Most lilacs get powdery mildew to some degree. Resistant varieties will help prevent this. Use an appropriate fungicide when you see the first signs of white specks on the leaves, usually in July or August. Or better yet, think of it as fall color and ignore it. Lime regularly.

Companion Planting and Design

You may not want your lilac front and center in your yard, since it doesn't have much to offer when not in bloom. Try it in view of a kitchen or family-room window where you will see it while in bloom, but it can blend into the background at other times. Lilacs add beautiful color to the south side of an evergreen border. Use different varieties of lilac to extend the season. Use as cut flowers and for the subtle differences in scent.

Did You Know?

There is a lilac grove at the Rutgers Gardens in New Brunswick. It is very old and had been neglected, but it recently began to undergo renovation. Some of its varieties have been discovered to be very rare.

Lilacs are romantic flowers. Their scent is full of spring and warm sunshine. Common lilac is not native to North America but was brought over with the early settlers. If you visit Colonial homes, you can often find original plantings. There are many varieties, and new ones are always being introduced. Some of the earliest to bloom can get nipped by late frosts, especially in the northwest part of the state. Most bloom late enough to avoid damage. By planting a variety of lilacs, you can extend the bloom to a full five weeks. They get no fall color, and their habit tends to be a little leggy, but you can get swept away to a magical place with each wonderful whiff of the flower.

Other Common Name
Common Lilac

Bloom Period and Seasonal Color
Upright panicles of white, pale yellow, pink, blue, lilac, wine, or purple flowers in May.

Mature Height × Spread
8 to 15 ft. × 6 to 12 ft.

Oak Leaf Hydrangea

Hydrangea quercifolia

The oak leaf hydrangea is a plant for all seasons. The eight-inch leaves look like oversized red oak leaves in a bright shade of green. In summertime, when many flowering shrubs have finished, oak leaf hydrangeas burst out in large panicles of white flowers up to twelve inches long. This display is appreciated in shady nooks where flower options are limited. As the flowers age, they develop a rose cast which deepens over time. Fall leaf color is a deep red to almost-bronze with hints of purple. This may be their most beautiful time of year. As the leaves drop, an exfoliating bark with a deep rich brown color is exposed. The skeletal shape is coarse with little side branching. The silhouette, bark texture, and color make for a bit of winter drama.

Bloom Period and Seasonal Color
Small white flowers in July; flowers age to pink; deep red fall foliage and rich brown bark.

Mature Height × Spread
4 to 6 ft. × 6 to 8 ft.

When, Where, and How to Plant
Plant in early spring or early fall. Oak leaf hydrangea prefers some shade and tolerates deep shade. It will endure full sun, but this plant needs moist, well-drained soil and requires a heavy organic mulch to keep the roots cool and retain moisture. The addition of organic matter during soil preparation is beneficial. It is an excellent choice for the edge of woods and under mature evergreens. Young plants are slightly delicate and may need winter protection. Use an organic mulch and a screen of burlap on the windy side until the plant is firmly established.

Growing Tips
Water at planting and whenever the soil dries. A light application of 5-10-5 fertilizer in early spring will keep plants full, especially after serious pruning.

Care
Oak leaf hydrangea has no serious pest problems. Prune right after blooming. You can pinch new growth to force side branching, but it is easier in the long run to let them be themselves. Overgrown individuals can be rejuvenated by severe pruning in the early spring. They can be cut back to about 6 inches but will probably not generate flowers that year. Occasionally, flowers do appear on the current year's growth. Propagate by division of the suckers in early spring. The long, upright branches sometimes snap at the base. This is not great for the overall shape, but the plants generally re-sprout and suffer no long-term consequences.

Companion Planting and Design
The bold shape of both leaves and branches stand out among delicate ferns which share its tolerance for a shady spot. The appearance also contrasts wonderfully with needled evergreens when hydrangeas are planted beneath the branches of mature trees. Mix with woodland wildflowers such as trilliums, bloodroot, and jack-in-the-pulpit for spring and impatiens for summer.

Did You Know?
A native of Georgia, Florida, and Mississippi, this plant can fill a niche in New Jersey gardens. The combination of shade tolerance and summer flowers make it a real pick-me-up for difficult spots at a difficult time of year. Don't try to force it into a sunny location—there are many more suitable choices.

Old-Fashioned Weigela

Weigela florida

When, Where, and How to Plant

Plant in early spring or early fall in full sun where there will be some room to spread out. This is one of the easiest plants to get started. It is very adaptable to a wide range of conditions. It can be started bare root, balled, or from a container-grown plant (see chapter introduction for planting instructions).

Growing Tips

Water at planting and whenever the soil gets dry. A light application of 5-10-5 in early spring or after a heavy pruning will keep it robust.

Care

Insects and disease are not serious. Pruning should be done right after bloom. It can take significant pruning, but do not use electric hedge shears. Remove some old growth at the base or close to it, then trim with hand pruners to keep it looking natural. Remove the occasional dead branch any time. While trimming things up a bit, you may come across rooted branches. These can be detached and transplanted or potted for sharing with a friend.

Companion Planting and Design

Weigela should not be used too close to the house or as a foundation plant. It is also not a great choice for a formal garden. Even when leafless, it is massive; however, it is a wonderful, easy care, free-spirited plant that can be used as a specimen or border plant. It gets so thick it is a good privacy planting. The worst thing you can do is try to squeeze this plant into a confined space. You will be unhappy with the result, and the plant will be miserable.

Did You Know?

For many years the idea of mixing a border planting of weigela, spirea, and forsythia has been very appealing. With this combination you can enjoy early yellow flowers, midseason white, and late-spring red or pink. All three have similar growth habits, but the combination allows you to eliminate the problems sometimes incurred with monocultures.

Full, tangled, and exuberant are the best words to describe weigela. This is not a plant for tight places or where you will view it up close (while beautiful in spring, the winter look is a little sad). The explosion of flowers in the spring is a riot of color and most dramatic when planted en masse or as a border. The arching branches will sweep the ground while covered in blossoms for major "drive-by" impact. Don't bother trying to force it into a formal hedge. The rigid pruning would destroy the wild elegance, and you would be left with just the tangled messy part. Weigela is tolerant of pollution, but its habit makes it tough to squeeze into most urban settings.

Bloom Period and Seasonal Color

Pink, rose, ruby, or purplish-pink flowers in late May and June; sporadic summer flowers.

Mature Height × Spread

6 to 10 ft. × 9 to 12 ft.

PeeGee Hydrangea

Hydrangea paniculata 'Grandiflora'

This is an old-fashioned faithful bloomer, although it is maligned in some of the literature as "overused." Perhaps it was at one time, but there is hardly one in every backyard now. Even if there were, big showy flower clusters in August are not exactly a hardship. PeeGee hydrangea normally grows as a large shrub, but you can train it into a tree form. Since it blooms on new wood, pruning can be done in early spring without shortchanging yourself in flower production. If you want really enormous flower heads, prune away everything but about ten primary branches. These will then produce panicles up to eighteen inches in length; they will be so massive they can weigh the branches down. This is a tough plant and easy to get established.

Bloom Period and Seasonal Color
White flowers appearing in August; blossoms age to pink, then brown.

Mature Height × Spread
10 to 25 ft. × 10 to 20 ft.

When, Where, and How to Plant
Plant in early spring or early fall. This is not a great choice for a small yard but is tolerant of urban conditions. It will do fine in full sun as a specimen plant but will do just as well tucked into the shade of a few evergreens. You can train the plant into a tree form by selecting a stem to be the trunk at the time of planting and removing the other stems. It adapts well to different soil conditions but prefers moist, sandy loam that is well drained. Incorporate organic matter into the soil at planting. The use of an organic mulch will help retain soil moisture, which will keep PeeGee fat and happy.

Growing Tips
Water at planting and when the soil gets excessively dry. A light application of 5-10-5 in early spring will encourage lush new growth, especially if it has been heavily pruned.

Care
Prune hard in the spring to control flower size or to keep it contained. Remove flower heads in late fall, or they will get brown and unattractive. PeeGee can get a few insects and diseases, as can other hydrangeas, but they are not usually serious.

Companion Planting and Design
Unfortunately PeeGee doesn't blend well with other plants. Its unrefined habit makes it stand out when planted as part of a bed or design. It looks better as a specimen plant or maybe a border planting. You may even consider tucking one here and there in an informal evergreen border planting. PeeGee can take a little shade and will break up the green with a splash of summer blooms. The flower clusters can be cut and dried.

Did You Know?
These plants will last for years. There is a lovely specimen on Main Street in Hightstown that is very large and appears very old. It is on the property of a building registered with the Historical Society. The flowers are magnificent every summer.

Rhododendron

Rhododendron catawbiense

When, Where, and How to Plant

Plant in late March or early April, but early September is a close second. Provide shade. Avoid southern and western exposures and windy locations. Avoid standing water as rhododendrons have no tolerance for wet feet. Check the location of downspouts. They can cause water to stand long enough to do damage. The addition of organic matter to the soil is beneficial. Do not add lime. Use an organic mulch to keep the soil cool and moist and to reduce weeds. Rhododendron roots are very near the surface. Careless cultivation can damage delicate roots.

Growing Tips

Water thoroughly at planting and whenever the soil is dry. This may include a deep watering in the fall (it is not wise to send a rhododendron io under water stress). Fertilize in early spring with 5-10-5, an acidic fertilizer, or a water-soluble fertilizer according to directions.

Care

Prune as necessary after bloom. Remove spent flowers which can make seeds and waste plant energy. Borers and black vine weevils can be problems. Control borers by spraying at ten-day intervals in May. Black vine weevils leave notches in the leaves, and the larvae feed on plant roots. You can try to control the adults, but you may need professional help. Your Cooperative Extension Service can assist you.

Companion Planting and Design

Rhododendrons with their colored flower clusters or "trusses" mix beautifully with their smaller cousins, the azaleas. Also consider oak leaf hydrangeas, skimmia, some of the viburnums, and the lovely mountain laurel as companions. As ground cover, try the evergreen sarcococca or the delicate sweet woodruff; ferns are a natural as are spring woodland flowers and impatiens for the summer.

Did You Know?

There is an old Rhododendron Garden at the Rutgers Gardens in New Brunswick. It is a lovely walk in the woods and warrants more than one visit as different varieties come into bloom at different times.

It is hard to imagine a yard without a rhododendron. The genus is very complex, with over nine hundred species that hybridize readily. Catawba hybrids are among the hardiest and best for New Jersey. They are native to the Allegheny Mountains down to Georgia and Alabama. There blooms are often six inches in diameter. They have large leathery leaves that are almost exotic in appearance. There is a theory that one can tell the temperature in winter by the degree of curling on the leaves (if the leaves are all curled up, it is probably below freezing). There are many colors available, and cultivars in different sizes—with new ones coming out all the time. Most yellows and oranges are not hardy, but hybridizers in California are attempting to cross tender varieties with those that are more cold tolerant.

Other Common Name
Catawba Hybrids

Bloom Period and Seasonal Color
May to June flowers in white, pink, rose, purple, or lilac colored clusters; evergreen leaves.

Mature Height × Spread
6 to 10 ft., some up to 20 ft. × 8 ft. or more.

St. Johnswort

Hypericum prolificum

Any woody ornamental that blooms in summer deserves a second look, and this one you can't miss. The first burst of St. Johnswort's summer flowers is usually quite spectacular, and the rest of the summer display is wonderful as well. It produces not just a single flower here or there but a significant number of sunny yellow blooms at any given time. A Saint Johnswort bloom has been compared to a single rose, although it is not nearly as fussy. St. Johnswort produces its blooms on new growth, so it can and sometimes should be pruned severely in the spring. St. Johnswort is native to the Garden State as well as south to Georgia and west to Iowa. Native plant material is generally well adapted to its environment.

Other Common Names
Shrubby St. Johnswort, Broombrush

Bloom Period and Seasonal Color
Bright yellow buttercup-like flowers in June, July, and August.

Mature Height × Spread
Up to 4 ft. × up to 5 ft.

When, Where, and How to Plant
Plant in late March or early April. Saint Johnswort likes sun but will do well in light shade. It is a good choice for dry rocky conditions. Several sources suggest using only container-grown plants, but Saint Johnswort suckers readily, and divisions made in early spring are almost always successful. While it is very tolerant of dry, rocky soil, it is still a good idea to prepare soil properly. Break up a hardpan with a pickaxe if necessary and add some organic matter. A layer of mulch will help retain whatever moisture the soil is able to hold.

Growing Tips
Water thoroughly at planting, especially when making divisions. Once established, it is very drought tolerant. A light application of 5-10-5 in early spring will help plants fill in, especially after a hard winter with serious die-back.

Care
This plant has no significant pests, which makes care easy. Prune hard in the spring to encourage a fuller plant that flowers with enthusiasm. If you want to divide St. Johnswort, that should also be done in the early spring.

Companion Planting and Design
St. Johnswort can be effectively used for mass planting or as part of a mixed border. With its mounded shape, St. Johnswort doesn't have enough character to be used a specimen plant, nor is it a great choice for a foundation plant since it is not very attractive in the winter. However, since it stays on the small side and can be pruned, you can try it as a foundation plant if soil conditions limit other options. It can be ideal in a rock garden.

Did You Know?
The species of St. Johnswort used as an herbal medication is *H. perforatum*. It is an herbaceous perennial that creeps along the ground, sending out roots. One of its key active ingredients is hypericin, which is not found in significant quantities in the ornamental varieties. *H. perforatum* was introduced into the United States from Europe and is now considered a serious weed.

Sand Cherry
Prunus × cistena

When, Where, and How Plant

Plant in late March or early April in a sunny location. Sand cherry is a nice choice for a specimen plant in a very small yard and is compact enough to do well in containers on patios and decks. It is extremely cold hardy but not pollution tolerant. Sand cherries are not particularly fussy about soil type or pH. They do require good drainage, so be sure to add organic matter to heavy clay soils. If you prefer a tree form, it may be necessary to select a dominant trunk at the time of planting and remove the other stems. Prune accordingly.

Growing Tips

Water at planting and whenever the soil gets dry. A light application of 5-10-5 in early spring will keep them thriving.

Care

Any pruning should be done after flowering, although this will remove developing fruits. Take any suckers from the base if you are trying to maintain a small tree. Older plants open up, so some pruning will keep them more compact if that is desired. Although a close relative of the purple leaf plum, it does not appear quite as susceptible to pests.

Companion Planting and Design

This sand cherry is considered a dwarf. It stays on the small side and maintains an attractive rounded shape. It is a good choice for container culture. A more important use for this gem is in exposed locations in the colder part of the state. The vivid leaf color is visible from a distance as are the massive number of flowers, but the beauty of the individual flowers should be viewed up close. They can also be cut for a vase.

Did You Know?

The name "cistena" comes from the Sioux and means "baby." It is surprising that this "baby" has taken almost one hundred years to become popular. Until about ten years ago, this sand cherry was almost unknown by local plant professionals. It can now be found readily, even if it is not yet available everywhere.

Sand Cherry is a wonderful shrub that can be trained as a small tree. It is a cross between P. pumila, the sand cherry, and P. cerasifera 'Atropurpurea', the purple-leafed plum. It has been around since 1909, when Dr. N. E. Hanson of South Dakota State University released it. The leaves are more dark red than purple, and the pale-pink flowers are spectacular against the emerging foliage. The overall shape of the crown is close to round, and the branches are upright to spreading but not drooping. Its greatest claim to fame is the rich leaf color which it maintains perfectly throughout the season. Its small blackish fruits are secretive, but the birds find them. The combination of later flowers and extreme cold-hardiness make this a dependable bloomer.

Other Common Names

Purple Leaf Sand Cherry, Dwarf Red Leaf Plum

Bloom Period and Seasonal Color

Pale pink single blooms in late April to early May; red foliage.

Mature Height × Spread

7 to 10 ft., up to 15 ft. × as wide as tall

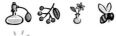

Vanhoutte Spirea

Spiraea × vanhouttei

The graceful way the branches of the Vanhoutte spirea arch up, over, and down until they sweep the ground is simply royal. The number of snow-white flowers is astronomical. The leaves are a subtle bluish green. Don't look for dramatic fall color, but the foliage may turn slightly purple. Vanhoutte spirea has been around since the mid-1800s. It has gone up and down in popularity and may not be receiving as much favor now as it did in the past. For a dependable, easy-care shrub, it is still a good choice. Vanhoutte spirea needs room to spread its wings and is not for small spaces. Plant it and let it be. There are other spireas that will stay compact and work well in tight places.

Other Common Name
Vanhoutte Bridalwreath

Bloom Period and Seasonal Color
Cascades of tiny white flowers in May.

Mature Height × Spread
6 to 8 ft., up to 10 ft. × 12 ft.

When, Where, and How to Plant
Plant in early spring or early fall. Give this plant a sunny spot with room to stretch out. It can be part of a group or used as a border or privacy planting or even as a specimen. Moist, well-drained soil is preferred, but it is very flexible regarding soil type and pH. Improve your soil before planting, as needed. The addition of organic matter is always helpful.

Growing Tips
Water at planting and when the soil becomes excessively dry. A light application of 5-10-5 fertilizer in early spring or after a major pruning will keep it full.

Care
This shrub has no significant pest problems and is virtually trouble-free. Every two or three years it is a good idea to selectively prune out the oldest wood at the base right after it finishes blooming. Take a pair of long-handled loppers and cut out the oldest shoots right at or near the ground. When you do that, you will be thinning out the top at the same time. Use hand pruners to shape and thin the rest. Do not shear this plant; shearing cuts off all the grace and leaves only what is ugly. If you squeeze it into a formal hedge with shearing, it will survive but will be very ugly.

Companion Planting and Design
This spirea grows relatively quickly and can make a good privacy hedge or mass planting. Try planting Vanhoutte spirea, forsythia, and weigela together in a border planting or informal hedge. The three have similar growth habits and bloom sequentially.

Did You Know?
I have a great example for my battle to eliminate, or at least minimize, the use of electric hedge shears. I was amazed by a local spirea hedge. Homeowners on one side let it grow naturally and it was like a snowdrift of white flowers. The neighbors on the other side had sheared it into a flowerless box. When I approached it from one end of the street, it looked like a dream, from the other a nightmare.

Virginia Sweetspire

Itea virginica

When, Where, and How to Plant

Plant in early spring. Container material is not particular about planting time, but if you are transplanting suckers to propagate your planting, that should be done in late March or early April. Choose a moist to moderately wet site in full sun or partial shade. Be sure to add copious amounts of organic matter to sandy soil to hold on to the needed soil moisture. An organic mulch will help cut down on surface evaporation.

Growing Tips

Water thoroughly at planting. Hot, dry summers will warrant occasional deep watering. Keep the plants mulched to retain soil moisture. This sounds like a little work, but if the plants are in moist soil with some room to grow, you can mostly ignore them. No fertilizer is needed in better soils. In poorer soils, an application of 5-10-5 fertilizer in early spring is beneficial.

Care

Sweetspire does not require an excessive amount of maintenance. It has no significant pests. In the spring, a little shaping and pruning of dead wood may be required. That is also the time to remove any suckers if you want them contained or to transplant the suckers if you want them to spread.

Companion Planting and Design

Sweetspire spreads by suckers, so in some places it will form large patches yet is not too aggressive. The summer flowers and attractive, long-lasting fall foliage provides interest for much of the year, an important consideration when you have a plant by the front door. Sweetspire will also tolerate container culture. These plants can be massed together, or plant a few and let them fill in on their own. A good spot is at the water's edge, or try low spots in your yard or drainage swales. These plants are small enough to be useful in foundation plantings, especially near downspouts where they will tolerate the extra moisture.

Did You Know?

Until recently, you would find sweetspire only in the wild. It was almost unheard of in cultivation. The movement towards planting native plants has contributed to its slow rise in availability. It truly is a nice addition to the landscape, especially for wet spots where options are limited.

This is a lovely summer blooming, native shrub that requires little fussing and provides dependable flowers. It is still blooming when most woody ornamentals have finished, and it is well suited for the wet spots in your yard where most plants can't survive. It is a good choice for planting along the edges of ponds or stream banks. Sweetspire can be found in the New Jersey Pine Barrens and south all the way to Florida. Each leaf is about four inches long and dark green during the summer, but it turns purple-red or even brilliant red in fall. The leaves provide fall color for an extended period. This native is proof of the benefits of using indigenous plants for an environmentally sound landscape.

Bloom Period and Seasonal Color

White flowers in spikes up to 6 inches tall in June or July.

Mature Height × Spread

3 to 10 ft. × 2 to 12 ft.

Winged Euonymus
Euonymus alatus

The winged euonymus gets its name from the corky ridges that develop along the length of its branches. Since most of these species are grown from seed, there can be significant variation in the degree of corkiness from plant to plant. These curious branches add drama in both fresh and dried floral arrangements. One of the other common names, burning bush, is due to the fall foliage that is such a brilliant red it looks like a blaze of fire. The rest of the year, winged euonymus is an attractive easy-care plant, but without any features that capture the eye. The shape is gracefully spreading without ever getting the "tangled" look that some shrubs get. Winged euonymus is a landscape workhorse with major "zing" in fall.

Other Common Names
Burning Bush, Corkbush, Spindle Tree

Bloom Period and Seasonal Color
Brilliant red orange fall color and occasional small orange berries.

Mature Height × Spread
8 to 20 ft. × 10 to 20 ft.

When, Where, and How to Plant
Plant in early spring or early fall. Winged euonymus thrives in full sun, partial sun, or shade, but its fall color may not be quite as vivid in shade. It is flexible regarding soil types and pH. Avoid waterlogged soils. This is a very easy, adaptable plant that requires no particular fuss. Young plants, probably from seed, may appear beneath the spreading branches. Weed them out or transplant these in early spring for best results.

Growing Tips
Water at planting and whenever the soil gets excessively dry. Fertilize lightly in early spring, especially after pruning.

Care
Winged euonymus is never a problem in the landscape. It is virtually trouble free. The euonymus scale that affects many of its relatives has little interest in this winged version. Since it is slow growing, it rarely needs pruning more than every other year. Do this in spring before new growth emerges. While it can be sheared, you may lose its graceful vase shape and end up with an unnatural-looking box. Selective pruning with long handled loppers and hand pruners will produce a more attractive result.

Companion Planting and Design
It is an excellent choice for a hedge or border planting, especially as a backdrop for more colorful summer plantings. Winged euonymus also works well in front of an evergreen border where its fall color stands out like a neon sign. As a specimen plant, it might work better if pruned to maintain the form of a small tree, although a large shrub really glows with autumn color.

Did You Know?
The wood of winged euonymus was once used for specialty items such as spindles (hence the other common name), bows for violins, and until the nineteenth century, for piano and organ keys. "Euonymus" is often mispronounced. The correct pronunciation is "yew-ON-im-us." In the 1922 edition of *Bailey's Cyclopedia of Horticulture*, the species is listed under "Evonymus", and it is still occasionally written this old-fashioned way.

Winterberry Holly
Ilex verticillata

When, Where, and How to Plant

Plant in early spring or early fall. Winterberry holly is a great choice for a soggy spot in the yard or at the water's edge. It will do well in a sunny location or in a little shade. These plants are not particularly fussy and will adapt to drier soils than those of their native habitat. Since they prefer boggy soils rich in organic matter, give them a good start by adding organic matter to the soil. Leaf compost is an excellent source.

Growing Tips

Water at planting and thoroughly during hot weather when the ground gets dry. Fertilize in early spring with 5-10-5 or an acid-type fertilizer. Acid soil is best. If you want berries and space is limited, it is possible to graft a male branch onto a female tree.

Care

Winterberry holly is a slow grower but may need occasional pruning to keep it from getting leggy. It will eventually sucker itself into a patch if allowed. To keep fruit production at its best, prune in late winter by removing the oldest shoots. The leaves will show signs of chlorosis (a decreased amount of chlorophyll) if the pH gets too high. This is not usually a problem in New Jersey soils, but foundation walls sometimes leach lime, which raises the pH in the surrounding beds. Avoid the use of marble chips as a mulch as marble is compressed lime and will cause the pH to skyrocket. Winterberry holly has few, if any, pest problems.

Companion Planting and Design

The red berries are dramatic in front of evergreens or en masse in a grassy field. They are spectacular when the field is covered in snow.

Did You Know?

If you want to use the heavily berried branches for holiday festivities, cut them in early November. They can be stored outside in a bucket of water where there is some wind (and bird) protection. If you wait until the holidays are near, you may find that the birds have eaten the fruits and the sprays aren't as pretty.

There is nothing prettier than a mass planting of winterberry holly with its red berries sparkling against newfallen snow. This plant is native to the eastern United States where it can be found in boggy places, making it a good choice for those difficult wet sites. You will need a least one male plant to produce the copious quantities of berries that are this plant's claim to fame. The berries appear in large numbers and will sometimes last until January if the birds don't eat them. A flock of lovely cedar waxwings stopping for a meal on the fly can make quite a dent in the display.

Other Common Names

Black Alder, Coralberry, Michigan Holly

Bloom Period and Seasonal Color

Male and female flowers on separate plants in spring; red berries on females from August to January.

Mature Height × Spread

6 to 20 ft. × 6 to 20 ft.

Witchhazel
Hamamelis virginiana

Witchhazel is native from Canada to Georgia. It can be found in the deeper part of the woods growing in the shade of its taller neighbors. It is easily recognized, even without leaves, by its fuzzy beige buds shaped like a butter knife. The flowers appear in the fall, making it one of the last shrubs to bloom. Sometimes the bright-yellow color of the fall foliage masks the flowers, but not always; sometimes the flowers will not open until the leaves have fallen. Other species and hybrids wait until early February when they are the first shrub to flower in the new season. The time of flowering is an important characteristic since whenever it decides to grace us with its flowers it is usually the only woody ornamental blooming.

Other Common Name
Virginia Witchhazel

Bloom Period and Seasonal Color
Yellow flowers in late fall or early spring; bright yellow fall foliage.

Mature Height × Spread
15 to 30 ft. × 15 ft.

When, Where, and How to Plant
Plant in early spring or early fall. It thrives in shade but maintains an open habit. In full sun, it will be a much fuller plant, but you will have to pay more careful attention to its water needs in hot weather. The leaves may burn up under drought stress. Although a woodland native, witchhazel shows a significant tolerance for urban settings. It tolerates poor soil, but avoid dry conditions. Woodland soil is almost always high in organic matter from the falling leaves. By adding leaf compost, you can approximate witchhazel's native forest soil. An organic mulch will help.

Growing Tips
Water thoroughly at planting. Don't let the soil get overly dry. The sunnier the location, the more often you will have to water. This native plant will do well without fertilizer in most soils, but a spring application of 5-10-5 or use of a water-soluble fertilizer according to directions will encourage new growth.

Care
Occasional pruning in early spring after witchhazel blooms will keep it from getting gangly. Prune out suckers to keep this plant from becoming a thicket (unless you want a thicket, which can be very nice for creating a woodsy atmosphere). Witchhazel doesn't have any serious insect or disease problems.

Companion Planting and Design
Because it is so shade tolerant, witchhazel is a very useful shrub or small tree. It works well planted under the shade of taller deciduous trees or evergreens. In an urban or condo environment where space is limited and there is rarely a spot with blazing sun all day, witchhazel works well. It can thrive in tight spaces with little light, and a bit of pollution. Mix with azaleas for later spring color, lots of ferns for the woodland effect, and impatiens, coleus, or caladiums to brighten up summer.

Did You Know?
Witchhazel is the wood of choice for making "divining rods," those Y-shaped branches used to locate underground sources of water. The bark from the plant is distilled to make the extract "witchhazel" that is used medicinally. If you break off a twig and crush it, you can get a whiff.

When, Where, and How to Plant

Plant in early spring or early fall in sun or shade. Avoid extremely windy locations and wet sites. Yews are flexible regarding soil type, as long as they are well drained. They are significantly tolerant of urban conditions. Dig an extra-large hole and break up any hardpan. Be sure to avoid the "bucket" effect in heavy clay, where you amend the soil to backfill the hole (water will flow into the hole as it follows the path of least resistance and just sit there). If drainage is poor, prepare the entire bed adding a 2:1 mixture of organic matter and sand, or plant the ball a little high. Raised beds are another option.

Growing Tips

Water when planted and whenever the soil gets dry. Fertilize in early spring with 5-10-5, especially after a significant pruning.

Care

To keep the plant full, prune in the early spring before growth starts. Unlike many other evergreens, yew can take severe pruning and will re-sprout on dormant wood, but a little selective pruning now and then is really all you should need. Once established, they are hardy, easy-care plants that maintain their color throughout the winter. If you must have a formal sheared hedge, yews are an excellent choice. They are also suitable for topiary since they tolerate heavy pruning. There is a big difference, however, between the art of topiary and "meatball madness."

Companion Planting and Design

There are a zillion varieties of yew and tremendous variation among them. The narrowest is probably 'Flushing', developed by Pete Vermeulen, in Neshanic Station, New Jersey. When 'Flushing' reaches 8 feet, it is only 18 inches wide; when 'Wardii' is 6 feet tall, it will be 19 feet wide. Other yews may fall anywhere in between these extremes. The most important aspect is to choose one that fits into the allotted space. Keep in mind that deer like to eat yews. If deer are a problem in your area, put up a deer fence or plant something else.

Did You Know?

In the England of years past, yews were used to make bows (perhaps even those of Robin Hood and his merry men).

Yews are adaptable evergreens with soft one-inch needles that are a rich dark green on the upper surface and pale green below. The new growth is yellow-green and feather soft. The red berries on female plants are an added attraction. Seeds sometimes sprout, but these seedlings will probably differ significantly from the parent. Site selection and soil preparation are critical. The only other significant problem originates with the gardener wanting to use electric hedge shears on it. Yews are not meant to look like hockey pucks, meatballs, or snowcones. If one you have is constantly outgrowing its allotted space, move it or toss it and plant another variety that fits the spot. There are plenty from which to choose.

Other Common Names
Japanese Yew, Intermediate Yew

Bloom Period and Seasonal Color
Bright, light-green new growth in early spring; red berries in fall; dark green all year.

Mature Height × Spread
40 × 40 ft., or more

Small Flowering Trees *for New Jersey*

After planting large evergreens and shade trees, it is time to add small flowering trees. This is very exciting! Flowering trees add color and personality. Their inclusion is a major step in making your yard an ever-changing garden of delight. Flowers can appear from very early spring into the fall, drawing attention to many spots on the grounds like a roving spotlight. Once established, flowering trees bloom year after year with only routine maintenance.

How Do I Choose?

Choose your flowering trees as carefully as you choose any other tree. One major consideration is light. Since the shade trees and evergreens are probably already in place, they will affect the amount of light a location will receive. A classic gardening mistake is locating native flowering dogwood in the sun-drenched center of the front yard. Because dogwoods are native to New Jersey, many gardeners assume they will thrive anywhere they put down roots. Actually, when growing naturally in the woods, they are "understory" trees. This means they live in the shade of their larger neighbors. Center stage, in hot July sun, the leaves will crisp. A lilac, on the other hand, will not bloom in the shade.

Also consider the tree's blooming time. If your flowering plants are all dogwoods, it makes for a spectacular spring display but a boring summer. With the right mix of small flowering trees and shrubs, it is possible to have something in bloom or bearing decorative fruit for nine or even ten months of the year. Plant all the dogwoods your heart desires, then for added interest plant a stewartia for flowers in July. Goldenraintree (*Koelreuteria paniculata*) also blooms in July, with fountains of yellow flowers and

Kousa Dogwood

large lantern-like seed capsules in the fall. The mixing of evergreen material with deciduous plants requires some thought. Evergreen trees have a majestic beauty all their own, but "ever green" is all you get. You could add a cherry tree to the sunny side of a row of evergreens and use the shady side for all those dogwoods. If you have a small yard, it may be important to get more than one season of interest from a tree. Stewartia blooms in July and has magnificent peeling bark for a winter show. Franklinia blooms even later, often until frost; the rich red fall color is its second act.

To prepare for pruning, find out if flower production is on new wood or old. If a tree's blooms are set (formed) the previous year, they should not be pruned until after bloom. Trees that bloom on current season's growth can be pruned in early spring. Pruning at the wrong time could prevent flowering and defeat the purpose of flowering trees.

Planting and Maintenance

To plant, dig a much bigger hole than you think you need. Twice as wide and deep or larger will allow roots to stretch out more easily. Add organic matter such as leaf compost and possibly sand and lime. The amendments you need depend on the soil conditions you have and the preferences of the plant. (See individual plant information in this chapter.) Wait at least one year to fertilize, then apply 5-10-5 or a water-soluble fertilizer in the early spring if needed. Check individual plant entries for fertilization requirements that may be more specific to that species.

If the rootball is wrapped in plastic burlap, it must be entirely removed. Natural burlap will rot and won't be a problem. Remove all tags, ribbons, wires, strings, and especially ropes holding natural burlap in place—these will eventually girdle the tree. Fill the hole with amended soil until the plant can sit at the correct height. Then place the plant carefully and fill around it with amended soil. Tamp it down gently but firmly. Do not press hard on the rootball or you may tear precious roots. Water thoroughly. Consider the need for staking, especially for larger, dense trees and/or windy locations.

Planting container-grown material is always a bit easier. The roots are less disturbed in the process. Plant at the same height it was in the ground or container. The only exception is to plant high in very wet ground. Building up the bed or draining away the water may be more satisfactory in the long run.

If you worry about trees dropping things, be sure to find out about flower, fruit, and seed development before you plant. It should not surprise anyone that flowering crabapples produce crabapples, but often some gardeners want to spray a crabapple to prevent fruit development! Does this make sense?

After all is done, sit back and watch them grow. Flowering trees can bring years of joy. They mark the passing of time by becoming increasingly beautiful with every season.

Eastern Redbud

Cercis canadensis

Eastern redbud is a New Jersey native that can stand tall among the most lovely of garden plants. The heart-shaped leaves emerge reddish purple then mature to a dark green. The April blooms are deep pink, almost purple, in the bud stage and open to a paler pink tinged in purple. The top of the tree tends to be round with a graceful branching habit. Its smaller stature makes it suitable for yards of all sizes, but it is a natural for the edge of a wooded setting. Redbud is extremely adaptable to light and soil conditions. It, like forsythia and dogwood, plays a major role in dispelling the remnants of winter.

Other Common Name
Redbud

Bloom Period and Seasonal Color
Pink to red flowers in April into May; foliage emerges red, turns green and may become yellow in autumn; older bark has streaks of orange inner bark showing through.

Mature Height × Spread
20 to 30 ft. × 25 to 35 ft.

When, Where, and How to Plant
Plant Eastern redbud in early spring. They are sometimes tricky to get established, so it is best to start with a smaller tree. Choose a location in full sun or light shade. Redbud prefers well drained, deep soils but are not overly fussy. Always avoid standing water. It is flexible about pH so seldom needs added lime. Pay attention to soil preparation to help redbud get established; be generous with organic matter and prepare an oversized planting hole to make it easy for the roots to spread out. (See introduction for more planting information.)

Growing Tips
Water thoroughly at planting and throughout the season. An organic mulch will be beneficial. Once the tree is established, an application of 5-10-5 fertilizer every spring will keep it vigorous.

Care
Other than pruning the occasional stray or dead branch, pruning is rarely necessary. Canker may be the biggest problem and requires the removal of any infected branches 6 inches behind the infected portion of the branch. Be sure to sterilize pruners in a 10 percent bleach solution between cuts to minimize the spread. If infection is widespread, it may be necessary to remove the tree.

Companion Planting and Design
Plant redbud front and center or mixed into a sunnier part of a woodland setting. The early spring flowers are a joy after the long, cold winter, so consider that when siting your redbud. They flower at a young age, so you will not have to wait long. Mix with dogwoods in the woods or rhododendrons along the foundation. Any of the early spring bulbs will complement redbud and add to the pleasure they provide.

Did You Know?
The redbud is the state tree of Oklahoma. It is a member of the pea family. Like peas, the redbud seedpods are edible while they are green and tender. Serve with butter! The flowers are also edible and are said to have a slightly nutty flavor. They can be served fresh with salad, cooked as a vegetable, or added to pancakes. Some people enjoy them pickled!

Flowering Crabapple

Malus spp.

When, Where, and How to Plant

Plant flowering crabapple in early spring or early fall, in a sunny location. Choose a spot where you can enjoy the flowers. Soil should be well drained, although crabs are flexible in regard to soil type. A slightly acidic pH is desirable and should not be difficult to locate in New Jersey. Follow good planting practices. Crabs are easy to establish. (See chapter introduction for more planting information.)

Growing Tips

Water at planting and whenever the soil becomes dry. Crabapples will benefit from an early spring application of fertilizer, especially in a year following early defoliation. Use 5-10-5 or a water-soluble fertilizer according to directions.

Care

Crabs generally require little pruning, but remove any suckers. To enjoy maximum bloom, prune after flowering but before early June. Rust and scab are two primary disease problems. To control both, you must start spraying at budbreak and continue at ten- to fourteen-day intervals until two weeks after the petals fall. Check with your County Extension Service for current fungicide information. Cleaning up the leaves will reduce the chances of disease for the following year. Unless you are willing to battle leaf diseases annually, only buy crabapples listed as highly resistant to disease.

Companion Planting and Design

Crabapples are generally planted alone since they make such a statement while in bloom. 'Red Jade' is a slow growing weeper that works beautifully planted at the corner of a foundation. If you are interested in fruit, have two varieties for fruit set. A crabapple can often be used to pollinate an apple. You may read not to plant apples near eastern red cedars (or other junipers) to avoid cedar-apple rust. This is true; however, you should accept that eastern red cedar is virtually everywhere in the state.

Did You Know?

Some cultivars will bear flowers and fruit in alternate years. You may want to sacrifice some flowers if it means choosing between trees that are seriously susceptible to disease and those with cyclical bloom without disease.

The difference between a crabapple and an apple is only the size of the fruit. Fruit two inches or smaller is a crabapple; larger fruit is an apple. Larger crabapples are considered edible, but even the smaller or bitter fruits can be used for jams and jellies. Flowering crabapples can be very confusing. So far there are seven hundred named cultivars. If you have your heart set on a particular cultivar, you may not be able to find it in the trade. Since crabapples (and apples) require cross-pollination, seedlings are very diverse. The flower display is one of this tree's best characteristics, while disease problems are one of its most frustrating. Many a crabapple tree is leafless by midsummer, but in bloom it is breathtaking.

Bloom Period and Seasonal Color
White, pink, or red flowers in late April or as late as early June.

Mature Height × Spread
15 to 25 ft. × 15 to 25 ft.

Franklinia

Franklinia alatamaha

Franklinia is an under appreciated small tree. Its large, beautiful, simple flowers arrive when other woody ornamentals are not doing much flowering. Its deep red fall color is a bonus. In addition to its beauty, the history of this native tree makes it a featured attraction in any American garden. It was discovered in 1770 along the Alatamaha River in Georgia. John Bartram collected samples, but when he returned, the original grove had disappeared. It is unclear as to whether natural disaster killed it off or whether trees were collected by others until the source was finally depleted. This small treasure was named after Ben Franklin. No wild populations exist today. Mystery always adds to beauty. In spite of its relative obscurity, however, it is not difficult to find locally.

Other Common Name
Franklin Tree

Bloom Period and Seasonal Color
White flowers from late July until frost; red fall foliage.

Mature Height × Spread
10 to 20 ft. × 6 to 15 ft.

When, Where, and How to Plant
Plant in late March or early April. Plant in a sunny location in well-drained soil. Franklinia prefers acidic soil, which is easily supplied in New Jersey. Franklinia does not transplant easily, so is best to begin with a small tree. Improve the soil by adding organic matter such as leaf compost. Franklinia can be grown as either a small tree or a shrub. (See chapter introduction for more planting information.)

Growing Tips
Water at planting and whenever the soil gets very dry. After franklinia is established, apply fertilizer such as 5-10-5 in the early spring. Avoid excessive nitrogen that you find in lawn fertilizers. Too much fertilizer may inhibit flower formation.

Care
Phytophthora wilt can be a problem during propagation and in containers. This is all the more reason to be sure that you plant the tree in a place with good drainage. It should not need major pruning, but if light pruning is necessary, early spring is the best time, as franklinia blooms on new wood. If you prefer a tree form, you may want to choose a single shoot at planting and remove the rest of the shoots. The more trunks it develops, the more shrub-like it will become, but it often grows with a single trunk on its own. Multi-stemmed shrub franklinias keep the flowers lower where they can be better enjoyed.

Companion Planting and Design
Grown as a tree, franklinia may show best as a specimen plant, but the multi-trunked shrubs can be used to blend with other plantings. The late season blooms add interest when few woody ornamentals are in bloom. Mix it with spring blooming shrubs to give another season of interest or plant it with butterfly bushes to increase summer impact. Even tucked into a few low growing junipers, franklinia will provide diversity when least expected.

Did You Know?
Franklinia will occasionally still be in bloom when its leaves turn red. This is a particularly lovely sight. Franklinia is unique, although its 3 inch white flowers are similar to those of the stewartia.

Fringetree
Chionanthus virginicus

When, Where, and How to Plant
Fringetree does best planted in early spring in a sunny location. Fringetree is usually found growing along streams or the edges of swamps and does best in moist soil. It is more tolerant of air pollution than many other trees, so is a good choice for urban locations. Add organic matter to help maintain soil moisture. It can be persnickety about being moved, and doesn't like dry soil. If you intend to grow it as a small tree, do some selective pruning at planting to establish a dominant trunk. (See chapter introduction for more planting information.)

Growing Tips
Water well at planting and whenever soil begins to dry, especially for the first year or two. A layer of organic mulch will conserve soil moisture. In average soils, fringetree often needs no fertilizer, but an application of 5-10-5 in the spring may give it a boost.

Care
Fringetree requires little pruning. It is native to the area and therefore well adapted. It has no serious pests, though it may occasionally be bothered by scale. If you grow a specimen with multiple trunks, prune out any crossing branches while they are young. Remove suckers on tree types. Since the flowers are borne on the previous year's growth, prune after bloom so you don't miss the show!

Companion Planting and Design
A tree-form fringetree will show off better in a different spot than one growing as a shrub. Also, if you are growing it for the birds, you may want to view your guests but not easily disturb them. You will need more than one plant to ensure fruit set and if possible make sure one is a male. Fringetrees get as wide as tall, so provide ample space. They have flowers, fruits, and attractive fall foliage, so don't hide their light under a basket.

Did You Know?
Fringetree is very slow growing and very late to leaf out in the spring. Cuttings of this plant are extremely difficult to root. Most fringetrees are grown from seed, which accounts for the lack of gender-identified young trees as well as for the variation in fall color.

This large shrub or small tree is native to New Jersey but can be found as far south as Florida. Native trees are well adapted to their environment, making them tolerant of most endemic diseases and insect infestations. These trees are either male or female, and you need both to produce the almost-black fruits. Because they are mostly hidden by foliage, the fleshy fruits are not particularly showy, but they are a favorite of our feathered friends. If feeding the birds is one of your interests, this species is a good choice. If you purchase the plants while in bloom, you may be able to distinguish between male and female trees by comparing their flowers. Male flowers have significantly longer petals.

Other Common Names
White Fringetree, American Fringetree, Grancy Graybeard, Old Man's Beard

Bloom Period and Seasonal Color
White flowers, in May; brownish yellow to bright yellow fall color.

Mature Height × Spread
30 ft. × 30 ft.

Japanese Snowbell
Styrax japonicus

Japanese snowbell is a lovely tree that extends the bloom of spring into early summer. It should be planted where its enormous number of small flowers can be appreciated up close. The tree appears to be covered with delicate bells peeking out from beneath its leaves. They ring a gentle fragrance that is music to the senses. Young trees are pyramidal in shape; their growth habit becomes more open and spreading as they mature. The bark of Japanese snowbell is smooth and grayish brown with patches and streaks of orange that add a bit of winter interest. This tree is not easily established, but you will be rewarded for your effort. Japanese snowbell is virtually pest free and will provide many years of sweet smelling flowers every June.

Other Common Name
Japanese Styrax

Bloom Period and Seasonal Color
White, bell-shaped 3/4-inch blooms in June.

Mature Height × Spread
30 ft. × 30 ft.

When, Where, and How to Plant
Japanese snowbell can be fussy. You will have the easiest time getting it established if you plant in late March or early April. It prefers full sun but is happy in partial shade. In the northwest part of the state, Japanese snowbell will benefit from some protection from harsh winter weather. Tuck it among evergreens to provide a bit of shelter. Be sure to choose a spot where you can see this tree up close. The flowers are abundant but small. From a distance they get lost, and you receive no pleasure from the lovely scent. A small plant will tolerate transplanting much better than a larger tree. If the tree is container-grown, there will be even less stress to the root system. Add copious amounts of organic matter to the soil. This will be helpful in getting the finicky roots established. (See chapter introduction for more planting information.)

Growing Tips
Water at planting and whenever the soil begins to dry. Fertilize in early spring in poorer soils with 5-10-5 to encourage more rapid growth.

Care
Japanese snowbell is practically pest free. Perform any necessary minor pruning in winter when the temperature is above freezing.

Companion Planting and Design
Japanese snowbell makes a stunning combination with richly colored rhododendrons and late-blooming azaleas. Their bloom periods overlap for a breathtaking display. The variety 'Pendula' is a graceful weeping form. 'Carillon' also weeps but is hardy only to Zone 7. 'Rosea' is pink with an upright habit.

Did You Know?
The leaves of Japanese snowbell appear lightly poised on its branches, exposing the dangling flowers that hang below them. If the tree is planted so that you can look up into the branches while it is in bloom, you will get a spectacular view. The common practice of using berms in today's land-scapes, or locating the tree partway up a slope, may create the perfect setting.

Kousa Dogwood

Cornus kousa

When, Where, and How to Plant

All dogwoods fare better with spring planting. Late March or early April is ideal. Plant Kousa dogwood where its flowers can be appreciated. These trees tend to spread, so give them plenty of room. Kousa prefers more sun than the flowering dogwood, but light shade is fine. It does best in acidic, well-drained soil with plenty of organic matter. Start with a young tree and do not add lime. Take extra care not to disturb the roots. (See chapter introduction for more planting information.)

Growing Tips

Water thoroughly at planting. Keep well watered, especially during the first summer. Fertilizer, such as 5-10-5, applied in the early spring will encourage more rapid growth but is often not necessary.

Care

Kousa dogwood has few pest problems. It is resistant to the multiple problems that are affecting the native species. It does not like to be pruned, though you should remove suckers and crossing branches if any appear. The fruits are edible and tasty but with a less than wonderful texture. The birds really enjoy them, so leave a few for your feathered friends.

Companion Planting and Design

Many homeowners choose dogwood to be the focal point of the front yard. The sun-loving Kousa is a better choice than the native species since it is more tolerant of strong sun. It is also an excellent choice for the corner of the house. Its spreading habit softens the house while making it appear larger. Locate this tree where you can look down on it, such as beneath a bedroom window. The flowers are magnificent by morning sun or moonlight. Mixed into an evergreen border, Kousa dogwood adds year-round interest. Since many problems with dogwood begin with injury to the trunk, leave a grassless area around the base that will eliminate the need for mowing close. Ground cover is a good alternative to grass in that area.

Did You Know?

There are magnificent mature specimens of Kousa dogwood at Longwood Gardens and some beautiful dogwoods, of many different varieties, at the Rutgers Gardens in North Brunswick.

Kousa dogwood is the ideal substitute for Cornus florida *(common flowering dogwood). Though the flowering dogwood can be found in local forests, it is in a state of decline due to a combination of factors including pollution. Kousa dogwood blooms in very early June, about one month after C. florida. The creamy white bracts are pointed at the tips, not notched like the bracts of the flowering dogwood, but the overall effect is similar. Some trees produce so many of these bracts that they resemble a snowdrift. The display lasts for up to six weeks. Its flowers are followed by bright red fruits that resemble pudgy raspberries. Birds love them. Kousa dogwood's red fall color lasts up to five weeks. Exfoliating bark adds a little winter zing.*

Other Common Names

Chinese Dogwood, Japanese Dogwood

Bloom Period and Seasonal Color

Usually white, sometimes pink, showy bracts in early June; red fruits in fall with red fall foliage; exfoliating bark for winter interest.

Mature Height × Spread

20 to 30 ft. × 20 to 30 ft.

Kwanzan Cherry
Prunus serrulata 'Kwanzan'

Kwanzan cherry is part of the fabulous display each spring in Washington, D.C. Its profusion of flowers is quite spectacular. This tree is available in two distinct forms: grafted trees and those grown on their own roots. Grafted trees are all very uniform in size and shape. The graft is high on the trunk so the branches start five or six feet off the ground. This makes them popular street trees. Specimens grown on their own roots have a more interesting form and reach up to forty feet. The upright habit opens up with age. Leaves appear with the flowers or just after, emerging bronze, turning green as they mature, then becoming orange bronze in fall. The Kwanzan cherry is a short-lived tree that lasts only fifteen to twenty-five years.

Other Common Names
Kwanzan, Sekiyama, Hisakura

Bloom Period and Seasonal Color
Double pink flowers, in late April or early May.

Mature Height × Spread
20 to 25 ft. or more × 20 ft.

When, Where, and How to Plant
Plant Kwanzan cherry in early spring. Late March or early April is the best time to plant. Choose a sunny location where its abundant flowers can be appreciated. Avoid heavy or wet soils, but keep the soil moist. Follow thorough soil preparation practices. In heavy soils, plant the rootball slightly higher than usual to avoid root rot. The addition of a 2:1 mixture of organic matter and sand will be beneficial. (See chapter introduction for more planting information.)

Growing Tips
Water thoroughly at planting. Water during hot, dry weather, especially the first year or two. Fertilizer is seldom necessary, but an application of 5-10-5 in the early spring will be beneficial in poor soils.

Care
Prune only the occasional rebellious branch. If you prune during bloom, the flowers can be used indoors. Tent caterpillars can be a problem in May; spray as soon as you see their silken tents forming. Control with *Bacillus thuringiensis* (Bt). If you learn to recognize the egg masses, you can remove them before they even hatch. Tent caterpillar eggs resemble a wad of granular charcoal stuck on the branch.

Companion Planting and Design
'Kwanzan' cherry is often used as a specimen tree for a focal point in the front yard. It is a better choice for that spot than the popular dogwood since it can take the hot sun. Choose a spot where you pass close enough to enjoy the scent. The grafted versions are gaining in popularity as street trees. They are beautiful and stay smaller than the more common shade trees, which keeps them out of utility wires. Branches pruned during the tree's dormant season can be forced into bloom, bringing a bit of spring ahead of the season.

Did You Know?
The name "Kwanzan" comes from the Chinese character that represents a sacred mountain. The tree may produce very small fruits, but they are inconspicuous and neither add to nor detract from the appearance. Birds enjoy them.

Purple Leaf Plum

Prunus cerasifera 'Atropurpurea'

When, Where, and How to Plant

Plant purple leaf plum in late March or early April in full sun. It is not overly fussy about soil but it should be well drained. Plant the rootball slightly higher in heavy soils. Add a 2:1 mixture of organic matter and sand to improve clay. If you obtain a bare-root specimen, first soak the roots for several hours, then plant ASAP. Dig your hole and place a mound of soil in the bottom for root support as you carefully spread roots out. Plant at the same depth it was growing previously. Gently work the soil in around the roots. Water when the hole is half filled and again when full. (See introduction for more planting information.)

Growing Tips

Water when the soil gets dry. During its first year, pay extra attention to the watering of a bare-root tree. The root hairs responsible for water uptake are traumatized during digging and planting. Apply 5-10-5 or a water-soluble fertilizer in the early spring if the soil is poor.

Care

Prune lightly in winter. Pruning during or immediately after bloom will reduce fruits. The black knot fungus loves plum trees causing black thickened areas on the branches that are easily identified. Prune branches 4 inches behind the swelling. Dip pruners in a 10 percent bleach solution between cuts. Spray in spring before the buds open, three times at seven day intervals. Aphids, tent caterpillars, scale, and borers can be problems. Contact your County Extension Service for current pesticide recommendations.

Companion Planting and Design

Purple plum is not a good choice for an urban environment since it is sensitive to pollution and has a short life expectancy. Select a spot, perhaps in front of a row of evergreens, where you can enjoy its advantages without being devastated if it declines.

Did You Know?

In 1880, this tree was discovered in Persia (Iran) by Mr. Pissard, gardener to the Shah. It was a sport which was later introduced into France. Other varieties have resulted from the selection and hybridization of the original.

The small pale pink flowers of purple leaf plum are not long lasting but are very pretty against the emerging cherry-red foliage. The leaf color darkens into a deep wine purple which it retains throughout the summer. Dark purple fruits, which are edible but taste awful, develop in July and August. You probably won't eat them unless you're starving. The birds are not quite as picky and enjoy them. It is true that ornamental plums are short lived and often bothered by pests, but the purple leaves are striking in the landscape. If you grow a purple leaf plum, enjoy it while it is beautiful and then replace it with something else. These trees last up to twenty years, but often less. Plums do not tolerate pollution.

Other Common Names

Cherry Plum, Myrobalan Plum, Pissard Plum

Bloom Period and Seasonal Color

Light pink flowers in late April; red to purple foliage spring through fall.

Mature Height × Spread

15 to 30 ft. × 15 to 25 ft.

Red Buckeye
Aesculus pavia

The red buckeye is a small tree that really needs a second look. It is a close relative of the gorgeous horse chestnut but is suitable for smaller yards and blooms at a very young age. The palmate leaves provide wonderful interest all by themselves, but the spikes of flowers in May are stunning. It is native from Virginia to Florida and does not appear to suffer from the blight that affects the horse chestnut. Red buckeye is generally grown from seed, so there is variation in flower color. It sometimes blooms in containers so you can evaluate the color if you find it at the right time of year. Red is classic, but the shades of pink are also lovely.

Other Common Name
Scarlet Buckeye

Bloom Period and Seasonal Color
Three- to six-inch panicles of red or reddish pink flowers in May.

Mature Height × Spread
10 to 20 ft. × 10 to 20 ft., larger in the wild

When, Where, and How to Plant
Plant in early spring or early fall. Using a container-grown plant gives an even broader range of effective planting time (almost any time the ground is not frozen, but 100 degree days and the dead of winter may be trouble). Blooms in light or even dense shade but produces the fullest plant in full sun. Red buckeye prefers moist, well-drained soil but is not too picky. Avoid very dry soils. Adding organic matter such as compost will be helpful. Generally this beauty is flexible and easy to establish. (See chapter introduction for more planting information.)

Growing Tips
Water at planting and whenever the soil gets dry. Keep well watered in the heat of summer, especially until the plant becomes established. These lovely trees do well without additional fertilizer, but an application of 5-10-5 or a water-soluble fertilizer in early spring will encourage new growth.

Care
When you have very dense growth, prune crossing branches and those growing toward the middle to keep good form. This light pruning can be done while dormant or right after bloom. The round top requires little further attention. Red buckeye can be subject (rarely) to the blotch that affects horse chestnut. Generally it maintains a lovely shape and has few if any pest problems.

Companion Planting and Design
This is a great small tree for smaller yards but pretty enough to go anywhere. Mix with dogwoods and stewartia in a woodland setting or place front and center as a focal point. It won't add much to an autumn garden since it has no fall color and may lose its leaves earlier than other trees. Consider a location where you can see it bloom from the house since the individual red flowers attract hummingbirds.

Did You Know?
The nuts and leaves of all the *Aesculus* genus are poisonous. Wildlife avoids them. Even so, the American Indians would roast the nuts then mash them, then soak the mash in water for several days to leach out the poisonous compounds. The meal was then used as flour to bake into bread.

Saucer Magnolia

Magnolia × soulangiana

When, Where, and How to Plant
Early spring planting of balled-and-burlapped trees should be done in late March or early April before new growth begins. If planting in fall, do it in early September and try to plant container-grown material to lessen root disturbance. Saucer magnolia prefers full sun, but avoid sunny, warm, protected, south-facing locations. Planting there may cause the tree to warm up and bloom prematurely, only to have its flowers blackened and killed by a late frost. Add plenty of organic matter to the soil; you will probably not need lime. Avoid planting saucer magnolia too deep. (See chapter introduction for more planting information.)

Growing Tips
Water thoroughly at planting and whenever the soil gets dry. Fertilizer is seldom necessary in good soils, but an application of 5-10-5 or use of a water-soluble fertilizer will encourage new growth.

Care
Prune after flowering if necessary, checking at the base for potentially troublesome crossing or rubbing branches. Insects and diseases may move in, but they are rarely serious.

Companion Planting and Design
Location is very important. Different varieties reach different sizes. 'Brozzonii' reaches 30 feet but blooms late so it may avoid frost problems. 'Lilliputian' is much smaller. Choose a spot where the flowers show to advantage, but if they are the only flowering tree dead center in your yard, it will be a sad year when they get frosted. Try on the eastern edge of the property. Scatter daffodils underneath or a sea of grape hyacinth for spring color.

Did You Know?
This hybrid is a cross between *M. denudata*, a Chinese species, and *M. liliiflora* from Japan. According to Donald Wyman's *Gardening Encyclopedia*, the hybridizer was a retired soldier from Napoleon's army. The cross was made in 1820, and the first hybrid flowered in 1826 in Fromont, France. A personal note: This is the first tree I learned to identify as a very young child. I rubbed the velvety petals on my cheek and was enchanted by the sensation. It seemed all was well with the world.

Saucer magnolia trees have the classic look associated with magnolias. Their enormous dark buds open up to spectacular goblet-shaped flowers that can be five to ten inches in diameter. The tree branches close to the ground and spreads. While in bloom it resembles a soft white cloud at rest. The large petals are silky smooth. When they float down from the tree, it seems as though the ground is covered in a sea of large pearls. Flowering is initiated when the tree is only two to four feet tall. Trees will occasionally produce a pineapple-like aggregate of bright-red fruits. A serious problem with the species is its susceptibility to late spring frosts. Once every three or four years, the entire crop is killed back due to weather.

Other Common Names
Chinese Magnolia, Tuliptree

Bloom Period and Seasonal Color
Pink to purple blooms on the outside, white on the inside, appearing March to April; occasional red-fruited pods in the fall.

Mature Height × Spread
20 to 30 ft. × 20 to 30 ft.

Scholar Tree
Sophora japonica

Scholar tree's profusion of creamy-white flowers in August are so delightful that this tree doesn't need much else. The compound leaves have seven to seventeen leaflets each, which may be rounded or pointed. The green three-inch-long seedpods turn brown in winter. Seedpods hang from the tree throughout the winter like dried string beans. Once established, scholar tree tolerates heat and drought. It is also exceptionally tolerant of urban conditions, including pollution. Scholar tree grows at a medium rate and often flowers after ten to fourteen years, but it sometimes takes twenty-five years. The trunk on older trees often becomes wonderfully contorted and twisted, enhancing the scholar tree's other attributes. The foliage has no fall color, but the dark-green branches add to the winter appeal.

Other Common Names
Pagoda Tree, Japanese Pagoda Tree, Chine Scholartree

Bloom Period and Seasonal Color
Creamy-white pea-like flowers in July and August.

Mature Height × Spread
50 to 75 ft. × 50 ft.

When, Where, and How to Plant
Plant scholar tree in early spring or early fall in a sunny location. A young tree makes establishment easier. It does best with some winter protection while young. Choose a well-drained site with loamy soil and add organic matter. Wrap with burlap in winter for the first few years and hope for a mild winter. (See chapter introduction for more planting information.)

Growing Tips
Water thoroughly at planting and whenever soil gets dry until it gets established. Scholar tree tolerates some drought after that. An application of 5-10-5 or a water-soluble fertilizer in early spring may be beneficial, especially on young trees, but wait until the tree has been in the ground at least one full growing season.

Care
Prune scholar tree in the fall. Pay extra attention to pruning to ensure that the tree develops a strong leader and a nice shape. Some winter damage may need attention in the spring, but it is usually minor. Powdery mildew and leaf hoppers can be problems, though occurrences are not usually serious. This tree needs TLC when young to insure good establishment and development of a nice shapely framework. After that, it requires little attention.

Companion Planting and Design
The flowers and fruits of scholar tree are a little messy. They may discolor pavement and parked cars with a yellow stain, but they do fine in a lawn area. Scholar tree is in quiet mode in spring and has no fall color, so choose something else for an early focal point. Locate in a "secondary" spot where you can still enjoy the summer blooms, the winter trunk, the seedpods, and the green branches. It is a great tree to provide interest in the two "off" seasons. 'Regent' grows rapidly and bears flowers earlier than the species. It has a more upright habit and will bloom in six to eight years. It was developed and patented at Princeton Nurseries.

Did You Know?
A natural yellow dye can be made from the flowers. Bake the flowers until they are brown and then boil to extract the colorant.

When, Where, and How to Plant

Plant these hybrid dogwoods in late March or early April. Unlike the flowering dogwood, these prefer full sun. Choose a place safe from lawn mower damage or other bark injury. The crown of these trees will spread, so plant at least 20 feet apart in well-drained acidic soil. Add a 2:1 mixture of organic matter and sand to heavy clay soil. Sandy soils in the southern part of New Jersey can be improved with plenty of organic matter such as leaf compost. Provide a 2-foot-wide grass-free area around the trunk and cover this area with an organic mulch. (See chapter introduction for more planting information.)

Growing Tips

Water deeply at planting and whenever the soil begins to dry. Fertilizer is seldom necessary in better soils, but 5-10-5 or a water-soluble fertilizer applied in early spring will encourage new growth.

Care

Rutgers dogwoods need not be pruned, so remove only suckers and crossing branches as necessary. These hardy trees are resistant to the problems that plague *C. florida.* Take care not to injure the trunk with power tools or even bicycles.

Companion Planting and Design

By planting both species and all six hybrids it is possible to have blooms for up to two full months. Put *C. florida* in the shady nooks, *C. kousa* in less shade, and fill the sunny spots with the hybrids. Mix with redbud (*Cercis canadensis)* in natural settings, fothergilla near the house, and rhododendrons for spring impact. Hybrids, in order of bloom, are 'Rutlan' (Ruth Ellen), 'Rutfan' (Star Dust), 'Rutcan' (Constellation), 'Rutdan' (Celestial), and 'Rutban' (Aurora). The final hybrid to bloom is 'Rutgan' (Stellar Pink), the only pink-flowering variety in the group.

Did You Know?

The two parents of these hybrids, *C. florida* and *C. kousa*, are distinct species that evolved on two different continents, so successful hybridization was iffy. To make things more difficult, the flowering dogwood finishes blooming completely before the Kousa even gets started. Pollen from *C. florida* was saved for when *C. kousa* came into bloom, and it was then hand pollinated.

The Stellar series of hybrid dogwoods have a wonderful history that make these beautiful trees particularly special for New Jersey gardens. They were developed by Dr. Elwin Orton at Rutgers University. These are a cross between the native dogwood, C. florida, *and the Kousa dogwood,* C. kousa. *It took twenty-five years of waiting, testing, and culling to select six superior varieties. The native dogwood blooms around May 1 and the Kousa around June 1, with the hybrids blooming between those times. It is interesting to note that two hybrids, whose bloom period is closer to that of the native dogwood, also have its spreading habit. The other four hybrids grow more upright, like the Kousa. Unfortunately, the hybrids are sterile so there is no fruit for winter interest. The lovely red fall foliage provides a great late-season display.*

Other Common Name
Rutgers Dogwood

Bloom Period and Seasonal Color
Large showy bracts in white or pink in May into early June; red fall color.

Mature Height × Spread
25 ft. × 25 ft.

Stewartia

Stewartia pseudocamellia

I once met a landscaper who said he wished he could find an abandoned grove of old stewartias. It would make his fortune. It is certainly true that these fabulous garden plants become more wonderful with age. Stewartias are slow growing and pyramidal in shape. The peeling bark with patches of red becomes increasingly intricate and interesting as the tree matures. Stewartia's large summer flowers are truly elegant in both purity and simplicity. They are abundant enough to have impact at any time of year, but they appear when few other woody ornamentals are in bloom. Fall color is brilliant and comes in shades from bronze to red to purple. Stewartia is truly a tree for all seasons.

Other Common Name
Japanese Stewartia

Bloom Period and Seasonal Color
Large white flowers in July and August; fall foliage in bronze, red and purple; attractive peeling bark in many shades of green and hints of red.

Mature Height × Spread
30 to 40 ft. × 20 ft.

When, Where, and How to Plant
Plant stewartia in late March or early April. Locate in sun but with a little shade from the hottest part of the day. Transplanting larger trees, and even young ones, is difficult. Start small and plant a tree in its permanent location. A container-grown plant will have the best chance to thrive, as root disturbance is minimized. Add large amounts of compost or other organic matter to enrich the soil. Stewartia does best in acidic soil, so do not apply lime. (See introduction for more planting information.)

Growing Tips
Keep stewartia well watered in the first year and during hot, dry summers. Fertilizer is seldom necessary, especially in good soils.

Care
Stewartia is virtually pest free and requires little or no pruning. Remove the occasional crossing branches or ones growing toward the center. Apply a thick layer of organic mulch to protect the roots from drying out and to moderate soil temperatures.

Companion Planting and Design
Stewartia's small stature and multi-season appeal makes it an excellent choice for smaller yards. This tree does well as part of a woodland garden. Plant lots of spring bulbs or woodland wildflowers such as trillium or bloodroot at the base. Tuck stewartia into an evergreen border along with dogwoods and redbud. It will provide summer blooms and autumn color.

Did You Know?
There seven species of stewartia. Few people know about all of them. Korean stewartia, *S. koreana*, is slightly smaller than *S. pseudocamellia*, but its flowers are slightly larger. *S. sinensis* is the Chinese stewartia. It has a more bushlike habit, with smaller flowers. *S. ovata* var. 'grandiflora', showy stewartia, is less common. This Georgia native is only 15 feet tall but has 4-inch white flowers with purple stamens. *S. ovata*, mountain stewartia, is also 15 feet tall. Tall stewartia, *S. monadelpha*, reaches up to 75 feet and is hardy to Zone 6. Virginia or silky stewartia, *S. malacodendron*, reaches 18 feet and is hardy only to Zone 7. Fairweather Gardens, a mail-order nursery located in Greenwich, New Jersey carries some of these unusual species.

Weeping Japanese Cherry

Prunus subhirtella 'Pendula'

When, Where, and How to Plant

Plant weeping Japanese cherry in late March or early April. Choose a sunny location with good drainage. The soil may require the addition of organic matter, such as leaf compost, during the soil preparation process. Add a 2:1 mixture of compost and sand to improve the soil aeration. Since root rot is an occasional problem, thorough soil preparation is important, especially in heavy clay soils. (See introduction for more planting information.)

Growing Tips

Water thoroughly at planting and whenever the soil gets dry. While these cherries need good drainage, they also do not want to dry out. Fertilizer is seldom necessary.

Care

Little pruning is required; but remove the occasional offending branch. You may want to enjoy some of the branches indoors. Pruning the branches straight across creates a very artificial look. If you must shorten the branches, vary the heights so that the tree retains a natural look. All flowering cherries are beautiful, and all struggle with a variety of pests. Watch out for tent caterpillars. Other problems include leaf spots, fall webworm, and peach scale. An application of organic mulch will help retain soil moisture and moderate soil temperatures.

Companion Planting and Design

These small and compact trees make them a natural for smaller yards and courtyards. Weepers do well as specimen trees where their graceful habit can be fully appreciated. They are lovely in all seasons and a good choice in places where you can have only one ornamental tree. Choose only low growing shrubs, ground covers, or early spring bulbs around the base. Since the graceful branches hang low, you do not want to detract from their charm.

Did You Know?

This variety was introduced from Japan in 1862. It is far more popular than the species. I once knew a family that was short on cash when it came time for their daughter's wedding. The date coincided with the blooming of the cherry trees. To decorate the tables, they pruned the cherry trees and arranged the branches as stunning centerpieces.

Its blizzard of small flowers in early spring and its ground-sweeping branches make the weeping Japanese cherry irresistible. Most trees are grown on tall, straight trunks as "standards." The weeping part is grafted onto the trunk about six feet up. Some plant people grow them on their own roots. 'Pendula' produces small black fruits that are tucked away under the leaves and therefore not very apparent, though the birds can always find them. Weeping Japanese cherries are not considered long-lived trees, but thirty to fifty years is a reasonable expectation. Foliage turns an attractive yellow to bronze in the autumn. In winter the arching branches, devoid of leaves, are like a work of modern art; their strong lines are woven together to create a compelling effect.

Other Common Names

Weeping Higan Cherry, Single Weeping Cherry

Bloom Period and Seasonal Color

Pale pink flowers in late April; yellow to bronze fall foliage.

Mature Height × Spread

15 to 30 ft. × 15 to 30 ft.

Vines *for New Jersey*

Vines add a new dimension to your garden. They can be manipulated in ways that woody ornamentals cannot. Vines are flexible in the most literal sense as well as in their usefulness. They can be trained over archways, up cinderblock walls, to screen an ugly view, or to draw attention to something beautiful.

A plant is defined as a vine by the way it grows. Vines can be woody, perennial, or annual. The key characteristic is that they need some sort of support to grow upright or they will ramble along the ground. Most vines continue to grow from the end in a long, continuous shoot. Some root along the way if left on the ground; this tendency can be useful for bank stabilization or erosion control. Sometimes small, sticky roots attach to walls. Some vines have tendrils with cuplike suction tips that are amazingly strong and hold the plant firmly. Others have curly tendrils that latch onto any support the vine touches. There are also twisting vines whose growing shoot spirals around whatever is holding it up. Finally, some vines have no way of attaching themselves and must be tied to a support.

What Are Your Goals?

Choosing the right vine requires a careful evaluation of your goal as well as the plant characteristics. Vines that cling by roots or suction cups may not be the best to climb up a wooden house as they might damage the surface and get under the siding. The same vines are fine growing up a wooden fence or covering a ramshackle shed. Vines with curling tendrils cling easily to a chain-link fence but have nothing with which to hold onto a cinderblock wall.

Clematis

If you are attempting to block a view, you may need an evergreen vine to keep it blocked all year long. While waiting for a woody or perennial vine to get big enough to do the job, plant a functional, attractive annual vine. Vines also have an important application in a small yard. They allow the use of vertical space to build diversity and character. The creative use of vines can turn tight quarters into an intimate nook.

Vines may produce flowers or fruits. For summer shade, plant pole beans or scarlet runner beans and get a harvest at the same time. Annual flowers that vine include morning glory and its close relative, moonflower. The cheerful black-eyed Susan vine, *Thunbergia alata*, grows thick and tall in a single season. It will be covered in dark-yellow flowers with black throats. Grape vines do triple duty. They provide thick cover for summer shade; if properly tended, they may produce a luscious crop of fruit; and stuffed grape leaves are a Greek and Lebanese delicacy.

Japanese Wisteria

Trellises present another set of variables. Use treated lumber so the trellises hold up for a while. Some trellises are now available in plastic, and under some circumstances, metal will work. Be wary of heavy wood vines. They twist and turn and get very interesting, but they can also pull down the trellis or wooden porch that holds them up. Wisteria will eventually "crush" a wooden support. It is a good example of a vine that benefits from a metal trellis. Metal pipes can be screwed together to make a very durable but unattractive support. Once vines are dense enough, the ugliness will not matter.

After all the practical aspects of growing vines have been appropriately weighed and measured, there is another very real benefit to consider: vines are "magical." As they wind up old wrought-iron gates and fences, they create an instant romantic aura. Is there anything more lovely than walking under an arch of climbing roses? In Frances Hodgson Burnett's *The Secret Garden*, it is vines that cover the long hidden door to the forbidden garden. And ivy-covered halls add character to any institution of higher learning. That is, after all, how schools became "Ivy League."

Caring for Vines

Choose, plant, and care for vines with all the careful discrimination you would use in planting anything else in your garden. Match the planting location to the growing requirements of the vine. In most cases you will want to purchase plants in containers to make getting your vines established as easy as possible. Some vines have aerial roots that make taking cuttings relatively easy, but that depends on the individual vine you choose. Growing from seed is slow and in some cases is avoided. For example, growing wisteria from seed may result in a plant that is extremely shy about producing flowers. You are better off with a cutting of a plant already proven to have satisfying flowering potential than risk years of growing time with no results.

If you want to propagate your own cuttings, do some research on the time of year and conditions necessary for the vine you have chosen, or just go and buy a container grown plant for almost instant (well, at least quicker) gratification. Amend the soil as determined by both the plant's needs and the existing conditions. That applies to fertilizer as well (see individual plant entries). Dig an extra large hole, plant at the same height as the plant was in the ground or container. Always removes wires, tags, ropes, string, and plastic burlap. Fill the hole around plant, tamp down gently but firmly, and water deeply. Then watch them grow. You will treasure them for their expressive personality and their enchanting qualities.

Clematis

Clematis hybrids

Clematis is grown primarily for its spectacular flowers. Up to eight inches in diameter, they are usually single but are sometimes double, in a wonderful range of colors. The large whites are stunning, but the bright colors are irresistible. The thin vines are brittle and somewhat delicate, but once established, they just keep growing. Some types bloom from their old wood in the spring and occasionally put out a bloom or two through the summer, but don't count on it. Others flower only on new growth in the summer and may bloom from July until frost; a few produce double flowers on old growth and single flowers on new. With the right collection of clematis, it is possible to have flowers all season, from spring until frost. The decorative seedpods of some varieties provide interest into the winter. Clematis provides vertical interest without taking up a lot of space.

Bloom Period and Seasonal Color
Flowers in a large range of colors, from spring to fall depending on the variety.

Mature Length
18 ft.

When, Where, and How to Plant
Plant in late March or early April. Clematis prefers sun on the leaves, but keep the roots in shade. Avoid very hot and wet areas. Clematis likes moist, well-drained soil with a thick layer of organic mulch. While not particular, they prefer a pH of 6 to 7.5, so a little lime may be beneficial; perform a soil test to be precise. Add lots of organic matter. Container plants establish most easily. Provide support that is thin enough for the tendrils to cling.

Growing Tips
Water at planting and whenever the soil gets dry, especially in hot weather. An application of 5-10-5 in early spring will encourage new growth and more flowers. Apply lime whenever pH dips below 6.

Care
Pruning can be tricky, and proper technique is dependent on variety. If you prune clematis that blooms on old wood in the early spring, the flowers will be gone for the year. Stem rot can be a problem. If the vine appears to be dead or dying, look for decay on the stem at the soil line. Control it by removing infected shoots below the soil line and treating the plant with an appropriate fungicide. (Read the fungicide label to be certain it is labeled for both the disease and the plant before spraying.) It is also subject to white fly, mites, scale, and borer although they are rarely serious. Check with your Cooperative Extension Service for current control measures.

Companion Planting and Design
Where clematis are not clinging to every vertical surface, a vine adorning a lamppost or mailbox can be lovely. But remember that there is room to expand one's horizons; clematis can grow up trellises and pergolas, gazebos and dead maples. Its slender vines soften the corner of your house or cover a chain-link fence.

Did You Know?
It's important to understand that dormant wood on clematis looks *very* dead. Even healthy stems are so brittle they tend to snap. Look for healthy buds. If you don't know the type of clematis you have, observe it carefully for a year. Wait to prune until you can see what is growing, and then you should be able to figure out if it is blooming on new growth or old.

Climbing Hydrangea
Hydrangea anomala ssp. *petiolaris*

When, Where, and How to Plant

Plant in early spring or early fall in full sun to part shade. Climbing hydrangea needs support but can cling to any rough surface with its aerial roots. Choose a spot where the plant can grow in rich, fertile soil that has an acidic to neutral pH. Add lots of organic matter, such as leaf compost, to the soil prior to planting. Newly transplanted climbing hydrangeas take several years to show much growth, but once the plants settle in, they will grow steadily and are worth waiting for. It is possible to propagate this vine by laying a side branch on the surface of potted soil. Secure it in place with a wire pin, and after it roots, the branch can be cut. Give the young plant some TLC in its container before transplanting, and you will have as many new plants as you desire.

Growing Tips

Water thoroughly at planting and whenever the soil gets dry, especially in hot, dry summer weather. A light application of 5-10-5 fertilizer in early spring encourages new growth.

Care

Once established, climbing hydrangea is a maintenance-free plant. It requires little pruning and has few, if any, insect or disease problems.

Companion Planting and Design

Climbing hydrangea can turn an ugly cinder-block wall into a vertical jungle of flowering vine. Plant it in tight spots to utilize vertical space or let it trail along the ground as a lovely ground cover. It will grow upwards when it runs into a suitable support. Plant with lacecap hydrangeas for a fabulous display or mix with ferns in a shady spot for a woodsy effect. Have it follow azaleas and rhododendrons to continue the magic and add oak leaf hydrangea for summer bloom.

Did You Know?

There has been some confusion between this species and *Schizophragma hydrangeoides*. They have a similar appearance, but the petals of the flowers on schizophragma are less showy, and its leaves are not as shiny. The hydrangea is considered the superior of the two plants.

The climbing hydrangea is a magnificent plant. It clings with small aerial roots that attach to any rough surface. It has the ability to grow quite large, up to seventy-five feet. The flower clusters are flat and up to eight inches across. They appear in late June and last about two weeks. The flowers are white with a light, pleasant scent. The branches extend from a wall in such a way that the plant has a layered look, which is particularly effective while the plant is in bloom. The leaves are usually heart-shaped, but quite wide, making them look almost round. They are dark green, extremely shiny, and very close together, giving a rich, lush appearance. The leaves stay green well into fall. The cinnamon red bark exfoliates on mature plants providing winter interest.

Bloom Period and Seasonal Color
Flat clusters of white flowers in late June to early July.

Mature Length
75 ft.

Fiveleaf Akebia

Akebia quinata

This deciduous vine has a number of appealing characteristics. It is a twining vine that needs support. The almost blue-green compound leaves are composed of five leaflets arranged "palmately," or like an umbrella, two to three inches across. Each leaflet is rounded with a notched tip, giving it an attractive, delicate appearance. The leaves persist late into fall but have no noticeable fall color. Each May, the vine produces small rosy-purple male flowers and one-inch eggplant-colored female flowers on the same flower spikes. The female flowers sometimes produce purple, edible fruits up to four inches long which ripen in September. This plant grows quickly with dense leaves and can become invasive in warmer climates, but it can be controlled by cutting it to the ground in late winter.

Other Common Name
Chocolate Vine

Bloom Period and Seasonal Color
Small purple male flowers and larger rosy female flowers in May.

Mature Length
40 ft.

When, Where, and How to Plant
Plant in late March or early April. Give this plant room to climb, and provide support to give the vine something to twine around. It does well in sun or shade but prefers rich, fertile soil. It is most useful for covering up a fence or ugly wall, and it can be magnificent growing up a dead tree. Avoid locating it near small plants that can be easily smothered. This plant can be divided or grown from seed or cuttings, although container-grown stock is recommended. Pinch repeatedly to encourage multiple stems for fullness. Add abundant organic matter, such as leaf compost, especially to poorer soils.

Growing Tips
Water at planting. Once it is established, water only when the ground is excessively dry. Fertilizer will only encourage rampant growth, so it is seldom necessary.

Care
The biggest maintenance chore with fiveleaf akebia is to prune it regularly to keep it from getting aggressive. It can be thinned routinely to keep it from becoming overwhelming, or you can simply cut it to the ground. It has no serious pest problems. Watch out for suckers that can pop up where you don't want them. The vine may require a little hand pollination to help it along if you want it to bear fruit. Simply tickle a bunch of different flowers with a soft artist's paintbrush to pollinate the female flowers. You can hum like a bee, if you think it will help.

Companion Planting and Design
This very fine foliage vine is useful for covering fences, walls, or trellises. As with all vines, take advantage of its ability to grow vertically. Use it to create magical garden "rooms" or to create a jungle feel in a tight space. Locate it where it will not smother smaller garden treasures.

Did You Know?
In the South, fiveleaf akebia is evergreen and is sometimes considered a weed. It grows far more slowly in cold-winter areas. The variegated form is slower, still. This is a very pretty vine and very useful, but choose your location carefully. New Jersey winters should be sufficient to contain this enthusiastic plant, but keep an eye on it and don't be afraid to prune it hard.

Japanese Wisteria
Wisteria floribunda

When, Where, and How to Plant
Plant in early spring or early fall. Wisteria will tolerate partial shade, but if you want flowers, drench the vines in sunlight. Prepare the soil, adding large quantities of organic matter. Deep, moist, well-drained loam will provide the best specimens in the long run. An application of lime will be beneficial. If you are planting in heavy clay, add a mixture of 2 parts organic matter and 1 part sand to the soil. Apply organic mulch to help retain soil moisture.

Growing Tips
Water thoroughly at planting and whenever the soil becomes dry. Fertilizer will encourage rampant growth and inhibit flower formation. Only fertilize if a soil test indicates the need.

Care
Failure to bloom is this plant's most frustrating problem. Root pruning sometimes jump-starts blooming. Prune vigorous shoots back to three or four buds and follow with an application of superphosphate. With luck, you will get flowers. Careful planning and guidance of the twining shoots can prevent these plants from wreaking havoc on your home. Prune immediately after bloom. Wisteria is susceptible to a variety of insects and diseases. Notches in the leaves may indicate that black vine weevil adults are feeding at night; this means the larvae are feeding on the roots as well. Scale can also be a problem. Check with your Cooperative Extension Service for current pesticides.

Companion Planting and Design
Twining wisteria vines are very powerful. Left unattended, it can strangle even an enormous shade tree. (The tree's ghost, dripping in flowers, is magnificent.) Metal pipe may be the best material for support, since wisteria can crush wood over time. You can also use severe pruning to develop a free-standing small tree. You will need to support the trunk, but not for long.

Did You Know?
Twining is Japanese wisteria's method of attachment. If you look closely, you will see it always twists in a clockwise direction. This is an identifying characteristic. Although very similar in appearance, Chinese wisteria can easily be distinguished from the Japanese species by its counter-clockwise twining.

Wisteria may be the queen of flowering vines. There is nothing that can top the splendor of a mature vine, twisted and gnarled, covered in trailing panicles of violet blooms that fill the air with an intoxicating scent. There comes a point when beauty touches a place that is not quite real, and wisterias can sometimes reach that place. Few species have the ability and even fewer specimens actually get there, but when they do, there is magic in the air. One of the biggest wisteria problems can be failure to bloom. Be sure to start with named cultivars rather than seedlings, and provide plenty of sun.

Bloom Period and Seasonal Color
Violet to white panicles in late April to early May.

Mature Length
30 ft. or more, depending on support

Kolomikta Vine
Actinidia kolomikta

Kolomikta vine is related to the fuzzy kiwi (grown mostly in New Zealand) and the hardy kiwi (grown both as an ornamental vine and for the small, smooth fruits similar to its fuzzy cousin). The foliage is about five inches long, emerges with a hint of purple, and matures dark green. The leaves of the male plant are particularly ornamental. It looks as if it was dipped into white paint and then pink. On some leaves just the very tip has color, while others are more than half pink. The color is graduated, with the deepest color along the edge. It is very beautiful. Female plants show some variegation, but not as pronounced. These twining vines will stay beautiful most of the year and produce an almost pest-free edible crop in the fall.

Bloom Period and Seasonal Color
Fragrant but inconspicuous white flowers in May and June; foliage variegated with white and pink.

Mature Length
20 ft.

When, Where, and How to Plant
Plant in early spring. In hotter climates, it requires shade to produce its color; in colder climates, it does best in full sun. It will produce the best color in soils high in lime, so add this during soil preparation. Kolomikta vine is flexible about soil type, but avoid wet ground. Since it is a twining vine, it needs something to hold. Kolomikta will grow from seed planted in the spring, but you will not be certain of the male-to-female ratio for some time. Cuttings taken in June are only moderately successful at rooting. Your best bet is to purchase container-grown material with the sex clearly identified.

Growing Tips
Water thoroughly at planting and during hot, dry weather. Don't be too quick to fertilize this vine, as excessive feeding may reduce variegation.

Care
Once the plant is big enough, you may be able to propagate it by layering. If pruning is necessary, it can be done at almost any time unless you are growing the plants for fruit production. Prune sparingly in early spring if you want small kiwis in the fall. *A. kolomikta* blooms and fruits on old wood. It is generally pest free.

Companion Planting and Design
Kolomikta vine produces fruits that resemble the hardy kiwi but are even smaller, about 1 inch. You should grow at least one male for every three to four females to ensure fruit set. The fruit will ripen in September and October. To get the best effect, consider alternating males and females. Kolomikta can cover a chain-link fence and with support can hide an ugly wall or block a view.

Did You Know?
According to the Oregon Extension Service, the fruit of *A. kolomikta* has 700 to 1000 mg. of Vitamin C per 100 grams of fruit. This is ten times higher than the amount of vitamin C in the fuzzy kiwi and twenty times higher than the amount in citrus.

Silver Lace Vine
Polygonum aubertii

When, Where, and How to Plant
Plant in early spring or early fall in a place that receives sun or just a little shade. This attractive vine needs something to twine around and is useful for covering an old fence. Since it clings loosely to its support, it is less likely than other vines to damage a porch or deck. It is a good choice for dry soils but is very adaptable to various soil conditions. Silver lace vine transplants easily. It can be propagated by dividing rhizomes in early spring; dig up a clump of roots and cut with a sharp knife. The larger the pieces you replant, the faster your vine will establish. Cuttings root easily, and plants are generally available in containers. There is nothing tricky about this one. If planted in spring, it will flower its first year.

Growing Tips
Water thoroughly at planting. Silver lace vine is drought tolerant once established. It grows so fast you may not want to fertilize unless soil conditions are very poor.

Care
Since it blooms on new wood, this plant can be pruned severely in early spring to control its high speed growth. It can even be cut to the ground, although such a practice will delay bloom significantly. The flies it attracts for pollination can be annoying, but they do no damage to the plant and are not worth controlling. Japanese beetles can be a problem, and they warrant control when you see them. Consult you local garden center or County Extension Service for the latest controls.

Companion Planting and Design
Growing a trellis over the front gate with silver lace vine would be lovely, or perhaps over the front steps. It can be very useful to cover a ramshackle shed or ugly fence.

Did You Know?
We have a silver lace vine at Blooming Acres. Its vines twine up the pergola to provide shade. It tolerates the abuse young children give it and blooms for an extended period with very little attention. The flies are annoying, but they do not overshadow this vine's beauty and function.

Silver lace vine is a rapidly-growing plant that produces copious flowers when not many woody ornamentals are in bloom. It can grow twenty-five to thirty feet its first year. The leaves emerge reddish-bronze but mature to a bright green, are almost heart-shaped, and are evergreen in the southern part of the plant's range. They have no noticeable fall color. The tiny flowers are truly lacelike. They cascade down the entire length of the vine, like lace "curtains" blowing in a breeze, and they have a slight, pleasant fragrance. This plant is pollinated by flies, so you may not want to plant it by an outside dining table. Silver lace vine is accepting of city conditions and is also recommended for the shore area.

Other Common Names
Silver Fleece Vine, Silvervine, Fleeceflower, China Fleece Vine, Mile-a-Minute Vine

Bloom Period and Seasonal Color
Off-white flowers, July to frost.

Mature Length
35 ft.

Places to Go of Horticultural Interest

Cape May County Gardens

http://www.capemaytimes.com/nature/gardens.htm

Cape May Bird Observatory Backyard Habitat Garden

This gorgeous garden demonstrates how to create wonderful backyard habitat for butterflies and birds that looks great! During the summer and early fall, butterflies cover every flower in sight. Free. Daily 10:00 A.M. to 5:00 P.M., Cape May Bird Observatory Center for Research and Education, Route 47, Goshen 609-861-0700

Hereford Inlet Lighthouse Garden

For inspiration and location, the perennial and herb gardens at Hereford Inlet can't be beat. Right on the edge of the sea, hollyhocks and hydrangea in the summer and asters in the fall surround the picturesque lighthouse. Free. Daily, 9:00 A.M. to 5:00 P.M., Hereford Inlet Lighthouse, Anglesea, North Wildwood, 609-522-4520

Leamings Run

The largest annual garden in the United States is right here in Cape May County. The red sage and cardinal flowers draw in the hummingbirds in August and early September. Admission fee. Daily, 9:30 A.M. to 5:00 P.M. until October 20. 1845 Route 9 North, Cape May Court House (609) 465-5871

The Frelinghuysen Arboretum

Headquarters of the Morris County Park Commission
53 East Hanover Avenue,
P.O. Box 1295
Morristown, NJ 07962-1295
973-326-7600

http://www.parks.morris.nj.us/parks/frelarbmain.htm

Open year-round 8:00 A.M. to dusk except for Thanksgiving, Christmas, and New Year's Day. The Frelinghuysen Arboretum 127 acres featuring a magnificent Colonial Revival mansion, the woodlands, meadows, beautiful gardens, and distinctive collections of trees and shrubs. The Frelinghuysen Arboretum is also a regional center for horticultural activities, including educational programs and a comprehensive collection of botanical literature.

The Gardens at Duke Farms

80 Route 206 South
Hillsborough, NJ 08844
908-243-3600

http://fdncenter.org/grantmaker/dorisduke/dukefarms.html

Greenhouse gardens open afternoons from September through May with the exception of Thanksgiving, Christmas, and New Year's Day. Reservations suggested for individuals and required for groups. The Grounds are open year round but vary seasonally. Advance reservations required. Admission Fee. Italian, English, Colonial, French, Chinese, Japanese, Indo-Persian, Jungle habitat, and desert environments make up the individual greenhouse displays. The Grounds include over 700 acres with both landscape and architectural features developed throughout the 20th century.

Howell Living History Farm

101 Hunter Rd.
Titusville, NJ 08560
609-737-3299
FAX 609-737-6524
http://www.howellfarm.com/index.htm

Open Saturdays 10:00 A.M.–4:00 P.M., programs from 11:00 A.M.–3:00 P.M. Open Sundays
Noon–4:00 P.M., April through November for self-guided tours only. Open weekdays 10:00 A.M.–4:00 P.M.
February through November Tuesday–Friday Closed on Mercer County holidays; Easter. Free admission
and parking. Fee for Children's Crafts, and Maze. Reservations required for groups only.

Howell Living History Farm takes you back to the turn of the last century. You can help plant or
harvest crops, tend the animals, make soap, or shell corn and bake cornbread.

Morven

55 Stockton Street
Princeton, NJ 08540
609-683-4495
FAX 609-683-3740
http://www.historicmorven.org/index.html

Grounds open May through October. Call for hours and garden tours. Gardens include entrance lawn,
Colonial Revival-style garden, and the Horse Chestnut walk. Parts of the Georgian style house pre-date
the Revolution. Morven has been home to a signer of the Declaration of Independence, five Governors,
and hosted President John F. Kennedy, Princess Grace, and Fidel Castro.

The New Jersey Botanical Garden at Skylands

Skylands Association
P.O. Box 302
Morris Road
Ringwood, NJ 07456
973-962-7527 or 973-962-9534
Fax 973-962-1553
E-mail info@njbg.org
http://www.njbg.org/contact.html

Skylands' gardens are open from 8:00 A.M. to 8:00 P.M. every day. Entrance to the gardens is free. On
weekends from Memorial Day through Labor Day, there is a modest parking charge. The Gardens consist
of the 96 acres which surround the Tudor-style manor house built in 1922. The botanical showplace was
developed by Mr. Clarence Lewis with design assistance from prominent landscape architects of the time.
Mr. Lewis spent over thirty years collecting plants from around the world to showcase in his gardens.

The New Jersey Museum of Agriculture

103 College Farm Rd.
North Brunswick, NJ 08902
732-249-2077
FAX 732-247-1035
http://agriculturemuseum.org

The Museum is open to the general public Tuesday through Saturday 10:00 A.M. until 5:00 P.M., and Select Sundays. Small admission fee. The Museum is closed on Mondays, Easter, Fourth of July, Thanksgiving Day, Christmas Eve, Christmas Day, New Year's Eve, and New Year's Day. On Mondays, the Museum's business office is open as most staff are at work.

The Museum's modern 30,000 square feet building is surrounded by the Cook College research farm. It contains permanent and changing exhibitions about the evolution of agriculture from New Jersey's first farmers—the Lenape Indians—to the present and future. The Museum maintains an extensive collection of historic agricultural artifacts second in importance and scope only to that of the Smithsonian Institution.

Presby Memorial Iris Garden

474 Upper Mountain Avenue
Upper Montclair, NJ 07043
973-783-5974
FAX 973-783-3833
http://community.nj.com/cc/presbyiris

Open mid-May through mid-June daily 10:00 A.M. to 8:00 P.M. Free admission but donations accepted. The Presby Memorial Iris Gardens opened 1927. The gardens feature over 2,000 varieties of irises, some from 1500s. Some rebloom in September or October. The Victorian Garden by the house is on display at all times. During the iris season, the gift area is open with irises and other gardening items available. An unidentified bag of six rhizomes can be reserved for $15.

Reeves-Reed Arboretum

165 Hobart Avenue
Summit, New Jersey 07901
908-273-8787
Fax 908-273-6869
http://www.reeves-reedarboretum.org

Open 7 days, year-round, from dawn till dusk. The Reeves-Reed Arboretum is 5$1/2$ acres of formal gardens including a trademark daffodil display, rose gardens, a rock garden, azaleas, a butterfly walk and a 100-year-old home available for rent.

Rudolf W. van der Goot Rose Garden at Colonial Park

    Somerset County Park Commission

    Horticulture Department

    Colonial Park (Lot A)

    156 Mettlers Road

    Somerset, NJ 08873

    732-873-2459

    Fax 732-873-3896

    http://www.park.co.somerset.nj.us

Open 8:00 A.M. to sunset (Daily but closed Wednesdays until noon). The Rudolf W. van der Goot Rose Garden is one acre in size and contains more than 3,000 roses of 325 varieties. As an accredited All-America Rose Selections (AARS) display garden, it is entitled to display AARS award-winning roses one year before their release to the public.

The Rutgers Gardens

    Cook College, Rutgers University

    112 Ryders Lane

    New Brunswick, NJ 08901

    732-932-8451

    Fax 732-932-7060

    http://aesop.rutgers.edu/~rugardens/

Open year round during daylight hours. The Rutgers Gardens cover over fifty acres just off of Ryders Lane in New Brunswick. The Gardens contain many collections including the Donald B. Lacey Display Garden, American Hollies of the World, The Rhododendron and Azalea Garden, and more. The Gardens adjoin the lovely virgin forest of Helyar Woods and feature the Log Cabin which is available to the public for special events on a seasonal basis.

Van Vleck House and Gardens

    21 Van Vleck Street

    Montclair, NJ

    973-744-0837

    http://www.vanvleck.org

Gardens open to the public April 15 through October 31 10:00 A.M. to 5:00 P.M. daily. The Van Vleck House and Gardens includes 5.8 acres of home and gardens. The house was built in 1916 in the style of a Mediterranean villa, and the gardens feature ericaceous plants, primarily rhododendrons and azaleas.

More on Rhododendrons

Name	Hardiness Zone	Height × Width	Color
Large Leaved Evergreen Rhododendrons (Elepidotes)			
Hybrids			
Cadis	-15°F	5' × 5'	Pink/Lavender Yellow
Calsap	-25°F	5' × 3'	White with Maroon Blotch
Capistrano	-15°F	4' × 5'	Yellow
Caroline	-20°F	5' × 5'	Light Orchid Pink
Catawbiense Grandiflorum	-25°F	5' × 4'	Blue/Lavendar
Catawbiense Album	-25°F	5' × 4'	White/Yellow Flare
Fantastica	-15°F	4' × 3'	Red with White Center
Ingrid Mehlquist	-20°F	2' × 4'	White
Janet Blair	-20°F	5' × 5'	Soft pink with hint of Pale Lavender
Ken Janeck	-25°F	3' × 5'	Apple Blossom Pink/White
Maximum Roseum	-25°F	6' × 4'	Light Pink/Orchid
Mist Maiden	-25°F	3' × 5'	Apple Blossom Pink/White
Nova Zembla	-20°F	5' × 4'	Red/Hint of Blue
Pearce's American Beauty	-20°F	6' × 4'	Rose Pink
Roseum Elegans	-25°F	5' × 4'	Lavender Pink
Scintillation	-15°F	5' × 4'	Pink
Solidarity	-15°F	5' × 5'	Pink
Tom Everitt	-15°F	6' × 5'	Luminous Pink
Wyandanch Pink	-25°F	6' × 4'	Pink
Yaku Prince	-10°F	3' × 4'	Pink
Species			
R. fortunei	-15°F	6' × 4'	Pink
R. maximum	-25°F	6' × 5'	Pink and White Forms
R. metternichii	-15°F	3' × 4'	Pink
R. yakusimanum	-15°F	2' × 3'	Apple Blossom Pink
Small Leaved Evergreen Rhododendrons (Lepidotes)			
Hybrids			
Dora Amateis	-15°F	4' × 3'	White
Faisa	-20°F	4' × 3'	Lavender Blue
Ginny Gee	-15°F	1' × 2'	Apple Blossom Pink
Mary Fleming	-15°F	4' × 4'	Yellow/Touch of Pink
Olga Mezitt	-20°F	5' × 4'	Bright Pink
Pikeland	-15°F	2' × 3'	Apple Blossom Pink
Pioneer Silvery Pink	-15°F	5' × 3'	Pink
PJM Group	-25°F	5' × 3'	Lavender Purple
Weston's Aglo	-20°F	5' × 4'	Pink
Weston's Pink Diamond	-20°F	5' × 3'	Pink
Wyanokie	-20°F	5' × 4'	White

Name	Hardiness Zone	Height × Width	Color
Small Leaved Evergreen Rhododendrons (Lepidotes) *(continued)*			
Species			
R. dauricum	-25°F	4' × 3'	Bright Lavender Purple
R. keiskei	-15°F	2' × 3'	Light Yellow
R. minus v. *carolinianum*	-20°F	5' × 3'	Pink to White
R. mucronulatum	-25°F	5' × 3'	Pink/Lavender/White
Deciduous Azaleas (Drops Leaves in Winter)			
Hybrids			
Gilbraltar	-20°F	6' × 4'	Orange
Klondyke	-20°F	6' × 4'	Yellow
Marydel	-10°F	4' × 6'	Pink
Northern Lights Group	-30°F	5' × 5'	Various colors
Weston Hybrid Group	-20°F	Varies	Various colors
Species			
R. arborescens	-15°F	5' × 5'	White to Pale Pink
R. atlanticum	-20°F	3' × 5'	White
R. calendulaceum	-20°F	6' × 8'	Yellow to Gold to Red
R. canescens	-15°F	6' × 3'	White to Pink
R. periclymenoides	-20°F	3' × 4'	Pink
R. schlippenbachii	-25°F	6' × 6'	Pink or White
R. vaseyi	-20°F	6' × 4'	Pink or White
R. viscosum	-20°F	6' × 4'	White or Pink
Evergreen Azaleas			
Hybrids			
Ben Morrison	-10°F	4' × 5'	Orange Center, White Edge
Elsie Lee	-15°F	5' × 4'	Lavender
Garden State Glow	-10°F	4' × 4'	Rose
Girard's Hot Shot	-15°F	4' × 4'	Orange Red
Hardy Gardenia	-10°F	4' × 4'	White
Herbert	-15°F	4' × 4'	Purple
Helen Curtis	-15°F	3' × 4'	White
Hino-Crimson	-10°F	4' × 4'	Red
Koromo Shikibu	-10°F	3' × 5'	Lavender
Linda Stuart	-10°F	5' × 3'	White Center, Pink Edge
Nancy of Robinhill	-10°F	3' × 4'	Pink
Opal	-5°F	3' × 3'	Lavender/Pink
Stewartstonian	-10°F	5' × 4'	Red
Species			
R. kiusianum	-15°F	2' × 4'	Various, White, Lavender, Pink, Red

Developed by Hank Schannen, Rare Find Nursery, Jackson, New Jersey. Reprinted with permission. **http://www.rarefindnursery.com**

Growing with Blooming Acres

An Array of Roses and Pansies

Our home, Blooming Acres, once laid claim to being the smallest farm in the Farmland Preservation Program in our state. It is just shy of ten acres. The view out our front door is of a cornfield as far as the eye can see, which on occasion gifts the viewer with a perfect double rainbow. The soils are rich and deep. For many years the farms for miles around produced potatoes, a crop which demands only the best ground for growing. Our home is full of growth and change and new life all the time. There are moments when we are moved by the breathtaking beauty of a rose-colored sunset or the donkeys silhouetted in the pasture. The day the baby goats came into the world is a most precious memory. It's easy to think that we have cornered a tiny piece of heaven, but sometimes that feeling is tested.

The land here is flat, almost like a pancake, with the exception of a small hill beyond the western edge of the farm. The wind whipping across the flat terrain is brutal during winter snow shoveling or early spring pruning. It penetrates all the layers we can wear and chills right to the bone. In summer, the constant blowing is a relief to the sun beating down because there is hardly enough shade for a mouse. It also keeps the insects away.

Starting From Scratch

In our first year on the farm, one of our first projects was to plant trees. Having just purchased the farm without yet selling our previous home, there was no cash for tree shopping. We had an older gentleman friend, Lou, who knew someone who had planted thousands of seedlings of deciduous trees and evergreens. They almost all took, but unfortunately they were growing only about three inches apart. We were invited to take all we wanted; they were desperate to get some of them out of there. So off we went to dig and haul. If plants could cry, this field of trees was gently weeping. They were so crowded that they had stretched out with huge gaps between each side branch. A single scoop no more than a spade's width would pull out three or four trees and damage several more to either side. It took careful scanning of the trees to find those with the best chances of survival. After making our choices, we had to dig each tree out so that it came away in the middle of the clump, carefully pruning away the ones on the sides so as not to disturb the roots of the targeted tree.

I felt a bit cruel killing off so many to save a few, but these trees would have killed themselves completely within another growing season. We salvaged five tuliptrees to plant along the road. I had always admired the straight, regal trunks of tuliptrees, the unusual and interesting leaves, and the tuliptree's spring flowers. (Don't expect too much from the blooms. The trees are fairly large by the time they produce flowers so they are a bit lost up in the branches.) I knew the beautiful yellow autumn color could bring another element of beauty, but it was doubtful that these pathetic trees would ever amount to much of anything. We kept our fingers crossed anyway, watered faithfully, and went back to conquer more.

The evergreens we saw consisted of mostly Norway spruce and white pine. "Spindly" would be about the only word to describe these specimens, and that would be kind. They were each about five feet tall, with a tuft of green on the top, and maybe three or four other tufts here and there. We planted them in clusters in the back field and used a few to extend an evergreen row that marked the edge of the property and the vacant lot that adjoined it. They looked exactly like Charlie Brown's Christmas tree before his friends decorated it. Many of the evergreens didn't make it, but quite a few did.

Years before purchasing Blooming Acres, I had been given a contorted white pine as a gift from Conover Nurseries in East Brunswick. It wasn't much more than a rooted cutting in a six-inch pot, but the twisted needles were fascinating. At that time, I thought I was about to move to a different house and had planted it in the front yard. When the deal fell through, I went back to dig it up again. The little tree lived in an oak tub for about five years and got to be about two feet tall and very full. We planted it at Blooming Acres while the house was empty. It was early fall, a good time for planting. The only deer damage we have ever suffered occurred that fall. A deer came right up to that little tree and ate all the green of one year's circlet of branches. This poor little tree that had been pampered to survive in a container finally had its first crack at being a real tree, and it got eaten! Once we moved in, the deer never returned, but it took about five years before the gap was sufficiently hidden by abundant healthy growth. It has now reached about twenty feet and is a beauty all year long, but especially in winter with a dusting of snow. It is during the grayest of seasons when the competition is low that visitors notice the unusual contorted needles. This is when the white pine's subtle elegance can be best appreciated.

As we meander through the many, many trees and shrubs scattered about today, I always smile as I stand in the shade of tall tuliptrees or admire the naturalized look of the random evergreens in the field. They may not be the most unique plants on the farm, or even the most perfect, but they are all treasured because they were planted with the most heart.

An Unexpected Guest

Full of Surprises

Another early project was the planting of one hundred feet of rose-of-Sharons as a border planting on the south edge. These summer flowering small trees are amazingly generous with the number of flowers they produce with only a minimum of attention. However, crammed into a tight space, they create a nightmare of seedlings and outlandish growth. It becomes a never ending battle to keep them from looking like a really bad hair day, but used along the property border, about one-hundred-fifty feet from the house, they can be as enthusiastic as they want. The seedlings only help fill in the gaps, and a tangled mess of branches covered in summer flowers is a problem everyone should have. We received buckets of seedlings from my boss and dear friend Tony Marano, then general manager of WCTC 1450 AM, the station where I broadcast "The Garden Show." The seedlings were four to five feet tall and straight up. That's how they grow when all the seeds germinate in one spot. It was one of those years when winter's chill switched over to a tropical heat wave in the blink of an eye. In early May, it was over

90 degrees Fahrenheit, and we were trying to plant about thirty-five bare-root trees. The heat was brutal, and the poor wilted things didn't look like they stood much of a chance. It is a testimony to their durability that just about every one survived. Over the years, one has died out here and there, but there are always plenty of seedlings to fill in the gaps. These plants cannot lay claim to being refined or elegant. They are more like colorful but ragtag gypsies that do what they please but with definite style.

The year of the gladiolus was another event to remember. It is possible to order many kinds of bulbs in bulk at a significant discount per bulb. In our case we had to figure out what to do with one thousand gladiolus bulbs. Two hundred immediately went to a friend, leaving only eight hundred bulbs to plant. The plan was to plant one hundred every week for eight weeks, starting at the beginning of May. We did pretty well the first few weeks, then skipped a week or so, and, ended up planting four hundred in mid-July, which is just about the latest time you can plant. Even with that, the several varieties of the last planting came into bloom at different times so the display throughout the season was nothing short of spectacular. To be able to visit friends with enormous armfuls of gladiolus in every imaginable color was glorious. And these cuttings didn't even make a dent in the show.

Digging and storing all these bulbs was just too daunting a task. My dear friend Lou had always left his glads in the ground with almost continual success, so we cut back the leaves and mulched a bit and just took our chances. Well, they all came back. The great revelation came like a shock when we realized that all eight hundred were going to bloom at just about the same time. We did not have the advantage of even an imperfect staggered planting. For about three weeks, the number of blooms was amazing. Then all at once they were done—finis! It did seem rather sad after all that color. Years later a few glads continued to pop up here and there, but the last few seemed to have succumbed to the evil winter of February 2003. We are due to replace them but will probably stick to the one- to two-hundred range. That should be plenty.

A Place in My Heart

No tree or shrub gets planted at Blooming Acres without a good reason. It has to have something special to earn a spot. Flowers are always acceptable, of course, but weeping, twisting, outrageous fall color or even beautiful bark can all be a qualifier. In the case of the weeping mulberry, it is strictly sentiment, as it has a special place in my heart. Most people think of them as weeds, but the ripe berries are yummy if you can tolerate the very persistent green stems. Even so, people don't usually plant them; they just ignore them and let them grow.

In my youth, it was the magic of the weeping mulberry that became my sanctuary. As a small child, I was a bit lost as the youngest of eight children. My closest sibling was a brother five years older. It is not hard to understand how growing up with five older brothers can be tough on a little girl. Carving out my own space was nearly impossible. Under the weeping mulberry, in the tiny cavern created by the arching branches that reach all the way to the ground, a small person can be safe in her own little world. I remember shafts of light would filter through the leaves, and there was the extra bonus of eating as much of its fruit as I could hold, while staining my fingers purple. Countless hours were spent under that tree, and I can never see one without smiling and remembering.

The Weeping Mulberry, a Sentimental Favorite

Years later I wrote about this experience in my newspaper column and made copies for all my siblings. My oldest brother, Barry, read it in my presence and asked if I had taken the story from his book. It was as though he had stabbed me in the heart! These were my personal, private memories on paper! But there in his book, was his telling of the same story, his version of the same magic, under the same tree twenty years earlier.

Finding a weeping mulberry for Blooming Acres was no small task. It took about five years, and then the one we planted was a male tree that would bear no fruit. I had wanted my children to capture the same joy, but it seems the messiness of the fruit impacted them more than the sweetness. Only male (and thus fruitless) trees are readily available, and even those are few and far between. Recently I bought one tied with a pink ribbon, optimistically hoping that pink indicated it was a female. But, alas, I was wrong.

In spite of the lack of berries, the first tree is a beauty now. I don't think the kids ever needed the sanctuary like I did; however, the dogs appreciate the cool shade on a hot summer day. It is a sight to see them stick their heads through the branches when they need to check out a car in the drive or investigate a noise. Meanwhile, I look at the tree and think I can hear my mother calling, and I remember the sweet juicy fruits.

A Work in Progress

In the spring at Blooming Acres the many lilacs scent the air with romance, while lilies add their fragrance in the heat of summer. There is one snowdrop plant in the window well that is the first to flower every year, and the Franklinia is probably the latest to bloom in the fall. We failed about five times to establish a crapemyrtle as the focal point in the front yard. The winter wind was just too much. There are four now, all well established, but each is tucked into a nook to protect it from the harsher weather. The Harry Lauder's walking stick was the first to join the contorted white pine in being twisted, but now you can find the weeping Norway spruce, the weeping European beech, the corkscrew willow, the fantail pussy willow, and even a fabulous contorted mulberry to entice us out in the winter.

Rhododendrons are lacking since we are still mostly in blazing sun, but the tuliptrees have grown enough to start a few rhodies in their shade. Roses come and go. They don't like the winter wind much either. We don't have the time to wrap each one so they have to take their chances. The kousa dogwood marks the grave of Tasha, the most wonderful dog friend that ever put paws on this earth, and a weeping pussy willow marks the place where lots of kitties rest. We have planted a Christmas tree each year we have lived here. Not all made it through the stress of an indoor holiday followed by midwinter planting, but most did.

Blooming Acres is a work in progress and is no longer a blank canvas. It's not perfect or finished and probably never will be. It holds doorways for us with peeks at the past and the future, and it is a place to grow.

Glossary

Alkaline soil: soil with a pH greater than 7.0. It lacks acidity, often because it has limestone in it.

All-purpose fertilizer: powdered, liquid, or granular fertilizer with a balanced proportion of the three key nutrients—nitrogen (N), phosphorus (P), and potassium (K). It is suitable for maintenance nutrition for most plants.

Annual: a plant that lives its entire life in one season. It is genetically determined to germinate, grow, flower, set seed, and die the same year.

Balled and burlapped: describes a tree or shrub grown in the field whose rootball was wrapped with protective burlap and twine when the plant was dug up to be sold or transplanted.

Bare root: describes plants that have been packaged without any soil around their roots. (Often young shrubs and trees purchased through the mail arrive with their exposed roots covered with moist peat or sphagnum moss, sawdust, or similar material, and wrapped in plastic.)

Barrier plant: a plant that has intimidating thorns or spines and is sited purposely to block foot traffic or other access to the home or yard.

Beneficial insects: insects or their larvae that prey on pest organisms and their eggs. They may be flying insects, such as ladybugs, parasitic wasps, praying mantis, and soldier bugs, or soil dwellers such as predatory nematodes, spiders, and ants.

Berm: a narrow raised ring of soil around a tree, used to hold water so it will be directed to the root zone. Also a large mound or small hill of soil, used as an alternative to a fence, generally planted with ornamentals for both privacy and beauty.

Bract: a modified leaf structure on a plant stem near its flower that resembles a petal. Often it is more colorful and visible than the actual flower, as in dogwood.

Bud union: the place where the top of a plant was grafted to the rootstock; often refers to roses.

Canopy: the overhead branching area of a tree, usually referring to its extent including foliage.

Cold hardiness: the ability of a perennial plant to survive the winter cold in a particular area.

Composite: a flower that is actually composed of many tiny flowers. Typically, they are flat clusters of tiny, tight florets, sometimes surrounded by wider-petaled florets. Composite flowers are highly attractive to bees and beneficial insects.

Compost: organic matter that has undergone progressive decomposition until it is reduced to a spongy, fluffy texture. Added to soil of any type, it improves the soil's ability to hold air and water and to drain well. It also increases the soils ability to hold nutrients.

Corm: the swollen energy-storing structure, analogous to a bulb, under the soil at the base of the stem of plants such as crocus and gladiolus.

Crown: the base of a plant at, or just beneath, the surface of the soil where the roots meet the stems.

Cultivar: a CULTIvated VARiety. It is a naturally occurring form of a plant that has been identified as special or superior and is purposely selected for propagation and production.

Deadhead: a pruning technique that removes faded flower heads from plants to improve their appearance, abort seed production, and stimulate further flowering.

Deciduous plants: unlike evergreens, these trees and shrubs lose their leaves in the fall.

Desiccation: drying out of foliage tissues, usually due to drought or wind.

Division: the practice of splitting apart plants to create several smaller-rooted segments. It is commonly used on perennials, bulbs and some shrubs. The practice is useful for controlling the plant's size and for acquiring more plants; it is also essential to the health and continued flowering of certain ones.

Dormancy: the period, usually the winter, when perennial plants temporarily cease active growth and rest. Some plants have their natural dormancy period in summer.

Established: the point at which a newly planted tree, shrub, or flower is growing at a healthy rate, with good color, expected flower and fruit production for its age, and tolerance for its environment. This is an indication that the roots have recovered from transplant shock and have to grown sufficiently to support continued growth.

Evergreen: perennial plants that do not lose their foliage annually with the onset of winter. Needled or broadleaf foliage will persist and continues to function on a plant through one or more winters, aging and dropping unobtrusively in cycles of three or four years or more.

Foliar: of or about foliage—usually refers to the practice of spraying foliage, as in fertilizing or treating with insecticide; leaf tissues absorb liquid directly for fast results, and the soil is not affected.

Floret: a tiny flower, usually one of many forming a cluster, that comprises a single blossom.

Germinate: to sprout. Germination is a fertile seed's first stage of development.

Graft (union): the point on the stem of a woody plant with sturdier roots where a stem from a highly ornamental plant is inserted so that it will join with it. Roses are commonly grafted.

Hardscape: the permanent, structural, nonplant part of a landscape, such as walls, sheds, pools, patios, arbors, and walkways.

Herbaceous: plants having fleshy or soft stems that die back with frost; the opposite of "woody."

Hybrid: a plant that is the result of intentional or natural cross-pollination between two or more plants of the same species or genus.

Low water demand: describes plants that tolerate dry soil for varying periods of time. Typically, they have succulent, hairy, or silvery-gray foliage and tuberous roots or taproots.

Mulch: a layer of material over bare soil to protect it from erosion and compaction by rain, and to discourage weeds. It may be inorganic (gravel, fabric) or organic (wood chips, bark, pine needles, chopped leaves).

Naturalize: (*a*) to plant seeds, bulbs, or plants in a random, informal pattern as they would appear in their natural habitat; (*b*) to adapt to and spread throughout adopted habitats (a tendency of some nonnative plants).

Nectar: the sweet fluid produced by glands on flowers that attract pollinators such as hummingbirds and honeybees for whom it is a source of energy.

Organic material, organic matter: any material or debris that is derived from plants. It is carbon-based material capable of undergoing decomposition and decay.

Peat moss: organic matter from peat sedges (United States) or sphagnum mosses (Canada), often used to improve soil texture. The acidity of sphagnum peat moss makes it ideal for boosting or maintaining soil acidity while also improving its drainage.

Perennial: a flowering plant that lives over two or more seasons. Many die back with frost, but their roots survive the winter and generate new shoots in the spring.

pH: a measurement of the relative acidity (low pH) or alkalinity (high pH) of soil or water based on a scale of 1 to 14, 7 being neutral. Individual plants require soil to be within a certain range so that nutrients can dissolve in moisture and be available to them.

Pinch: to remove tender stems and/or leaves by pressing them between thumb and forefinger. This pruning technique encourages branching, compactness, and flowering in plants, or it removes aphids clustered at growing tips.

Pollen: the yellow, powdery grains in the center of a flower. A plant's male sex cells, they are transferred to the female plant parts by means of wind or animal pollinators to fertilize them and create seeds.

Raceme: an arrangement of single stalked flowers along an elongated, unbranched axis.

Rhizome: a swollen energy-storing stem structure, similar to a bulb, that lies horizontally in the soil, with roots emerging from its lower surface and growth shoots from a growing point at or near its tip, as in bearded iris.

Rootbound (or potbound): the condition of a plant that has been confined in a container too long, its roots having been forced to wrap around themselves and even swell out of the container. Successful transplanting or repotting requires untangling and trimming away of some of the matted roots.

Root flare: the transition at the base of a tree trunk where the bark tissue begins to differentiate and roots begin to form just before entering the soil. This area should not be covered with soil when planting a tree.

Self-seeding: the tendency of some plants to sow their seeds freely around the yard. It creates many seedlings the following season that may or may not be welcome.

Semi-evergreen: tending to be evergreen in a mild climate but deciduous in a rigorous one.

Shearing: the pruning technique whereby plant stems and branches are cut uniformly with long-bladed pruning shears (hedge shears) or powered hedge trimmers. It is used when creating and maintaining hedges and topiary.

Slow release fertilizer or Slow-acting fertilizer: fertilizer that is water insoluble and therefore releases its nutrients gradually as a function of soil temperature, moisture, and related microbial activity. Typically granular, it may be organic or synthetic.

Succulent growth: the sometimes undesirable production of fleshy, water-storing leaves or stems that results from overfertilization.

Sucker: a new growing shoot. Underground plant roots produce suckers to form new stems and spread by means of these suckering roots to form large plantings, or colonies. Some plants produce root suckers or branch suckers as a result of pruning or wounding.

Tuber: a type of underground storage structure in a plant stem, analogous to a bulb. It generates roots below and stems above ground (example: dahlia).

Variegated: having various colors or color patterns. The term usually refers to plant foliage that is streaked, edged, blotched, or mottled with a contrasting color, often green with yellow, cream, or white.

White grubs: fat, off-white, wormlike larvae of several types of beetles the most common of which is the Japanese beetle. They reside in the soil and feed on plant (especially grass) roots until summer when they emerge as beetles to feed on plant foliage.

Wings: (*a*) the corky tissue that forms edges along the twigs of some woody plants such as winged euonymus; (*b*) the flat, dried extension of tissue on some seeds, such as maple, that catch the wind and help them disseminate.

Bibliography

Anglade, Pierre, ed. *Larousse Gardening and Gardens.* New York, NY: Facts on File, Inc., 1990.

Bailey, L.H. *The Standard Cyclopedia of Horticulture.* New York, NY: The MacMillan Company, MacMillan & Co., Ltd., 1922.

Barton, Barbara J. *Gardening by Mail.* Boston, MA: Houghton Mifflin Company, Tucker Press, 1997.

Beales, Peter. *Classic Roses.* New York, NY: Holt, Rinehart and Winston, 1985.

Bradley, Fern Marshall, and Barbara W. Ellis, eds. *Rodale's All-New Encyclopedia of Organic Gardening.* Emmaus, PA: Rodale Press, 1992.

Bubel, Nancy. *The New Seed Starter's Handbook.* Emmaus, PA: Rodale Press, 1988.

Burrell, C. Colston, et. al. *Treasury of Gardening.* Lincolnwood, IL: Publications International, Ltd., 1994.

Clausen, Ruth Rogers, and Nicolas H. Ekstrom. *Perennials for American Gardens.* New York, NY: Random House, 1989.

Coon, Nelson. *Using Wild and Wayside Plants.* New York, NY: Dover Publications, Inc., 1980.

Cox, Jeff, and Marilyn Cox. *The Perennial Garden.* Emmaus, PA: Rodale Press, 1985.

Crockett, James Underwood, and the editors of Time-Life Books. *Annuals.* New York, NY: Henry Holt and Company, 1971.

—. *Bulbs.* New York, NY: Henry Holt and Company, 1971.

Crockett, James Underwood, Oliver E. Allen, and the editors of Time-Life Books. *Wildflower Gardening.* New York, NY: Henry Holt and Company, 1977.

Cutler, Sandra McLean. *Dwarf & Unusual Conifers Coming of Age.* North Olmsted, OH: Barton-Bradley Crossroads Pub. Co., 1997.

Dirr, Michael. *Manual of Woody Landscape Plants.* Champaign, IL: Stipes Publishing Co., 1983.

Dobelis, Inge N., ed. *Reader's Digest Magic and Medicine of Plants.* Pleasantville, NY: The Reader's Digest Association, Inc., 1986.

Durant, Mary. *Who Named the Daisy.* New York, NY: Congdon & Weed, Inc., 1976.

Elias, Thomas S. *The Complete Trees of North America.* New York, NY: Times Mirror Magazines, Inc., Book Division, Van Nostrand Reinhold Company, 1980.

Ernst, Ruth Shaw. *The Naturalist's Garden.* Emmaus, PA: Rodale Press, 1987.

Gardner, JoAnn. *The Heirloom Garden.* Pownal, VT: Storey Communications, Inc., 1992.

Harlow, William M., and Ellwood S. Harrar. *Textbook of Dendrology.* New York, NY: McGraw-Hill Book Company, 1958.

Heriteau, Jacqueline. *The National Arboretum Book of Outstanding Garden Plants.* New York, NY: Simon and Schuster, The Stonestrong Press, Inc., 1990.

Hertzberg, Ruth, Beatrice Vaughan, and Janet Green. *The New Putting Food By.* Lexington, MA: The Stephen Greene Press, 1984.

Holmes, Roger, and Frances Tenenbaum, eds. *Taylor's Guide to Container Gardening*. Boston, MA: Houghton Mifflin Company, 1995.

Jimerson, Douglas A., ed. *Successful Rose Gardening*. Des Moines, IA: Better Homes and Gardens Books, Meredith Books, 1993.

Kelly, John, ed. *Reader's Digest A Garden for all Seasons*. Pleasantville, NY: The Reader's Digest Association, Inc., 1991.

Kowalchik, Claire, and William H. Hylton, eds. *Rodale's Illustrated Encyclopedia of Herbs*. Emmaus, PA: Rodale Press, 1987.

Liberty Hyde Bailey Hortorium (staff). *Hortus Third*. New York, NY: MacMillan Publishing Company, Collier MacMillan Publishers, 1976.

Loewer, Peter. *The Annual Garden*. Emmaus, PA: Rodale Press, 1988.

Ortho Books (editors). *Enjoying Roses*. San Ramon, CA: Ortho Books, 1992.

Ortho Books (editors). *The Ortho Home Gardener's Problem Solver*. San Ramon, CA: Ortho Books, 1993.

Phillips, Roger. *Trees of North America and Europe*. New York, NY: Random House, 1978.

Pickles, Sheila, ed. *The Language of Flowers*. New York, NY: Harmony Books, 1990.

—, ed. A Victorian Posy. New York, NY: Harmony Books, 1987.

Pickston, Margaret. *The Language of Flowers*. London: Michael Joseph Ltd., 1968.

Powell, Eileen. *From Seed to Bloom*. Pownal, VT: Storey Communications, Inc., 1995.

Riotte, Louise. *Sleeping With A Sunflower*. Pownal, VT: Storey Communications, Inc., 1987.

Rossi, Rosella. *Simon & Schuster's Guide to Bulbs*. New York, NY: Simon & Schuster Inc., 1989.

Roth, Sally. *Attracting Butterflies and Hummingbirds to Your Backyard*. Emmaus, Pennsylvania: Rodale, 2001.

Sanders, Jack. *Hedgemaids and Fairy Candles*. Camden, ME: Ragged Mountain Press, 1993.

Schenk, George. *The Complete Shade Gardener*. Boston, MA: Houghton Mifflin Company, 1984.

Schuler, Stanley. *How To Grow Almost Everything*. New York, NY: M. Evans and Company, Inc., 1965.

Sunset Books and Sunset Magazine (editors). *Sunset National Garden Book*. Menlo Park, CA: Sunset Books, Inc., 1997.

Taylor, Norman. *Taylor's Guide to Annuals*. Gordon P. DeWolf, Jr., ed. Boston, MA: Houghton Mifflin Company, Chanticleer Press, 1961.

—. *Taylor's Guide to Bulbs*. Gordon P. DeWolf, Jr., ed. Boston, MA: Houghton Mifflin Company, Chanticleer Press, 1961.

—. *Taylor's Guide to Ground Covers, Vines & Grasses*. Gordon P. DeWolf, Jr., ed. Boston, MA: Houghton Mifflin Company, Chanticleer Press, 1961.

—. *Taylor's Guide to Ornamental Grasses*. Gordon P. DeWolf, Jr., ed. Boston, MA: Houghton Mifflin Company, Chanticleer Press, 1961.

—. *Taylor's Guide to Perennials*. Gordon P. DeWolf, Jr., ed. Boston, MA: Houghton Mifflin Company, Chanticleer Press, 1961.

—. *Taylor's Guide to Roses*. Gordon P. DeWolf, Jr., ed. Boston, MA: Houghton Mifflin Company, Chanticleer Press, 1961.

—. *Taylor's Guide to Shrubs*. Gordon P. DeWolf, Jr., ed. Boston, MA: Houghton Mifflin Company, Chanticleer Press, 1961.

—. *Taylor's Guide to Water-Saving Gardening*. Boston, MA: Houghton Mifflin Company, Chanticleer Press, 1990.

Tenenbaum, Frances, ed. *Taylor's Guide to Seashore Gardening*. Boston, MA: Houghton Mifflin Company, 1996.

—, ed. *Taylor's Master Guide to Gardening*. Boston, MA: Houghton Mifflin Company, 1994.

Van Hazinga, Cynthia. *Flower Gardening Secrets*. New York, NY: Time-Life Books, Inc., 1997.

Venning, Frank D. *Wildflowers of North America*. New York, NY: Golden Press, Western Publishing Company, 1984.

Wister, John C. *Bulbs for Home Gardens*. New York, NY: Oxford University Press, 1948.

Wyman, Donald. *Wyman's Gardening Encyclopedia*. New York, NY: MacMillan Publishing Co., 1986.

Zucker, Isabel. *Flowering Shrubs & Small Trees*. New York, NY: Michael Friedman Publishing Group, Inc., Grove Weidenfeld, 1990.

Photography Credits

William Adams: pages 115, 131

Liz Ball and Rick Ray: pages 11, 12, 15, 22, 42, 44, 46, 50, 63, 66, 67, 76, 77, 78, 79, 81, 84, 95, 107, 111, 146, 155, 158, 166, 171, 186, 188, 192, 199, 202, 203, 210, 222, 226, 227, 230, 231, 233, 235, 237

Cathy Wilkinson Barash: pages 61, 154

Pam Beck: page 134

Karen Bussolini: page 10

Laura Coit: page 214

Mike Dirr: page 238

Thomas Eltzroth: pages 13, 14, 19, 23, 25, 26, 27, 28, 29, 30, 31, 32, 33, 34, 35, 36, 37, 38, 39, 40, 41, 43, 45, 47, 48, 53, 55, 56, 58, 59, 64, 69, 73, 82, 83, 87, 89, 90, 97, 98, 99, 102, 103, 105, 106, 108, 109, 112, 116, 118, 124, 125, 135, 139 (bottom) 140, 141, 143, 147, 148, 150, 159, 160, 161, 165, 168, 174, 175, 177, 179, 180, 181, 182, 183 (bottom), 184, 191, 194, 196, 198, 205, 206, 208, 212, 219, 225, 228, 232, 239, back cover (first and third photos)

Peter Gentling: page 132

Pamela Harper: pages 16, 91, 92, 93, 104, 128, 173, 187, 189, 190, 197, 201, 221, 236

Pegi Ballister-Howells: pages 62, 74, 85, 164, 167, 172, 246, 248

Mary Irish: page 70

Dency Kane: pages 88, 211

Peter Loewer: page 126

Dave Mackenzie: page 133

Charles Mann: pages 129, 162

Jerry Pavia: pages 49, 51, 60, 71, 75, 80, 86, 94, 96, 110, 127, 130, 137, 144, 149, 151, 152, 153, 157, 169, 170, 183 (top), 193, 195, 204, 207, 209, 213, 215, 216, 218, 220, 223, 224, 250, back cover (second and fourth photos)

Felder Rushing: page 145

Ralph Snodsmith: pages 57, 101, 200, 229

Mark Turner: pages 54, 65, 72

Andre Viette: pages 8, 17, 24, 68, 122, 123, 136, 138, 139 (top), 142, 156, 234

Plant Index

Featured plant selections are indicated in **boldface**.

Meet the Author

Pegi Ballister-Howells

Pegi Ballister-Howells is well suited to write about New Jersey ornamental gardening. She received her bachelor's degree in Biology from Rutgers College and a master's degree in Horticulture from Rutgers University. She has worked with numerous organizations in the horticulture field, including the New Jersey Farm Bureau as marketing consultant since 1993, Herb Tech of New Jersey as regional manager, The New Jersey Nursery and Landscape Association, The Vegetable Growers Association of New Jersey, and the Rutgers University Cooperative Extension as an assistant professor and county agricultural agent. She is a member of the Board of Trustees for the New Jersey Museum of Agriculture, and takes agricultural photographs across the state.

Her expertise is shared with the public as host of the popular call-in radio program, "The Garden Show," on WCTC-AM 1450 in New Brunswick. Additionally, her 30-minute cable television show "At Home with Pegi," produced by EBTV, features gardening, agriculture, the animals she loves, and all the skills that go into running and maintaining a home. For each of the last five years Pegi has also spoken at the Philadelphia Flower Show, one of the largest flower shows in the world.

The writing of Pegi Ballister-Howells appeared for 15 years in the *Home News Tribune*. The author has also been published in many other periodicals, including *Garden State Home and Garden*, *The Star Ledger*, *The Courier News*, *Rutgers Magazine*, *Heresies*, *New Jersey Living*, *The Plant Press*, *Slow Food Central New Jersey*, and The Farm Bureau publications *The Update* and *Farm Bureau News*. She currently authors the newsletter for the Vegetable Growers Association of New Jersey. Pegi, her husband, family, and assorted creatures live on a ten-acre working farm, Blooming Acres, where they do extensive ornamental and vegetable gardening.